EAST LOTHIAN FOURTH STATISTICAL ACCOUNT
1945 – 2000

VOLUME THREE: THE PARISHES OF
Bolton, Gladsmuir, Humbie, Ormiston,
Pencaitland, Saltoun

Edited by Sonia Baker

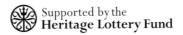

Supported by the
Heritage Lottery Fund

East Lothian Council Library Service
for
The East Lothian Fourth Statistical Account Society
2005

Published by
East Lothian Council Library Service for
the East Lothian Fourth Statistical Account Society, 2005

Designed by
East Lothian Council

Printed by
Howie & Seath Ltd

ISBN 1 897857 31 4
2005

Project Manager
Veronica Wallace

Web page design: Peter Gray

Web pages: www.el4.org.uk

VOLUME THREE: THE PARISHES *of*
Bolton, Gladsmuir, Humbie, Ormiston, Pencaitland, Saltoun

Contents

Additional Information

OVERVIEW

During the 52 years that have passed since the publication of the East Lothian volume of the third statistical account, great changes have occurred both in the situation in East Lothian and in the study of local history in Scotland. In this field there has been a great expansion with increasing recognition of its importance in university departments, in local authority library and museum services, and in the setting up of local history societies. There has also been increasing recognition of the importance of the three existing great statistical accounts, which gave reports of Scotland, parish by parish. They were produced at three critical stages in our history. The first was written when the work of the agricultural improvers was virtually complete, and proto-industrial changes were under way (1789-93); the second was written just at the beginning of a period of vast industrial change (1845), and the third when the country was coming to terms with the aftermath of large scale war (1953). All gave important analyses, both of stability and change.

As the new millennium approached, it became clear that the last, the third, account of East Lothian had become, like its predecessors, a historical document and that since its publication, the county had been subject to enormous social and economic change.

By 1997, there was a feeling that it was time to do the exercise again. The council of the East Lothian Antiquarian and Field Naturalists' Society, under their president, Professor Mitchison, decided to explore the feasibility of such a project. Professor Mitchison fully endorsed the proposal for a Fourth Statistical Account of East Lothian.

The account is presented in seven volumes: the county (Volume One), the parishes (Volumes Two to Six), and reminiscences of growing up in the county (Volume Seven). The countywide essays are complemented by the detailed parish contributions, which themselves vary in style and approach; some contain more oral material than others. Additional information and some longer versions of both are presented on the CD-ROM version of the work.

These volumes contribute to our understanding of the economic and social history of the county, 1945 to 2000; they should in no way be seen as the complete story of the period, as each topic could, in itself, be the subject of far more research and study. There are omissions too. Some topics have not been addressed, as there simply was no existing research available, at the required level. There is always more to discover; we have made a start. East Lothian is in many ways, Scotland in miniature; it has a wide range of landscapes, occupations and experiences. Inevitably, the county's experiences mirrored the Scottish and even the British picture; the difference lies in the detail.

This mammoth task has been a labour of love, but has been more testing than any love affair. East Lothian is worth such effort. We hope this Millennium landmark will be read, be useful, but above all be enjoyed, for a good part of the third millennium.

Stephen Bunyan   Sonia Baker
Chairman   Editor
East Lothian Fourth Statistical Account Society

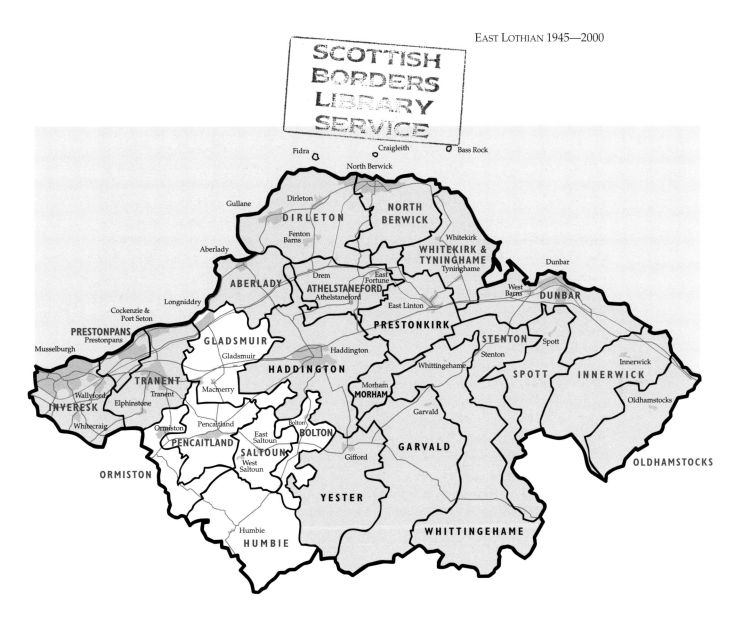

East Lothian 1945—2000

East Lothian Parishes
included in Volume Three

Bolton
Gladsmuir
Humbie
Ormiston
Pencaitland
Saltoun

ACKNOWLEDGEMENTS

On behalf of the society, I would like to acknowledge the support and help that we have received from a vast number of people.

First of all, we must thank the Heritage Lottery Fund without whose financial support we could not have begun. We are grateful for the extensive support of East Lothian Council, and for contributions from the following community councils: Cockenzie & Port Seton; Dunbar; Gullane area; North Berwick; Pencaitland; Prestonpans; Tranent & Elphinstone; West Barns; and from other organisations and individuals. We appreciated the support of East Lothian Council Library and Museums Service. *East Lothian Courier* and *Musselburgh News* back numbers proved to be a mine of information.

We were encouraged by the interest and support of 14 local history and amenity societies who provided representatives on the committee and who, by and large, took on the responsibility for the parish volumes. The Haddington Remembered group volunteered much useful information.

Where there was no such society in a parish, we managed to find volunteers in almost all cases. Their input was invaluable. It soon became clear that the changes in most parishes were greater than we had realised and we are grateful to the parish representatives and the many local volunteers who have produced such a range of material, and to those who have responded to a wide range of queries on a myriad of subjects.

Particular thanks must go to those who took on the role of parish representatives for this volume – namely Ralph W. Barker (Pencaitland), John P. Bolton (Humbie), Denise Brydon (Ormiston), Kathy Fairweather (Gladsmuir – Macmerry), Julie Murphy (Saltoun), David Robertson (Gladsmuir – Longniddry), Jean Shirlaw (Gladsmuir) and Michael Williams (Bolton). Each parish record contains a wealth of information, some of which might have been lost forever.

Many of the photographs used to illustrate the work came from East Lothian Council Library Service, supplemented by private photographs.

I must also pay tribute to our editor, Sonia Baker who has been indefatigable and whose perseverance has kept the show on the road. We are also grateful for the support and assistance of Veronica Wallace, Chris Roberts and Ray Halliday in the Local History Centre who solved many knotty puzzles and showed great patience, and also for secretarial help from Doris Williamson and Jackie Stevenson.

Stephen Bunyan
Chairman
East Lothian Fourth Statistical Account Society

Introduction

This volume covers the small rural parishes of Saltoun and Bolton, and the large but even more rural Humbie, together with the equally small but more urbanised designed village of Ormiston. The remaining two parishes of Pencaitland and Gladsmuir are of a similar size to each other, but very different in character. Pencaitland has become increasingly populous during the later years of the period, with the old village almost swamped with new houses. In contrast, Gladsmuir's population expansion has been accommodated in what is virtually a 'new town' – Longniddry, while the village that gives the parish its name has remained small and compact. Gladsmuir parish is also home to the Macmerry industrial site, together with the ex-mining settlement of Macmerry itself.

These parishes have an ancient link in the coal road, the B6363; this links Winton colliery at Pencaitland, to Penston, and then – crossing the A1 – on to Longniddry and down to the sea. There is also a dismantled railway that runs from Winton to Tranent.

The parish representatives who produced the material in this volume are:
Ralph W. Barker (Pencaitland) on behalf of the Local History Group
    (part of the Pencaitland Amenity Society)
John P. Bolton (Humbie)
Denise Brydon (Ormiston)
Kathy Fairweather (Gladsmuir - Macmerry)
Julie Murphy (Saltoun)
David Robertson (Gladsmuir - Longniddry)
Jean Shirlaw (Gladsmuir)
Michael Williams (Bolton)

John, Julie, David and Michael all produced their essays largely single-handedly. Jean wrote the material for the rural part of Gladsmuir, and then Kathy (in addition to taking on the main writing role for Macmerry) edited and collated the material collected. Ralph wrote much of the Pencaitland essay, with additional checking by Liz Strachan, and this was supplemented by contributions from several other contributors. The Ormiston report, in spite of there being no organised group in the parish, was a real group effort, under Denise's guidance.

The series editor, Sonia Baker, and Stephen Bunyan, David Moody and the Local History Centre team – Veronica Wallace, Chris Roberts, and Ray Halliday - carried out additional research.

Considerable effort has been made to check the information given in the account, but many facts proved elusive, hence the use of approximate dates. There is still more to discover about the history of these parishes 1945-2000; this account makes a start.

Bolton

Parish Representative: *Michael Williams*

Introduction

Bolton remains a rural parish covering some 1254 ha (3099 acres). It consists of a hamlet with a church and nine farm steadings: Under Bolton; Upper Bolton; Ewingston; Marvingston; Eaglescairnie Mains and Home Farm; Cauldshiel; Kirkland and Pilmuir (no steading); and Howden. The parish is undulating and well-wooded with the Birns Water providing the southern march and the Newhall Burn and Colstoun Water on the northeast march. These rather arbitrary boundaries and the fact that Bolton hamlet is in the far north of the area do not provide cohesion to the parish. Seven of the farms are family-owned, 300-650 acre holdings; Kirkland and Pilmuir are owned by Pilmuir, but rented to and worked by the farmer at Under Bolton.

Bolton village, 1983

Environment

The main change to the countryside has been the loss of hedgerow trees (mainly elms) and the creation of some very large fields (100 acres) at Under Bolton. Apart from this, the area has remained remarkably consistent over the period. A number of ponds have been created, some small woodlands replanted and some hedges replaced.

Land Ownership

Colonel Willoughby Peel sold Eaglescairnie in 1954. The steading was bought by Mrs Alison Greenlees. The house was first bought by the Duke of Hamilton then by James McIntyre (Leith) Ltd and occupied from 1957 by Ian McPhail and family. The house was sold to Mr and Mrs Robin Salvesen in 1965. The Duke of Hamilton sold the tenanted farms at Under and Upper Bolton to an insurance company; the tenants, William J Clark & Son and Allan and John Steven, later purchased both properties.

Townscapes, Buildings & Landscapes of Distinction

Membland House, just off the Bolton road from the B6355 from Gifford, was built in 1960 for Admiral Sir Peter Reid by the architect Schomberg Scott. The house is typical of the late Georgian/early Victorian style of farmhouse in the area. The most interesting aspect is the very unusual hexagonal service cottage to the south of the main house.

Population
By parish, from the General Registrar's office

1931	296	151M	145F
1951	239	124M	115F
1961	209	102M	107F
1971	180	86M	94F
1981	206	108M	98F
1991	254	116M	138F
2001	175	93M	82F

By parish, from ELDC   *By settlement, from ELDC*

1991	168			---
1997(est.)	170	81M	89F	39
2001	NO DATA			NO DATA

Population figures are difficult to compare, as no two sources extract data in the same way.

The change from a parish population of c239 in 1945 to c170 in 2000 has been mainly due to the radical reduction in farm labour. Most farm labourers' cottages have been sold, joined together and modernised changing the pattern and type of inhabitants. Very few tied cottages remain whereas, in 1950, Eaglescairnie alone had 13.

Belief

Bolton Kirk has remained the sole place of worship in the parish. The parish was linked with Saltoun (linked in 1929) throughout the period, and they shared the same kirk session. In 1945, there were 420 communicants noted; 300 in 1973; 252 in 1999 – for Bolton & Saltoun. The existing link was extended to Humbie and Yester in 1979. Services are held in Yester/Humbie/Saltoun or Bolton each Sunday – ie three each Sunday with Bolton and Saltoun alternating; this has been in operation since c1980. Previously both Bolton and Saltoun churches had held weekly services. The joint parishes' minister is based at the manse in Yester.

Ministers

1928-47	Robert N. Paisley
1948-58	Alexander Campsie
1959-79	George W.H. Louden
1979 Bolton & Saltoun linked with Humbie & Yester	
1979-84	Allan Scott
1985-97	John Wilson
1999-date	Donald Pirie

In 1982, Bolton church was closed because of structural deterioration, and remedial work carried out at a cost of £5000. The following year, the General Assembly refused their permission when asked if the kirk could sell two Canongate silver communion cups to raise funds for vital repairs to the building. Nonetheless these cups – dating from 1696 – were later sold.

The session clerk – Norman Murphy – set up a Bolton & Saltoun churches web page – www.ndhm.co.uk. The inscriptions in Bolton churchyard were recorded, and are given on the website. The SWRI parish description (c1974) is also reproduced there.

In 1994 on the 750th anniversary of the dedication of the church, a tree was planted in the churchyard to commemorate the event.

Homes

There has been little change in housing location. Six single-storey council homes – Orlits – were built in Bolton village in the early 1950s, and development of the steading at Ewingston was started. The schoolteacher, Mrs Fraser, was allocated the Orlit next to the school.

The main change in the parish has been the change in family accommodation. Most cottages in 1945 outwith Bolton were tied to agricultural workers and their families. By 2000 there remained only three tied cottages. Cottages were either sold or let, most were considerably upgraded and many joined to one unit. The significance of this was the development of an entirely different type of population. Most commuted to their work outwith the parish and did not have the ties to the land in the same way. This population also was more affluent and in most cases owned cars.

1930s thatched cottage, Bolton Muir, designed by Philip D Hepworth

Utilities

The whole parish is on the public water supply. There is no mains sewerage, and no mains gas. At Howden, there is a mobile phone mast. Bolton village has street lighting.

Shops & Services

There were no shops in Bolton during this period, though cigarettes and sweeties were sold from a corner of Tom Whitecross's living room in one of the Under Bolton farm cottages c1951-56.

However, a wide range of mobile shops served the area. The co-operative groceries and fleshing van called until the mid 1980s, and a milk round survived until 1998. Fruiterers and fish vans were regular visitors. Deliveries were made readily from Haddington and Edinburgh (John Lewis etc), and Tesco started an online shopping service in 1999.

Shops and Services (cont)

The mobile library was popular, travelling from East Lothian Council Library Service HQ in Haddington.

The small play area beside Bolton hall dates from 1990; there were swings and climbing bars in the playground to the rear of the hall when it was a school. There is a public telephone in the village.

Education

The primary school at Bolton, which had opened in 1913, was closed in 1967. One room was used for teaching, and was separated from the dining room by a wooden partition. Marks on the floor show where the fireplaces were; the cloakroom and teacher's toilet were behind the main rooms, and the children's toilets were, as was usual then, across the playground. Electric light was installed in 1951. School dinners were provided, but a copy of the log book noted that in 1953 when they increased in price from 7d to 9d, '…nine children have stopped taking them and go home or to friends for dinner.'

The children were taken to places of interest, such as the Highland Agricultural Show, 24 June 1955; Edinburgh Castle, the zoo, the Scotsman offices and the museum, 25 May 1956; the Haddington wool mills, 19 April 1957; and to Dunfermline, the abbey, Carnegie's birth place, Pittencrieff glen, Rosyth dockyard – 'Ark Royal etc' on 17 May 1957. They also went to the celebrations at Lennoxlove – fireworks and a bonfire – when the Marquis of Douglas and Clydesdale came of age.

Mrs Fraser and her pupils at Bolton School, c1952
(J & W Gray)

Left to right   *Front row: Colin Cranston; Twin 1? Allan; Twin 2? Allan; Ernie Coulter.*
2nd row: Ann Cockburn; Isabel King; May Cockburn; Mrs Fraser; Helen Litster; Maureen King.
3rd row: George Cockburn; Willie Gray; Margaret Sinclair; Amelia Campbell; Peter Whitecross; Mabel Bisset; ? Allan; Ian Huxley.
Back Row: Jock Litster; John Anderson; George King; James King; Robin Cranston; Alan Anderson.

Over the years there were a number of teachers. Mrs MacIntosh left on 24 December 1946; Mrs Turnbull followed her, until 29 June 1951; then came Mrs Fraser who left on 27 September 1957, and was replaced by the last teacher, Miss Taylor, on 10 January 1958. At times more than one teacher was employed, for example a Miss Robb was assistant teacher in 1955, and pupil numbers varied. In 1957, there were 31; 19 in 1960; there were just eight in 1966, and only five for the last term in summer 1967. From then on, Bolton children went to school elsewhere.

The school's closure had been approved back in 1962 (NAS ED 48/1650) along with that of Morham, Garvald and Gifford; a new school was to be built at Gifford (called Yester). In 1962, Bolton was a one-teacher school, catering for 20 pupils from the 'agricultural community'; the school building was deemed inadequate and below modern standards. Bolton itself was viewed as 'no real village… although …there are a few houses within sight of the school.' (NAS ED 48/1650 p3).

After closure, the pupils were sent to Yester or Haddington. Bolton remained in the catchment area of the Knox Academy for secondary education.

The primary school building was reopened as a village hall, having been sold to the Community Association for £1. A new access road was built to the rear of the Orlits, and the old school field at the back swapped for a piece of land to the west of the hall; this straightened the field boundary to the north, making life easier for the farmer.

Transport

The road network has remained identical throughout the period. Public transport (bus only) has remained poor and infrequent.

Leisure

Until 1967, the old school – which was attached to the old schoolhouse near the war memorial – was used as a village hall. In the early 1970s, the extensions on the side of the old school were demolished, and the remainder of the original building was incorporated into the schoolhouse. From 1967, the community took over the school building at the far end of the Orlits. By 2000, it was used by the Bolton Bowling Club, and for such as Christmas parties, BBQs 'in hall if wet', and other celebrations.

To celebrate the Millennium, villagers redecorated the hall, and a mural, *Bolton: 1913-2000 and Beyond*, was made for the inside. The mural was designed and the work organised by Sue Fraser; the children involved all 'signed' it with their handprints – Sean (4), Rosie (7), Eve (6), Eleanor (8), Amy N (11), Tom H (13), Thomas P (5), Amy H (11) – and Val (47) and Sharon (35) assisted. Various aspects of the village were portrayed: two children c1913, and two more c2000 (complete with mobile phone and personal stereo, standing in front of the Orlits). The school (now hall), the church, the war memorial and the main tool of the village, the tractor, were all included.

With a declining and ageing population, the village could no longer sustain the number of clubs it once had. The Bolton SWRI, established 1926, finally closed in 1987, when membership had dwindled to just nine.

A ladies' guild and Sunday school thrived as joint ventures with Saltoun, operating month or week about respectively. The guild ended in the mid 1970s, but the Sunday school continued.

Leisure (cont)

A youth club, again a joint venture with Saltoun – intended for the 11-16 age group, folded in Bolton during the late 1960s, having extended its age range well into the mid 20s! The club's equipment went to Saltoun.

Bolton's sole surviving club in 2000 was the bowling club. Established pre-war, by 2000 it was the only survivor out of about eight in the county that made up the East Lothian Scottish Carpet Bowling Association. The others were - Morham, Garvald, Longyester, Crossroads, The Boggs (Pencaitland), Haddington, and Athelstaneford. Eight players were required for league games. In 2000, Bolton had 16 members, although some came from outwith Bolton. They bowled on a carpet-covered, raised (perhaps 6") platform some 3' wide and 24' long, targetting a tacket or button, on the carpet. In its heyday during the 1950s-80s, the club had 24-30 members. Bolton members were the East Lothian Carpet Bowling Champions in 1944, and the League and Knockout Cup Champions in 1983.

Economy – Agriculture

This remains the main economic driver. The mixed farming of the 1950s developed to mainly arable farming with stock, which reflected the good years for arable units in the 1980s and 1990s. Stock numbers reduced throughout the period, as did the cropping acreage related to stock rearing (turnips etc). The switch to white cropping reduced the biodiversity potential of the farmed land. Horses were still used on farms until the mid 1950s but the mechanisation of agriculture was relentless. Mechanisation and in particular the use of hydraulic technology was directly related to the massive reduction in farm labour over the period.

The 1990s saw a serious decline in the financial fortunes of the agricultural industry, mainly due to low world commodity prices. This further reduced the need for farm labour and encouraged the use of part-time and contract labour.

Forestry: this has remained important to the economy of the area. One large block of commercial forestry south of the Saltoun/Gifford road owned by Hamilton and Kinneil Estate was rotationally felled and replanted throughout the period. The remaining forestry resource, consisting mainly of farm woodlands, largely remained neglected on a commercial basis but remained an important amenity and landscape resource. Extensive management of farm woodlands was carried out at Cauldshiel and Eaglescairnie under Forestry Commission schemes from 1990.

Local Government

Bolton is one part of Ward 16, the community council for Humbie, East Saltoun, West Saltoun and Bolton.

This account of Bolton parish was written by Michael Williams. Additional information was provided by the following:

Jimmy Gray   Education; Leisure - the Hall, the Bowling Club
Willie Gray   Education; Leisure - the Hall, the Bowling Club

FURTHER READING & REFERENCES
National Archives of Scotland, 25 October 1962, *Discontinuance of Rural Schools*, ED 48/1650

GLADSMUIR – *excluding* LONGNIDDRY

PARISH REPRESENTATIVES:
Jean Shirlaw – Gladsmuir & Kathy Fairweather – Macmerry
PARISH EDITOR: *Kathy Fairweather CBE*

Introduction

Gladsmuir parish (including Longniddry) covers some 2908 ha (7186 acres). Created in 1692 from parts of the parishes of Haddington, Aberlady and Tranent (which may account for its odd shape), Gladsmuir was something of a contrivance and always contained a mixture of coastal and inland, farming and industrial areas. After the war, the coastal settlement of Longniddry expanded and developed a life of its own; in 1967 this was recognised when it became part of the registration district of Prestonpans. For the purpose of this account, the parish of Gladsmuir includes Macmerry, Gladsmuir, and surrounding farmland. *A separate account is given on Longniddry – see page 35.*

Before, during and for a short time after, the war, a large area of land belonging to Hoprig Mains Farm was used as an airfield (see Economy). In 1945, parish life was dominated by the airfield; there were numerous huts and other buildings housing the military on Penston farm where around 1000 men were stationed. Today there are eleven of the original buildings remaining, which are used to store machinery. The effects on civilian life in the parish were considerable. Macmerry Primary School, for example, was closed for the duration of the war, and children had to attend schools in Tranent, Longniddry or Pencaitland.

By 2000, there were still some physical traces of these wartime activities, but the predominant changes were the building of roads, especially the new A1 expressway with its flyovers, slip roads and roundabouts, the development of the Macmerry Industrial Estate and the continued house building in Macmerry, which all had a major impact on the appearance of the parish. Rural areas of the parish changed relatively little over the 55 years. There has been little house building outwith existing settlements, and farmhouses, steadings, rows of cottages, trees and fields, mostly still enclosed by hedges, leave the farms easily recognisable. In 1945, land in the parish was used predominantly for agriculture and, although this was in decline throughout the period, by 2000 it still occupied the greatest area of land.

Environment

The climate of the parish, influenced by its proximity to the coast, meant that extremes of weather were rare. Wildlife abounds in Gladsmuir; otters are seen in the ponds at Woodside, and there is a badger sett in the pond area with another two setts about half a mile away. Over the period, there was a slight decline in foxes, but a definite increase in rats and frogs. Herons, buzzards, mistle thrushes, fieldfares, long-tailed tits, crows, wood pigeons, and seagulls have all increased in number, while curlews, skylarks, partridges and house sparrows all decreased. There was a big increase in red admiral butterflies, and a general decline in wild flowers; many elm trees succumbed to Dutch elm disease. Ferns, nettles, hogweed, ivy, honeysuckle and moss all increased.

The eventual nature reserve of Butterdean wood, an area of mixed woodland surrounding the site of the demolished Butterdean house between Gladsmuir and Hodges farm, changed hands several times. The Forestry Commission bought it in 1947 and, by the late 1960s much of the area had been cleared of broadleaved trees and planted with conifers. In 1982 the Ogilvy

Environment (cont)

family, earlier owners of the woodland, repurchased it and some of the trees were sold as Christmas trees. The local authority put on a tree preservation order to prevent felling for agricultural use.

In 1988 the Woodland Trust, with financial assistance from the local council, bought the wood. They have since carried out extensive thinning and opened up coniferous areas, thus releasing any existing broadleaves, and allowing for natural regeneration. In the broadleaved areas, the conifers have been removed. Since the Woodland Trust has been responsible for Butterdean, provision has been made for public access. There is a surfaced track at the northern end of the wood, signposts and explanation boards and within the wood itself, an extensive network of paths; there are three asserted and one confirmed public right of way, which connected to and/or passed through the wood; the wood is used regularly by local people for dog walking and so on. The quality of the woodland as a habitat for wildlife, much diminished as a result of the conifer planting, was gradually improving by 2000.

The proximity of the railway and the A1 road has meant continuing pressure on land in the parish for development. So far, both industrial and housing development have been restricted largely to the village of Macmerry, where 32 acres of land at the eastern end were zoned for industrial development in the early 1960s. The first industrial unit opened there in 1966; by the 1990s all the land was occupied and an extension was being planned.

Also in the 1990s, there were proposals for a large housing development at Greendykes, but these were resisted successfully.

Land Ownership

By 2000, much of the land in the parish was in private hands or belonged to the local council. The large estates - St Germains, Lamington, and Elvingston - had been sold and broken up into smaller units. In 1947 the trustees of Charles Stewart Parker Tennent sold St Germains estate in lots. James Rennie, the farmer at Greendykes, bought three lots. On Lord Lamington's death in 1954, the farms of Gladsmuir, Hoprig, Hoprig Mains, Penston and Westbank were sold to the tenant farmers. Many subsequently changed hands again.

The Ainslie family had owned the Elvingston estate since 1836; it was bought by Sir David Lowe in 1944 and was sold off in lots in the 1980s after his death. The last remaining 30 acres, along with the mansion house of Elvingston, were bought by Dr David Simpson and his wife Janice in 1987. Dr Simpson established a Science Park (1998) in the grounds (see Economy – Industry).

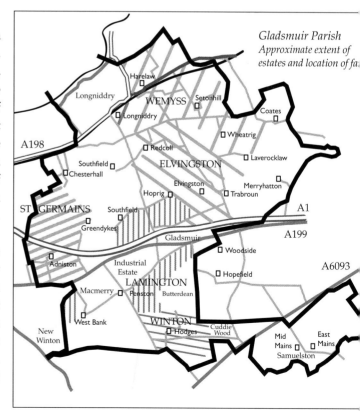

Gladsmuir Parish Approximate extent of estates and location of fa...

Aerial view of part of Gladsmuir parish, including Longniddry, 1988

(Crown Copyright: RCAHMS (All Scotland Survey Collection))

Land Ownership (cont)

Development in the different parts of the parish of Gladsmuir/Macmerry during this period was quite varied. The village of Gladsmuir changed relatively little. Macmerry expanded, with growth both in the areas zoned for industry and in housing, but still remained a self-contained and active working village rather than simply a dormitory suburb for Edinburgh. In the surrounding rural areas, farming continued, with some restoration and extension of former farm buildings into private homes. The airfield was decommissioned in 1955; since then the site has been used partly for agriculture and partly for industry.

Townscapes, Buildings & Landscapes of Distinction

Both the current parish church in Gladsmuir (originally built in 1839 and rebuilt after a fire in 1886) and the ruins of the earlier church (dated 1695), are B listed, as are the Elvingston house and lodges, and an 18th century doocot at Elvingston. The doocot was restored by Sir David Lowe, and contains 764 nesting boxes: Dr and Mrs Simpson have restored the house. From 1947, James E. Rennie owned the mansion house of St Germains (originally part of Seton estate); he sold it to J. N. Toothill, who divided it into flats in the 1950s.

Small areas of parkland surrounding the mansion houses of St Germains and Elvingston have been retained; Stephen Adamson carried out some restoration work on the Elvingston garden.

Aerial view of Gladsmuir village, c1960 (Jean Shirlaw)

Population

By parish* from the General Registrar's office

1931	1779	860M	919F	*By locality **– census –*			
1951	2001	1008M	993F	*ie Macmerry village itself*			
1961	2173	1094M	1079F				
1971	3039	1479M	1560F	1503	755M	748F	
1981	4349	2097M	2252F	1332	636M	696F	
				By Small Area Statistics ** – census			
1991	4383	2126M	2257F	1157	556M	601F	
2001	3894	1872M	2022F				

By Gladsmuir parish, from ELDC

				By settlement **, from ELDC	
1991	4069			1173 Macmerry	
1997 (est.)	4271	2087M	2184F	1207 Macmerry	*87 Gladsmuir*
2001		NO DATA		1113 Macmerry (ELC)	--

Population figures are difficult to compare, as no two sources extract data in the same way.

* these figures include Macmerry, Gladsmuir and Longniddry
** see p38 for Longniddry figures

The census data for the civil parish of Gladsmuir includes Longniddry, Macmerry and the small village of Gladsmuir. The population increase shown by these figures can be largely attributed to an increase in the population of Longniddry; meanwhile, the populations of Gladsmuir and Macmerry declined gradually but steadily throughout the period.

Belief

The Church of Scotland has been the only belief system operating in the parish during this period, although members of other religions live in the parish. Places of worship were the parish church in Gladsmuir and Macmerry village hall. In Samuelston, Gladsmuir church converted two old farm cottages into a church hall in 1938. A Men's Guild was held here until the 1950s when the hall was no longer used for church purposes, as the population of the village had dwindled. The building was handed back to the owner, J. Thomson, the local farmer who owned Samuelston West, Mid and East Mains. He sold it for conversion into a house.

A Men's Guild was also held in Gladsmuir church hall. The Woman's Guild continued to meet over the years, generally monthly in the manse dining room.

'There was an opening devotional prayer and a hymn, often by the minister, or the minister's wife – this was an expected part of her duties'.
Jean Shirlaw

The Sunday school and bible class met in the church hall after spending part of the service in the church. However, from the late 1970s, Gladsmuir church hall ceased to be used for church functions, due to its position on the south side of the A1 road; the traffic had increased to such an extent that it was dangerous for people crossing over to the hall, especially the children going to Sunday school and bible class. It was then decided that they should meet in three rooms of the manse.

Belief (cont)

These arrangements continued until the minister retired in 1984, when the charges of Gladsmuir and Longniddry were linked and the Gladsmuir manse was sold. Part of the glebe had been sold in 1948 to East Lothian County Council, to accommodate an extension to the graveyard, and a further part was sold in 1973. The walled garden too had been sold in 1973, and a house built there.

After 1984, the Sunday school met for a short time in the church and then, for the following 14 years, a small class was held in Macmerry village hall, when the twice monthly church services were held there. From c1997, due to little response, there was no Sunday school.

The Woman's Guild continued to be active, meeting monthly in Macmerry village hall. During the year it put on a sale of work and a concert with refreshments for the senior citizens.

Little development was possible in the church life because of the situation of the church and the lack of the hall. The linkage with Longniddry held good for 17 years but Gladsmuir church was finding the going hard by 2000. A faithful body of members gave valiant support, and pastoral work continued with the part-time assistance of Rev Laurie Underwood. Services were held every week at Gladsmuir and twice a month at Macmerry village hall.

Ministers

1914-50	William Reid Wiseman
1950-54	Crichton Robertson
1955-85	Robert S.S. Shirlaw
May 1984 linked with Longniddry under Longniddry minister	
1985-date	A. Graham Black

Here, Jean Shirlaw shares her recollections of church life at Gladsmuir

Pre-war, there was a common communion cup; individual cups were just coming in by 1955. The common cup contained fermented wine - port; the elders always used the common cup.

Disjunction Certificates were used by the Church of Scotland to keep a head count, and to introduce communicants to a new area if they moved. To "get your lines" became less common as the period progressed.

There were seat rent envelopes, where the rent was paid twice a year, but this was abolished in the 1970s. Where previously the church was divided into different estates and workers, no one could then claim the right to a certain pew, but a few of the older members felt they still had a right to their pew, and were none too happy if someone else sat in it! There was a separate manse pew. Cards were placed at the pew ends for guidance.

On funerals

The coffin was left in the house so that it could be viewed; most burials took place within four days. From the 1960s-1970s, instead of the coffin remaining in the house, it would be taken to a funeral parlour from where it would be taken to the church if the family wanted a service there before burial or cremation.

Women went to funerals only from the 1960s and 1970s; post-war, the men would gather at the graveyard. From the late 1970s, women would be invited to 'take a cord'. The interment of ashes became more common from the mid 1970s. There was one instance in the 1950s, at Trabroun, where there was a wake; prayers were said around an open coffin and a tipple taken. However, this appears to have been a one-off.

Belief (cont)

Weddings

Banns were read, or hung outside the registrar's or in church – on two Sundays. During the war, the banns were proclaimed at the church door.

Weddings took place in the church or in the vestry, and sometimes in the manse, with at least two held in our lounge.

Particular to East Lothian was 'a creeling' when somebody put a creel on the back of the bride, and a piper had a bottle of whisky.

Wendy Goldstraw (née Bruce) shares her memories on how her family were drawn to Gladsmuir church:

Apparently, when the family moved to Seton Mains in the 1920s, the family kept attending church in Edinburgh. Then my father won a couple of ducks in the Gladsmuir raffle, got friendly with the minister and started attending Gladsmuir - gradually the rest of the family followed. There were family pews and I remember at one time there were several rows of Bruces…

On the services

I remember services such as Harvest Festival and Remembrance Sunday; for example, Remembrance Sunday was for me the start of what war and sacrifice was all about. And wondering whether the Boy Scouts would hit the lights with their flag! The Christmas tree was always one of the biggest.

I remember thinking there must be something special about Communion because I wasn't allowed to go, but for every other service I was encouraged to go!

I got told off by my Aunt Mary for not wearing a hat - but my mother said it was OK because Mrs Shirlaw (the minister's wife) was not wearing one!

Bob's (Rev R. Shirlaw) voice filled the whole church – no need of a microphone! Yet when there was a christening – the babies just looked up at him in wonder.

On special occasions

The church fetes (as an adult too but especially as a child) – selling raffle tickets, the tombola, the wonderful baking, the wonderful vegetables gifted by Sir David Lowe and the delicious soup my mother would make with them afterwards.

And on attending Gladsmuir church as an adult:

Adult memories are more ordinary with the exception of our wedding, and the first Communion Brian and I attended after our marriage. Memories are of special services, and of gradually declining attendances.

The church is run by the Kirk Session with elders taking specific and general roles. There is also a Congregational Board (Brian is treasurer and I am clerk); Graham Black chairs both. I guess that is the linkage with Longniddry. The session, in particular, takes a more active role. Betty Jeffrey in particular is a very good session clerk; John Robertson is gift aid convenor and Bob McIntyre is fabric convenor and both do a lot of work. Because Graham has to divide his time between Longniddry and Gladsmuir, we usually have Rev. Laurie Underwood taking the services and she is very good – especially with the children.

The usual services happen of course - Christmas communion, Harvest Thanksgiving, Remembrance etc. There are also special ones such as Songs of Praise, one to celebrate the Macmerry Gala with the Queen and her Court present, an annual joint service with Longniddry, and occasional ones with perhaps a special choir or band present.

Belief (cont)

Macmerry has retained a strong sense of community. The gala was an annual event throughout this period, although it saw some changes. It used to involve tea and buns and races for the children, but in 1949 a gala queen was introduced and the crowning of the queen became a focal point for the event. The celebrations now take place over a weekend in the middle of June. A gala committee plans and organises the celebrations.

The community was very active in the 1970s and 1980s before the building of the bypass, in campaigning for road improvements after a series of accidents. The Macmerry Road Safety Action Group campaigned successfully for a pedestrian crossing in 1976.

Homes

Housing was confined largely to the two main settlements, the village of Macmerry, and a smaller hamlet at Gladsmuir.

Macmerry contains an older row of stone-built houses along the main road, but most of the houses were built between the 1930s and the 1980s by the council. As a result of the governments ' right to buy' policy introduced in the 1980s, many were bought by their tenants; by 2000, about one third of the houses were privately owned.

After the war the village of Macmerry began to expand. Prefabs arrived on the backs of lorries in the late 1940s, and twelve of them were erected in Merryfield Avenue (these were demolished around 1967/8). The Orlit homes in Whiteloch Road and Robin's Neuk were constructed at about the same time. The houses in Brierbush were built in the 1950s and those in Robin's Neuk in 1953. Brierbush Road was built up between 1954 and 1973, and Brierbush Crescent in 1973. Annfield Court (SSHA) and Westbank Gardens were built in 1977. Reid Housing built ten sheltered houses in the late 1980s, and there was some private house building to the north of the main street in the 1990s. Most of these were low-rise one or two storey houses, either semi-detached or four in a block or terraced.

Gladsmuir Coach House stables before conversion, 1970s (Jean Shirlaw)

The local authority had built 18 houses in Gladsmuir (ten pre-war at Lammermuir, and eight post-war at Lamington Road), but by 2000 nearly half of these had been sold into private ownership.

The small settlements at Samuelston and Penston both declined over the period to clusters of farm cottages, some of them derelict. There was some renovation and extension of cottages into family homes, especially at Samuelston, in the 1990s through a private developer. At Penston, the former inn was developed and extended into a large private home, but many of the cottages and farm buildings remained unoccupied and semi-derelict at the end of the period. In the rural areas there was some conversion of former agricultural buildings into private homes.

A rural home at Penston Gardens:

'The cottage was built in 1676, …

occupied by the Dobson family from 1890-1997. The walls of the cottage are three feet thick. Originally earthen floors, they are now either stone or floorboarded. The original red pantiled roof was replaced using wooden Canadian Shingle tiles in 1949 - in the years after the second world war, materials were in short supply, and therefore the choice of tile was based on availability. The wooden tiles are at present still on the roof, although in a very poor condition. A scullery and toilet were added to the original building in 1930 with cold running water. Hot water was added in 1942, and electricity in 1956.

Cottage at Penston (Fiona Dobson)

The fire, a Lothian Range, was fitted in December 1940 replacing an existing smaller range. The range fire is the only source of heating for the house and water.

Entering the house by the back door leads directly into a small scullery with a lino tile covered stone floor. Underneath the window is a porcelain sink with draining boards on either side. Next to the sink is an electric cooker. Against the opposite wall is a twin tub washing machine. Leading off the scullery is the toilet, comprising toilet pan and wooden dresser used for storage. A door leads off the scullery into a hallway, stone floored, carpeted with rugs. On the right is a shelved pantry concealed by a curtain for storing food and utensils. Next to the pantry is the bedroom. A square room furnished with a double bed, wardrobe, two chests, a large dresser, bookcase and chair. The wooden floorboards are carpeted. There is a double window on the south-facing wall. The living room is square with a single window facing north and a double window facing south. The fire range is situated opposite the entrance door on the east wall.

The living room doubles as a bedroom and is furnished accordingly with a double bed in the corner to the right of the door, trolley beside bed. The TV and fridge are placed underneath the double window; a large old-fashioned dresser is next to the fire range with a wooden four leg table in front. Chairs are around the table on two sides only. An easy chair is to the right of the fire (next to dresser). A kist (doubles as seat) sits to the left of the fire, in front of a wall cupboard. A treadle sewing machine sits

Homes (cont)

underneath the single window with an easy chair in front. A high-backed sideboard is against the wall to the left of the single window. A large double wardrobe is against the wall to the left of the door. The rooms are very cluttered with the furniture generally tightly packed. Lack of storage space means belongings are stacked in piles all around'.
Fiona Dobson

Utilities

Mains electricity and a public water supply have been available throughout this period. Mains drainage is supplied in the larger settlements, but properties in the rural areas rely on septic tanks. Mains gas is available in Macmerry, but not elsewhere in the parish.

Both terrestrial and satellite TV are available. Several mobile phone masts were constructed beside the new road works, so reception in the area is normally quite good. The main streets of Gladsmuir and Macmerry are lit.

The council provides regular rubbish collections throughout the parish. There is also a council-run waste disposal site at the rear of the Macmerry Industrial Estate, where members of the public can deposit their own rubbish.

Shops & Services

The small number of shops in the parish served the local area and immediate surroundings only, and by 2000 had been reduced to one Spar convenience store in Macmerry named The Village Shoppe. Macmerry was never a major retail centre, and by 2000 this was the only remaining retail outlet. Until the 1980s this included a post office, but this was closed and relocated in separate premises beside the village hall. Macmerry garage in the main street is used as a workshop for repairs.

Macmerry village shop and Post Office, 1950s

24

A public house called the Robin's Neuk was built at the western end of Macmerry in 1968, and was later renamed the Country Inn. It closed in 2000. The Miners' Welfare Institute and the bowling club were then the only licensed premises in the village.

In Gladsmuir village there was a post office run by Mrs G. Anderson from the 1940s until the 1960s, firstly in a house in Brick Row, and then in a house at the joiner's shop. Mrs Robson then took over the post office, and it was sited in her home at the old school house until 1975, when it closed.

There has been a garage on the site of the original blacksmith's shop in Gladsmuir since the 1930s. It changed hands a number of times, but in 2000, continued to sell petrol and undertake repairs and MOTs etc.

A joinery business has operated in Gladsmuir on part of the old Lamington estate since the early 18th century. When the estate was sold in the 1950s, the tenant George Anderson & Sons carried on the business, and the same family still ran the business in 2000. In the 1970s the joiner's shop, which fronted the A1 road, was converted into a dwelling house and the joinery work carried out in premises to the rear of the building.

James Smith ran a blacksmith's business in Gladsmuir until he retired early in the 1990s when the business closed. The work was varied - agricultural repairs, servicing lawnmowers, and all kinds of metalwork, railings, chain link fencing and gates were made. The bulk of the work was for the local council, but ornamental wrought iron gates were also made for Morham churchyard.

In the early part of the period, the parish was served by a number of mobile shops and delivery services. G.E. Livingstone (from Macmerry) had an ironmongery van, which came to Gladsmuir and the surrounding farms from the late 1940s until the early 1960s; the van was specially adapted to carry a tank containing paraffin for customers' paraffin lamps and heaters.

There was a fish van from Port Seton, a Co-op van and a butcher's van from Haddington. Between the 1950s and 1970s, a grocer from Longniddry delivered three times a week if requested. Milk was delivered by the Co-op and the Crown Dairy from Haddington, and newspapers could be delivered from the post office in Macmerry. By 2000 only a fruit and vegetable van, and a fish van, were still operating.

A mobile library run by the council served both Macmerry and Gladsmuir.

Healthcare

There was no medical practice in the parish. Residents looked to Haddington, Longniddry or Tranent for medical care. Home helps were available, and meals-on-wheels when required.

Education

There was no school in Gladsmuir, and the primary school in Macmerry was closed in June 1940 because of its proximity to the airfield. Pupils were dispersed mainly to Tranent public school, but some went to schools in Longniddry and Pencaitland. The headteacher was appointed head at Ormiston Junior Secondary School after 21 years at Macmerry. During the war the school premises were used for various military purposes, including military stores, and an HQ for the local Home Guard. Tents were at one stage pitched in the playground for soldiers, and officers occupied the head teacher's house.

Education (cont)

After the war, the future of the school was in some doubt but, after strong local objections, it was reopened on 27 August 1946, with a roll of 47 pupils, which had risen to 69 by the end of the school year. By 1953 the roll had risen to 119, and the pressure on accommodation was such that the dining hut was brought into use as a classroom, and the Miners' Institute hall was used for physical education. By Easter 1954, when the roll had reached 146, a class was also being held in the Miners' Institute, and pressure was being put on East Lothian County Council to extend the school. An extension was finally agreed and was completed by August 1959, by which time the roll had reached 213. This extension added a 2-storey block of six classrooms and cloakrooms, and an assembly/dining hall; the old school was reconstructed and brought into use for the infant classes. The school roll rose to a peak of 222 in 1964-65: in 2000, the roll was 104.

When the head teacher Mr Willie McIntyre retired in 1972, the schoolhouse was vacated. During the 1970s there were increasing concerns about the safety of the pupils because of the proximity of the school to the busy A1 road, and demands for effective crash barriers. An articulated lorry demolished the school railings in 1974, and a child was knocked down on the road also in 1974, and another in 1975.

Pupils from the parish travelled to Ross High School, Tranent for secondary education after it was opened in 1954. Before that, those that passed the 'quali' (qualifying exam) attended Preston Lodge School in Prestonpans, and those that did not attended Tranent Junior Secondary School.

In the late 1960s and early 1970s, an independently run playgroup was held in Gladsmuir church hall. In 1977, Macmerry Nursery School was opened, housed in a unit of its own in the south-west corner of the primary school playground. In 1989, the nursery became two nursery classes in the main school building.

Macmerry Primary School celebrated its centenary in 1989 with the publication of a centenary magazine, an open day and a concert and the burying of a time capsule in the playground. Money was also raised to dig a well in a village in India to commemorate the event.

Pat Moncrieff was the teacher of Primary 1 at Macmerry Primary School, 1952-69; here she recalls her time there:

The P1 classroom was large, with a high ceiling, and had the blessing of a cork tile floor which minimised the clatter. There were small desks with lids at first, then rectangular wooden tables with metal legs, which could be grouped together (groups of eight or ten). There were small individual black boards with white and coloured chalk, a large sink, and various cupboards. The windows were too high for the children to look out.

Across the passage we could use the General Purposes (GP) room for painting, woodwork etc. In the 1960s this was quite "advanced" learning.

There was no school uniform; infants' teachers often wore a smock overall (often floral) but graduates did not – they scorned to do so. It showed status, although teachers of the older children often wore their black gowns: this would have scared the wee ones!

Free milk was delivered in ⅓ pint bottles with straws. I used to take strawberry flavouring and made 'milk shakes' which the children took in the café (a table set up in the GP room) as they finished an assignment. This was very popular, even with those who didn't want milk at first. Children brought their own piece (jam and bread, or biscuit), which they ate with the milk or in the playground.

School lunches were cooked on the premises, and served 'en famille'. A P7 pupil served out at each table of eight or so. Those staff having lunch at school (if not taking a sandwich in the staff-room) sat at another table. There was no real need for lunchtime supervision. Meals were eaten on the 'stage' of the assembly hall.

Most children walked to school, even from nearby farms – accompanied by their older siblings, or mothers when in the infants' class. Staff lived in Macmerry or came by bus or later by car.

Lessons were the three Rs (reading, writing and arithmetic) plus nature study; physical education (PE); handwork and singing, stories and poems. I used "Two Years in the Infant School" by Enid Blyton as a guide in my early years of teaching. A week's activities eg stories, nature, handwork, handwriting were organised by themes eg homes, shops, spring. Reading schemes used were Radiant Way and Janet and John. Work cards were used for mathematics. Much work was done as a class from the blackboard and by repetition. PE was exercises and Music and Movement (Ann Driver on BBC Schools programme), singing games etc. There were playground games and snow activities (building a snowman, organised snow fights). Sports day was mainly races. Infants ran egg and spoon, sack, obstacle, and three-legged races. The school had a football and a netball team.

There were seven members of staff, including the headmaster, usually one other male, and the rest female - all university graduates. Usually there was one teacher per stage, depending on the numbers in the twice-yearly intake. I had Easter and summer entrants so group teaching was essential - and the older ones helped the younger to settle in more quickly: there was no pre-school provision. Class size was a maximum of 45.

Teachers taught all subjects in the curriculum – no specialists at first, then latterly an art teacher for the older pupils. Most staff were a little musical, some very musical. When the infants went home at 3pm the infants' teacher took the older ones for handwork, sewing, knitting until 3.45pm – or there was football practice (with the headmaster) or netball practice (me).

Playtime was a quarter of an hour. All ages played together. Playground games - ball games, skipping, peevers, statues etc, were taught in games times, and continued as playground activities.

Special events were a school concert, a play written and produced by P7 children, and a school sale held once a year in the evening. The whole village attended. It was a complete sell-out especially the cake and candy stall.
The School Club for P7 was popular. Once a week after school – games, walks, modelling with balsa wood, board games etc.

Transport

Although the goods service continued until 1960, the railway station in Macmerry was closed to passenger traffic on 1 July 1925. However, the parish is well served by good bus services to Edinburgh, Tranent, Haddington and Dunbar. Transport north and south by bus and car became much faster with the opening of the A1 Macmerry and Tranent by-pass in 1986, and the dualling of the carriageway between Bankton and Haddington in 1996, which by-passed Gladsmuir itself.

Since this road opened, there has been an attempt to encourage cyclists with the marking of cycle lanes on either side of the old road, now the A199, which traverses the parish.

The old railway line to the west of Macmerry has been turned into and maintained as a railway walk.

Transport (cont)

*A1 from
Macmerry
bridge, c1994,
before dualling*

Police

There was a police station and a house for the policeman's family in St Germains Terrace in Macmerry until the 1970s. Police are rarely seen in the parish now, but it is served by a community police liaison officer.

Leisure

Since the use of Gladsmuir Church Hall was abandoned c1970, the only leisure facility in Gladsmuir village is a small play park on ground that until 1968 belonged to Gladsmuir Farm. From 1945 until the 1970s, the hall was used for church dances, whist drives, Sunday school, Christmas parties and, occasionally, for wedding receptions. The 1st Gladsmuir Guide Company and the 1st Gladsmuir Brownie Pack were registered in 1948, following encouragement by Mrs Alison Greenlees of Huntingdon – one of the early Scottish guides. Both groups met weekly in Gladsmuir until c1968, when they moved to Macmerry school hall. The guide company disbanded in the 1990s; the brownie pack was still going in 2000.

During the 1960s, the Gladsmuir Racing Pigeon Club was popular.

A social club was formed in Macmerry in the Miners' Welfare Institute hall in the late 1950s. Originally all the committee members had associations with mining, but now membership has been extended more widely. There is live entertainment in the club most Saturday evenings and the club organises a variety of activities, including computer classes run in conjunction with Jewel and Esk Valley College.

In the Macmerry village hall, a playgroup operated for some years, but has now closed. There is however, a baby and toddler group. A youth club meets in the village hall, and an over-50s club in the Miners' Welfare Institute hall once a month. A lunch club for pensioners meets in the village hall twice a week; it also organises outings for pensioners in the summer and holds a Christmas party.

The bowling club in Macmerry was formed in 1963, and now has 60 members. The green operates from April to September and the club premises are licensed.

The Macmerry St Clair Football Club, which began in the late 19th century, was still active in 1960. They latterly played on a field situated between Whiteloch farm and Winton.

A model aircraft club operated in the north-east corner of Hoprig Mains Farm from c1966-90 before moving to Drem aerodrome.

Since 1990, both residents and visitors have been able to make use of the go-kart centre (see Economy).

Penston Brass Band got its name from the village of Penston on its foundation on 6 April 1842. The band was formed from the 300+ inhabitants of the mining communities, which flourished when coal was the leading industry in the Macmerry/Penston area. Naturally, most of the founder members were miners. Though Penston village has dwindled from a thriving village to a cluster of farm cottages, the band is probably as strong and as 'weel kent' as ever. Some household names to have been associated with the band over the years are the Gray, Watt and Ross families among others. At one time there were no less than 13 members of the Gray family involved with the band, with George Gray conducting between 1912 and 1954. John Gray and John Watt were awarded Life Membership medals.

Possibly the highlights of the band's accomplished history came when they qualified to compete in the national finals in London in 1962 and 1974. Walter Ross took over the band in 1954, maintaining one of Macmerry's finest and proudest traditions. The band, which is self-supporting, still rehearses in Macmerry and still plays at galas, fair days, and garden fetes.

Economy

At the end of the war, there were still about 15 men in the village of Macmerry employed in mining, either at Dalkeith or at Bilston, and until the 1970s a number of men from Macmerry continued to work in coalmines. Most of the other men worked in the building industry or in farming.

By 2000 many of the residents of Macmerry travelled to work in local towns or in Edinburgh. The companies that set up on the Macmerry Industrial Estate often brought a nucleus of their own workers with them, but they also employed some local labour. Some of them, such as Weber Marking Systems, employed mainly women.

Macmerry airfield was located at the east end of the village on land belonging to Hoprig Mains Farm where an air strip had been laid out for the Edinburgh Flying Club in 1935. In its first year, the club had a membership of 114, of whom 29 were qualified pilots. In 1937 Macmerry became a passenger airport on the route from Aberdeen, to Perth, Macmerry and then south to Newcastle and Doncaster. It operated a request service. During World War II, the RAF requisitioned the airstrip.

Afterwards, it was returned to the flying club (reopened 31 August 1946), which continued to use it until 1955 when its activities were transferred to Turnhouse, west of Edinburgh. The site has since been used for industry (the go-karting centre and Macmerry Industrial Estate) and agriculture.

The go-kart racing centre attracts people from quite a wide area. In 1990, go-karting started on part of the former wartime airfield; in 1992/3, Karting Indoors Ltd. erected a modern

Economy (cont)

Go-karting at Macmerry, 1992

building. The name was changed to Raceland in 1995/6 when an outdoor amenity was added. There are about 20 people employed at the facility, 90% of them from East Lothian. Go-karters come from the Lothians, Edinburgh, Central Region, Borders and England.

Economy – Industry

During the 1939/45 war, a factory was set up by the Air Ministry to the north of Gladsmuir village on part of the Elvingston estate. It repaired planes for the wartime aerodromes in the county.

Between 1946-59, Calum Grant & Partners Ltd set up a light engineering firm on the site of these wartime hangars; in 1959, they sold out to Ayrshire Dockyard Company. They changed the name to Lothian Structural Development Company (LSD); this firm manufactured pylons and towers, which carried overhead electric cables, and became one of Britain's main pylon producers. Various types of towers were made, such as those used to mount floodlighting of football grounds, and towers for supporting ski lifts in Scotland. At one time the factory employed around 350 workers and produced 350 tons of steelwork per week.

In 1976 W.N. Lindsay Grain Merchants, Leith took over the premises vacated by LSD. The buildings consisted of an office block and two hangars. Since then, four sheds have been built and three grain dryers installed. From 1982-91 the firm traded as Wholesale Grain Merchants. From 1991 to date, they have purchased two smaller companies and a farm as well; large transactions are negotiated with the agricultural industry. Local people and seasonal workers are employed.

Economy - Industry (cont)

On the Penston road to the west of Gladsmuir, planning permission was granted in 1975 to Truck Crete Ltd for a readymix concrete business. It was acquired by Aggregate Industries UK Ltd in 1989 and operates as a readymix concrete batching plant. It employs one full-time operator on the site with an average of four truck drivers and attendant maintenance and supervisory staff. The plant supports the sand and gravel quarry at Longyester.

From 1998 the Elvingston Science Centre (see Land Ownership), has provided accommodation for nine companies involved in electronics and the manufacture of software as well as Simpson Research Ltd. This was a collaborative venture between Scottish Enterprise, Edinburgh & Lothian (SEEL), East Lothian Council, Napier University and Simpson Research Ltd, a technology consultancy company.

Since the late 1950s, the council has encouraged industrial development at the Macmerry Industrial Estate, east of the village, which opened on 23 September 1960. In 1963, East Lothian County Council had agreed to build the first advance factory on the site. The intention was to attract industry to the area to provide jobs following the decline in mining. By 1965, the site had been serviced at a cost of more than £100,000, and the first project, a 20,000 square foot warehouse for the Scottish Grocers' Federation was opened in 1966.

Although it only provided 20 jobs, it was hoped that other enterprises would soon follow. The take-up of units on the site was slow, but an upholstery firm, Classic Upholstery Service moved in and a firm manufacturing mobile classrooms moved to the area from Peterborough. This was Elliotts (East Lothian) Ltd later Elliott Medway. Hart Builders also took up premises

Macmerry Industrial Estate, 1966 (A.G. Ingram Ltd)

Economy - Industry (cont)

on the site. By 1968 a fifth factory was being built for a precision engineering firm McKettrick-Agnew & Co Ltd who were moving from Musselburgh and employed 30-40 people. In 1971 United Sintering, a subsidiary of United Wire Ltd of Edinburgh moved in. They produced precision metal castings, and employed around 30 people.

In 1972 the Macmerry Industrialist's Association was set up. Bisset & Steedman moved their colour television servicing depot, employing about a dozen skilled men from Musselburgh, to a new unit at Macmerry and a small Musselburgh firm, Newhailes Plastics (which manufactured glass fibre products) moved in. Alande Designs, which employed up to 20 people in the production of modern clothing, moved from Haddington to one of the units in Macmerry.

In addition to providing more suitable premises for existing local firms, the estate began to have more success in attracting firms from outwith the area. Cookson & Zinn, specialist manufacturers of storage tanks, moved from Suffolk to Macmerry in 1972 because of the development of North Sea oil. They took over premises occupied for three years by Eastore, the only company on the site so far to have gone out of business, the result of the failure of a major contract. The company's workforce and the skills they had built up had, however, been instrumental in attracting Cookson & Zinn to the area. Weber Marking Systems, which manufactured stencils, ink and printers for use in industry, moved from Reading to Macmerry in 1973. By 1973 therefore only four of the original 32 acres of the site were still available for further development and the council was considering the acquisition of additional land for the building of advance factories.

With the industrial slow-down in the later 1970s and 1980s however, there was little new development on the site and some firms such as Elliott Medway were forced into staff reductions and redundancies. It was not until the 1990s that there was further growth, with Had Fab expanding their production of phone masts. By the end of this period the industrial estate was busy, although there was always some changeover in the firms occupying sites. There were also plans for further development on the site between the A199 road and the A1 dual carriageway to the north of the village.

The principal occupants of premises on the industrial estate at the end of the period were East Lothian Council with a base for vehicle and plant maintenance; Northcross Works, manufacturing fittings for museums, exhibitions etc; and Lothian Tractors, Numac Engineering, Bindery Machinery Services, McBirnie Coachworks, ITW Industrial Finishing, Had Fab Steel Fabricators, Pentair Enclosures, Scotprint, Hart Builders, CR Joinery, Reywood and David James Kitchens and Bathrooms.

Economy - Agriculture

Agriculture in the parish was devoted mainly to intensive cereal production, although there were some cattle and sheep; the Co-op kept a dairy herd at Adniston until the 1970s. The acreage of autumn-sown wheat expanded following the introduction of new improved high yielding varieties. Mechanisation made it feasible to sow larger acreages well in advance of winter and chemicals were available to protect the crop from disease and weed infestation throughout the long growing period. On the farm, grain driers had the capacity to reduce moisture to the required levels. The acreage of oats declined sharply, but some potatoes were still grown. Sugar beet was still being grown at Greendykes Farm until the closure in 1971 of the sugar beet factory at Cupar, Fife. Where winter keep for cattle was required, grass silage was the usual crop. Oil seed rape began to be grown from the late 1980s. Tractors and other farm implements became progressively larger and more powerful throughout the period. There was a growth in contracting work on farms. Clydesdale horses were bred and exhibited by the farmer at Greendykes in the 1970s and 1980s.

> *'When we moved through from the Borders to Greendykes Farm, Macmerry in December 1949, I was surprised to see that horses were still used on the farm. There must have been five or six pairs of horses working, from ploughing to pulling carts etc and each pair were looked after by one farm worker. Horses doing this sort of work were rarely seen in the Borders at that time'.*
> Arnott Craigs

In 2000, the farms in the parish are: Gladsmuir (59 acres), Hoprig, Hoprig Mains, Penston, Westbank, West Adniston, Greendykes and East Adniston, Chesterhall Hodges, Samuelston Mid Mains, Samuelston East Mains, Samuelston West Mains, Merryhatton, Coates, Redcoll (250acres), Trabroun + Laverocklaw (379 acres), Southfield, Chesterhall, Longniddry, Harelaw, Wheatrig Setonhill and Redhouse. All are owner-occupied except the Hodges (on the Winton estate), and Longniddry Farm, Setonhill, Wheatrig, Harelaw, Redhouse (all of which are on the Wemyss estate).

Jean Shirlaw describes the farms on the Elvingston estate, from 1944-80:

They were Redcoll, Trabroun, Laverocklaw and Hopefield (not in Gladsmuir parish). When the estate was bought in 1944 by David Lowe & Sons Ltd. (Musselburgh) it was mixed farming specialising also in horticulture. The firm also owned land in Prestonpans where vegetables were grown under special heated conditions. In 1962, the partnership was dissolved leaving David and his brother Arthur to form Elvingston Estate Ltd. David, the Chairman, lived in Elvingston House and Arthur (who is still alive) lives in Redcoll.

From 1944 until 1980, when Sir David died, quite a large part of the land was used for horticulture. Over the years, a large variety of vegetables were grown such as cabbage (Savoy, spring, red); cauliflower both early and late varieties; broccoli, curly kale, French and broad beans. There would be about eight-nine acres of celery, 30 acres of carrots and turnips, and 50 acres of cabbage lettuces were grown. They were famous for their own specially bred leeks (short and long) and sprouts, which would cover together about 40 acres. Among other vegetables grown were potatoes, marrows, courgettes, cucumbers and tomatoes.

Another venture was fruit growing. It was not unusual to see a field of rhubarb or blackcurrants and maybe five acres of raspberry canes. It was beautiful to see 20 acres of plum trees in blossom in the spring with some of their own specially bred daffodils blooming between the rows of plum trees.

Forestry Alba Trees Ltd occupied a site on the eastern edge of the parish beside Butterdean wood, which it bought in 1988 (formerly part of the Elvingston estate). It has since developed into the largest native tree nursery in the UK, specialising in raising native trees from seed in environmentally suitable conditions. It has supplied 60 million trees all over the UK and

Economy - Agriculture (cont)

abroad. Alba Trees Ltd has about 30 permanent employees and a further ten or more on contracts. It has recently received a Royal Warrant and an East Lothian Business Achievement award.

This account of Gladsmuir parish was compiled & edited by Kathy Fairweather. Additional information, research and essays were provided by Jean Shirlaw and the following:

David Sydeserff   Economy - Agriculture
David Welsh   General information
Margaret Welsh   General information
J. Wilson   Leisure - Penston Band

And the recollections of Arnott Craigs (agriculture – horses at Greendykes); Fiona Dobson (homes - Penston Gardens); Wendy Goldstraw, nee Bruce (belief); Pat Moncrieff (education – Macmerry Primary School 1952-69)

Additional assistance was given by: Dorothy Baillie, Jean Beveridge, Rev Graham Black, Alistair W Bremner, Tom Cameron, Margaret Fortune, Tim Hall, William Hogg, Mrs Jenkinson (Snr), Arthur Lowe, A Lindsay, Betty Livingstone, Calum Nisbet, Duncan Orr, Dr David Simpson, Edward Sommerville, Ian Thomson, John Wallace, Derek Wood and the Church of Scotland General Trustees.

FURTHER READING & REFERENCES
Blair, Catherine (1940) *Rural Journey: a History of the SWRI*
Land Use Consultants for the Countryside Commission for Scotland, CCS (later Scottish Natural Heritage, SNH) and Historic Buildings and Monuments Directorate, Scottish Development Department (first published c 1987, 1997 reprint) *The Inventory of Gardens & Designed Landscapes in Scotland: Volume 5: Lothian & Borders*
Macmerry Primary School (1989) *A Centenary Magazine*
Ramsay, J. *'Gladsmuir Parish' The New Statistical Account of Scotland (1845)* pp173-202
East Lothian Life (Summer 2000) edited version of Sharon, Monica 'First Lady of Mak'merry'
Scottish Home & Country (December 1987)
Shirlaw, Jean H. (1988/89) *A Short History of Gladsmuir*
Wiseman, W. E. (c1960) *Gladsmuir Parish*

There is a privately-held Catherine Blair archive; please contact the Local History Centre, Haddington for further information.

GLADSMUIR – LONGNIDDRY
PARISH REPRESENTATIVE: *David M. Robertson*

Introduction

The concept of Gladsmuir parish has now little relevance to Longniddry; by 1945 it was a parish in its own right. It remained in the registration district of Gladsmuir to 1967, but thereafter registrations took place in Prestonpans. As a council electoral ward, it was 'North Gladsmuir', then 'Gladsmuir'. The present Longniddry electoral ward excludes Gladsmuir and Macmerry, but takes in a large part of the east end of Port Seton. The postal address 'Longniddry' includes several farms at some distance from the village, as does the catchment area of Longniddry Primary School, and a number of these places lie outwith the boundaries of the old parish of Gladsmuir. The remainder of Gladsmuir parish is dealt with separately. *See p15.*

Longniddry village is bounded on the north by the Firth of Forth. To the west and south of the village lies rich agricultural land, growing mostly cereals and oilseed rape. The ground rises gradually to the south, to the Gladsmuir ridge some two miles away. On the east side, are the woods of Gosford estate. Apart from a few stone-built pantiled cottages on Main Street, Longniddry consists almost entirely of dwelling houses built in the 20th century.

In 1945, Longniddry was a medium-sized village in a rural setting, where many people still worked locally. Apart from the older Main Street cottages, the village could be divided physically and socially into three - the business and professional people in the private houses, the war veterans of the 'Garden City' who came from all over Britain, and the tenants of the council houses, mostly (but not all) working folk of more or less local stock.

Service personnel had been based nearby at Gosford, (where there was also a prisoner-of-war camp), and further off at Macmerry; wartime Longniddry was in a 'restricted area', making life difficult.

Environment

Longniddry lies just outside the East Lothian coalfield; in the 1950s-62, a small mine was operated at Glencairn, near Cantyhall. Blindwells opencast mine exploited a massive swathe of countryside between Longniddry and Tranent from the 1970s until the end of the century, approaching to within a mile of the south-west corner of the village.

Rainfall is low, the prevailing wind is from the west, and snow does not usually lie long. As far as wildlife is concerned, the most obvious newcomers are collared doves and magpies, which were unknown in 1945 but are now very common in Longniddry. Buzzards now nest in Gosford estate, and are now frequently seen around Longniddry and even over the village itself.

Grey squirrels, unknown in the 1940s and 1950s, now abound; foxes too are seen more frequently than before. Brown hares and partridges have declined, and the water hen seems to have disappeared from the local burns.

> *'…they'd have a hare shoot, and they would come from Cantyha' right along through towards Ballencrieff … and it wasnae unusual for them to shoot two hundred hares. Now I would hazard a guess that you'd be lucky to see two hundred hares in East Lothian!'*
Archie Mathieson

Many fine old trees around the village have now succumbed to old age or Dutch elm disease. One elm near the shops in Links Road so far remains miraculously unaffected. Two

Environment (cont)

ancient sycamore trees in front of Longniddry Primary School are of note because John Knox is traditionally said to have preached beneath them.

The foreshore acquired three large car parks (Tindall, F.P. (1998) pp37-40). The largest, at Ferny Ness (just in Aberlady parish), incorporates a network of permanent and semi-permanent tracks in an area formerly noted for its wildflowers. In the 1960s, East Lothian County Council carried out a programme of work to stabilise the sand dunes and check erosion along the foreshore. Sea buckthorn, marram grass and sea lyme grass were planted with remarkable success. By far the greatest visual impact on the foreshore environment was the construction of the Cockenzie Power Station across the bay.

Aerial view of Longniddry, 1946   *(Crown Copyright: RCAHMS (RAF Aerial Pdotographs Collection))*

Land Ownership (see Homes)

A century ago, the Earl of Wemyss owned almost everything; Wemyss & March Estates are in general, very reluctant to sell buildings, preferring to renovate and rent. With a few exceptions, most of the older property in and around the village is still in their hands. They still own Longniddry Farm, Harelaw, Redhouse, Wheatrig and Setonhill, all of which are tenanted.

Other farms in the Longniddry area are Seton East, Seton Mains, Chesterhall, Southfield, Redcoll, the Coats, Harelaw, the Spittal, and Lochhill. The farmers of Redcoll and Southfield own their farms. Elsewhere the picture is confusing. The Spittal has been divided up among neighbouring farmers, as has much of Lochhill. There is no longer a resident farmer at Seton Mains, Seton East or Chesterhall, and the land is farmed from elsewhere. The land within Gosford policies is let out to various farmers, while the adjacent Harelaw fields are farmed by the estate itself. The steadings at Chesterhall and Seton Mains have been converted into housing. Harelaw steading is now an equestrian centre. Seton East steading has been almost entirely demolished, and the remaining building houses a farm shop.

Few cottages are now needed for farm workers, so they have been renovated and either sold or rented out. Thus, for the first time in history, only a tiny minority of the population of the farms in the Longniddry area is actually engaged in farming.

In Longniddry itself the estate has released land for development. From 1916 on, the Scottish Veterans' Garden Cities Association built houses for war veterans on estate land near the station – the Garden City. East Lothian County Council acquired land and, between the wars, three streets of council houses were built – Elcho Terrace, John Knox Road and Amisfield Place. By 1945, six streets of private housing had also appeared – Links Road, Elcho Road, Seton Road, Douglas Road, Kings Road and Gosford Road.

In the early 1960s the Wemyss estate began selling feus on 68 acres of land to the west of the village. Meanwhile, the fields lying between Wemyss Road and Gosford Road also filled rapidly with private housing.

Until the mid 1960s, a roughly equal balance was maintained between owner-occupied and rented houses. That changed with the advent of massive private building. The right-to-buy for council tenants skewed the situation even further in favour of private ownership. Council housing stock in 1975 was 189; 37 houses have been built since then, but at 31 March 2001 council housing stock was only 113. Since 226 council houses have been built in Longniddry, and only 113 remain in council hands, 113 must therefore have been sold. Thus, exactly 50% of former council housing in Longniddry is now owner-occupied.

Townscapes, Buildings, & Landscapes of Distinction

Several buildings have been awarded B listed status by Historic Scotland. Longniddry House (B listed) is supposedly 18th century, but its origins are obscure. The West Lodge is Longniddry's most eye-catching building, and is A listed. The school (B) was completed in 1931, designed by county architect F.W. Hardy. A modern extension was completed in 1978.

The 18 houses for war veterans in the 'Garden City', begun in 1916 (architects Henry and MacLennan) are all B listed; also worth a mention are the council houses in Elcho Terrace (Dick Peddie and Walker Todd 1921). Of the 20th century villa development, two houses in Gosford Road – 'Harmony' (Tarbolton and Ochterlony 1933), and 'The Cottage' (Basil Spence c1955) –

Townscapes, Buildings, & Landscapes of Distinction (cont)

are of note as is the B listed 'Eventyre', Lyars Road (Ian G Lindsay of Orphoot, Whiting and Lindsay 1936).

Some local farm steadings have been partially demolished to accommodate modern farm buildings. Others have been converted into housing. At Longniddry Farm the original steading is more or less complete, and it and the farmhouse are B listed. At Harelaw, the farmhouse and cottages have been tastefully restored (B listed). The steading, now housing riding stables, is entered under an interesting little tower with a pointed roof, which contains a doocot.

Population
By Gladsmuir parish*, from the General Registrar's office

				By locality – census – ie Longniddry itself		
1931	1779	860M	919F			
1951	2001	1008M	993F	780**		
1961	2173	1094M	1079F	928**		
1971	3039	1479M	1560F	1490	703M	787F
1981	4349	2097M	2252F	2901	1394M	1507F
				By Small Area Statistics - census		
1991	4383	2126M	2257F	2786	1350M	1436F
2001	3894	1872M	2022F	--	--	--
By Gladsmuir parish, from ELDC				*By settlement, from ELDC*		
1991	4069					
1997 (est.)	4271	2087M	2184F	2924		
2001	NO DATA			2613 (ELC)		

Population figures are difficult to compare, as no two sources extract data in the same way.

* *the parish figures include Longniddry and Macmerry.*

** *figures for 1951 & 1961 supplied by Anne Blackwood, Population Statistics Branch, General Register Office for Scotland.*

After 1945, a number of German prisoners of war and Polish servicemen settled in the area.

Here and throughout the text, David Robertson comments on Longniddry life:

In the main the Poles and Germans integrated well with the community, and were accepted by it. No better illustration of this could be given than the fact that a former soldier of the German army has carried the colours of the Longniddry branch of the Royal British Legion at their annual Remembrance Day parade.

Only a handful of Longniddry residents are of black/Asian origin, and seem to have no problems in the community. The 'sectarian divide', so obvious in the west of Scotland, is completely foreign to Longniddry. A substantial number of Longniddry residents are English and mildly anti-English remarks are sometimes heard. These should perhaps be treated as 'anti-incomer' sentiments rather than truly anti-English. There is still a feeling in some quarters that Longniddry has been 'swamped' or 'taken over' by incomers. This is more mild discontent rather than burning resentment however, and could not be said to be a real problem. Such thoughts are expressed in private mutterings, and not in overt hostility.

Irish potato workers were a necessary part of the agricultural work force until around 1980. At Longniddry Farm the granary was adapted to house them and a small empty cottage utilised as a cookhouse. A squad of Irish agricultural labourers was based semi-permanently in the farm cottages at Harelaw in the 1960s and 1970s. A few of them lived there all year round, and their numbers were augmented by new arrivals of both men and women in the potato season. They tended to keep themselves to themselves, and were kept very much at arms' length by the local community. Several of the long-term Harelaw residents were 'poor souls' deeply addicted to drink, and only a step above down-and-out status. When Wemyss & March Estates renovated the cottages, the remnants of the squad scattered to goodness knows where, and the contractor, their boss, settled in a neighbouring community.

In recent years, the coastal car parks have become a frequent stopping place for travelling people – 'gypsy travellers', as opposed to 'New Age' travellers. Usually they come in small groups, stay two or three days, and cause no problems. However, in 2000 an exceptionally large contingent stayed several weeks and caused much local indignation by leaving rubbish and excrement lying around, and by supposedly verbally abusing innocent dog-walkers.

Any overview of the population of Longniddry at the beginning of the 21st century reveals it to be overwhelmingly 'middle class'. Most householders are owner-occupiers employed in 'white collar' jobs in a professional or managerial capacity. Very few work in Longniddry itself or the immediate area, and large numbers commute to work in Edinburgh.

In the 1940s and 1950s it would have been obvious that Longniddry was not a homogeneous community. Many of the private houses were large and separated from the rest of the village by fields, and were typically owned by business or professional people who sent their children to private schools. Many of them were speakers of the 'Morningside' brand of Scottish English, which is nowadays fading towards extinction.

The council house tenants were more likely to be manual workers or tradesmen of local origin, more likely to be speakers of local dialect, and almost certain to send their children to the local secondary school. It must be stressed however that Longniddry's streets of council houses bore no resemblance to the modern conception of a 'housing scheme', which in the minds of many is synonymous with crime, fecklessness, and multiple social problems. Longniddry's council tenants were respectable working folk with a substantial mixture of office workers, engineers, teachers, small businessmen, and others who would nowadays no doubt consider themselves 'middle class'. The tenants of the Garden City war veterans' houses came from a variety of backgrounds, but were mainly 'working class' folk, many of them with urban rather than rural roots.

In the 1960s and 1970s the whole physical and social structure of Longniddry was drastically altered by massive private building. Large numbers of people arrived in Longniddry from all corners of the British Isles and beyond, most of them young or in early middle age, and most of them in the professional/managerial bracket; well educated, intelligent, and ambitious for themselves and their families. These people did not carry the social or political baggage of 1950s East Lothian. If there was any driving philosophy it was that of meritocracy where it was up to the individual to progress and succeed by his own efforts. The pretensions of 'toffs' and the complacency of 'villagers' were likely to be treated with impatience or amusement.

Since the sale of council houses began, many of them have been sold on to a new generation of incomers, thus spreading the 'suburban' ethos even further through the community. Longniddry still has dyed-in-the-wool proletarians and wealthy upper-echelon types, but

Population (cont)

nowadays the social levels seem to shade into each other much more than before. Nowadays we all seem to be middle class suburbans.

Housing in Longniddry is expensive. An ex-council house in Forthview Road was recently (2000) put on the market at 'offers over £79,000'. Young people who wish to live locally are more likely to buy a house in Port Seton or Tranent, where property is cheaper.

Throughout Longniddry, the situation is one of a constant stream of young people leaving, and a constant stream of incomers arriving. It is almost certain that the people of each passing generation in Longniddry will be succeeded not by their own progeny but by the children of others, like themselves, from elsewhere. The prevailing culture is therefore likely to be that of middle Scotland (or middle western world) rather than recognisably local.

Belief

Longniddry during the last half of the 20th century certainly contained Roman Catholics, Episcopalians, members of many other Christian sects and denominations, and a handful of Muslims. However, the only religious organisation in Longniddry with a place of worship was the Church of Scotland; members of other denominations and faiths in the village go elsewhere for worship.

Longniddry Parish Church was originally a 'chapel of ease' under Gladsmuir Parish Church; from 1937 it was a church extension charge, and then erected into a parish in 1944. A new manse was completed next to the church in 1985. Gladsmuir is still the usual burial ground for Longniddry. The parishes of Longniddry and Gladsmuir were linked in 1984. Each retains its own church and Kirk Session, the minister serving both, but living in Longniddry.

Ministers

1940-59	John Ford McLeod
1959-70	Robert Inch Johnstone
1972-2000	Andrew Graham Black

May 1984 linked with Gladsmuir under Longniddry minister

A wide variety of activities and organisations are centred on Longniddry parish church. There is Sunday school, TYC (Today's Young Christians) for teenagers, Woman's Guild, Young Women's Group, theatre bus and Traidcraft. The Wednesday Club for pensioners, the WRI and playgroup also meet in the church hall.

George Millar, former session clerk, comments on matters to do with Longniddry Parish Church:

The growth of the village since 1945 has resulted in a radical change in the social and economic character of the church. In 1945, when the Kirk Session numbered 15, there were two farmers, two policemen, two village grocers, the stationmaster, the postman, one schoolteacher, three manual workers, and three who worked in the town. Today (2000), there are 43 elders in the church, of which 13 are women, twelve are men who are retired, and the remaining 18 are all engaged professionally or hold positions in national or international companies.

And a further personal view of changes in the church from David Robertson:

The minister in the 1950s was Mr McLeod, a stout ba'-faced man with a very upper-crust mode of speech. He was a powerful preacher and would thump on the book-board of the pulpit with his fist. He made a majestic entry into the body of the kirk down the central aisle preceded by the beadle bearing the pulpit bible. In those days the bell was rung for a full ten minutes before services. Worship began with the singing of a metrical psalm, and ended with a paraphrase before the benediction. Singing was slow and solemn, and 'amen' was sung at the end of every hymn. The authorised version of the bible was used, and prayers were couched in the same archaic language.

In the 1960s the minister was Mr Johnstone, who was very keen on youth work and local politics. He had an artificial leg, a prominent nose, a 'hingin lip' and a lantern jaw, and was called 'Ahab' by the youths of the village. Some of his congregation were unhappy about his involvement in politics and the fact that his wife worked. During Mr Johnstone's time evening services were replaced by an early morning service. Mr Johnstone was a pedestrian preacher, and church attendances fell away inexorably, and while the church was increasingly deserted by the original residents of the village, incomers seemed disinclined to make up the deficit.

By contrast, Mr Johnstone's successor Graham Black, a man of consummate goodness and sincerity, drew large numbers of new Longniddry residents into the church, to such an extent that 'natives' are now very much a minority in the congregation. The Good News Bible is used, modern hymns are much in vogue, lengthy and flamboyant children's addresses feature strongly, and the Apostles' Creed has staged a comeback from the middle ages. Non-alcoholic wine is used at communion, psalms are almost never heard, and informality has become a cardinal virtue. Attitudes are very much more liberal and tolerant than in the 1950s, and the common media stereotypes of dour Scottish Presbyterianism bear little resemblance to the church in Longniddry.

Most Longniddry people are well-disposed towards the church, but only a tiny proportion of the total population ever attend services. This seems enough, however, to keep the church flourishing.

Some views on baptism:

'Baptisms within the church occur on a regular basis, although many parents, especially those without a church connection, decide not to have their child baptised, but to leave any church involvement to be decided by the child as he reaches maturity'.
George Millar

On confirmation:

'Fifty years ago, becoming a member of the church was for many an automatic thing, as part of the process of growing up in the community. However, today this commitment is not seen as something teenagers wish to embrace as a matter of course, and it would appear that nowadays the majority of young people have in fact switched worlds, stepping out of the communal world of the church, which of course is often identified with their parents, in search of an alternative social world'.
George Millar

On marriage:

'Within the church a number of marriage ceremonies are conducted each year. However, the church has also come to accept that living with a partner is no barrier to church membership and involvement with the church organisations'.
George Millar

Belief (cont)

A crowd of local women and children always gathered on the pavement outside the church. Confetti was thrown with liberal abandon, and lay in drifts in the gutter for days after. As the wedding party drove off, coins were scattered for the children. The reception would usually be in a hotel in a neighbouring town or village, as there were no facilities for wedding receptions in Longniddry. This would usually include dancing to a 'live' band, usually a Scottish country dance band. When Gordon Morrison, the farmer of Longniddry Farm, married around 1950 the reception took the form of a 'kirn' in the farm granary.

It sometimes happened that pregnancy was the cause of the marriage. This was supposedly frowned upon, but was more often a cause for quiet amusement than condemnation. The birth of a child to an unmarried mother was a fairly rare event, but such children were never discriminated against in any way.

Waiting for the bride. The women of the village spectating at a wedding in 1951 (A&J Gordon)

Attitudes to courtship and marriage seem to have changed greatly since the 1950s and 1960s. Teenagers seem much more inclined to play the field than to 'go steady'. It is now more or less taken for granted that both boys and girls will be sexually experienced by their late teens, and it has become common for established couples to move in together. Whereas in the 1950s and 1960s the usual age for marriage was in the early or mid 20s, now it is occurring much later, and almost all couples who marry will have lived together first. It is also not unusual for partners living together to have children. From being a near-compulsory requirement of society, marriage seems to be on the point of becoming an optional extra.

Whereas in the 1950s and 1960s pre-marital sex tended to be a furtive business of discreet fornication behind hedges, it has now come to be regarded almost as a right akin to 'Life,

Belief (cont)

Liberty, and the Pursuit of Happiness'. Parents whose sons or daughters are living with partners may not wholeheartedly approve, but the usual attitude is, 'What can you do? You don't want to lose them'.

Anecdotal evidence suggests that a great deal of 'high jinks' went on during the war years and immediately thereafter. Similarly, teenagers growing up in the early 1960s gained the impression that there had been more scope locally for sexual adventure in the 1950s than in their own time. The official consensus of opinion in Longniddry in those days was that sexual activity outside marriage was 'wrong'. In fact of course a great deal of it did go on, but was mostly conducted discreetly. Respectable girls were supposed to say no, although sometimes respectability could be more a case of succumbing only after lengthy persuasion instead of participating enthusiastically from the outset. All the same, the ideal of the virgin bride was probably often enough attained in reality. The 'sexual revolution' which is supposed to have been the hallmark of the 1960s probably took a little longer to arrive in Longniddry. Certainly, virginity in both sexes persisting for several years beyond the age of consent was not unusual in the Longniddry of the 1960s.

Adultery was not unknown in the 1950s and 1960s. This was always roundly condemned but at the same time the gossip was greatly savoured and was often a source of much amusement. No matter how discreet the participants tried to be, the whole village seemed to be party to what was going on.

Homes

Longniddry has become by far the largest settlement in the old parish of Gladsmuir. A mile to the west the farm of Seton Mains has itself become a small village centred on a converted steading and renovated cottages. Chesterhall nearby has been similarly reinvented.

Longniddry grew only very slowly in the 20 years after the end of the second world war, a trend not continued thereafter; the land built on between 1945 and 2000 was all prime agricultural land.

After the second world war, the council extended Amisfield Place with a street of prefabs, prefabricated metal temporary houses containing the unheard-of luxuries of fridges and partial central heating. More council houses were built in the 1950s in Wemyss Road; the first stage - all Orlits - was built of rather ugly concrete blocks. These council houses all had large gardens, since it was expected that families would wish to grow their own vegetables.

'I always made porridge in the morning. Dinner was always at night. Always soup - all kinds of vegetables, lentil soup. Stovies. We loved our stovies ... Steam puddings, well, dumplings - clootie dumplings ... Lots of plain cooking. They really liked that. We had loads of vegetables because we had the allotment. Cakes, scones of course, biscuits, fly-cakes ... We grew all our own fruit - blackcurrants, redcurrants, strawberries, raspberries of course. I think sometimes it was healthier living than it is nowadays.'
Mrs J Robertson

'It was mainly soup. And we all grew our own vegetables of course. Everybody had a garden. The meal was at night. Just the usual - stew, and mince, mince and tatties. What else? We would have fish ...'
Anon

Homes (cont)

In the post-war years there were no houses in Longniddry without hot and cold running water, a bath, and an indoor lavatory.

Nevertheless,

A bath once a week was still deemed sufficient for some children in the 1950s, and if you ventured too close in the classroom your nose would tell you that this was more than one or two fellow-pupils got.

The council replaced the prefabs with Church Way in 1967, and built Forthview Road in several stages in the 1960s and 1970s. The last council houses to be built were Park View and, in 1985, the pensioners' houses in Wemyss Place.

Young couples embarking on marriage in the 1940s and 1950s did not usually have much spare money, and the innovation of hire purchase took a while to catch on, furniture was often second-hand, or donated by or inherited from relatives.

'Well, at that time most people had second-hand furniture, if I can remember. They couldnae afford to buy anything else … Most of mine was my mother's.'
Anon

'It [furniture] was rather sparse, I would say. No carpets of course. Only lino … Well, when I look back we had iron bedsteads. But these are all fashionable nowadays, aren't they?
… This living-room was used as a bedroom. And we lived in that. We had a bed settee eventually, which was great, wasn't it?'
Mrs J Robertson

Cooking was a much more labour-intensive operation in post-war Longniddry than it is today. In the years immediately after the war not all of the Main Street cottages had electricity, and although all the council houses built before the war in Longniddry did have electricity, not everyone had an electric cooker. The houses had a large cast-iron range in the living room/kitchen. Trivets allowed the housewife to cook over the open fire, and flues heated an oven built into the range.

Labour-saving devices and luxuries came slowly:

'I remember getting a 'carpet square'. Oh, I thought that was wonderful. And that led to a hoover. So I got a second-hand old-fashioned Hoover. That was something!'
Mrs J Robertson

'We had a wireless, and Tom Greig (the garage proprietor) used to - ken these accumulators? There were two of these accumulators, and every week one was put into the garage to be charged … Tom Greig was the first to get a television. And then Billy's mother and father. They got the television for … the Coronation.'
Anon

A handful of households had television in time for Queen Elizabeth's coronation in 1953. Children would gather in the evenings to watch television in the houses of their more fortunate neighbours. However, the open-house policies and generous invitations to come in anytime soon became less freely offered. Television quickly gained in popularity, and by 1960 probably most households had it.

Homes (cont)

Glassel Park advances over Mitchell's fields, c1970

(A&J Gordon)

Advertisement for Cruden which appeared in The Scotsman, 13 September 1970

(Cruden Investments Ltd)

Private house building picked up in the 1960s. Gap sites between the 1920/30s villas were filled after the second world war, and latterly some owners of houses with spacious gardens began to sell off plots for further building.

Meanwhile in the early 1960s building in earnest took off to the west of Links Road, on 68 acres of land that the Wemyss estate earmarked for development. Glassel Park began as an estate of individually designed houses. However, the ground was sold to Cruden, and the fields around Longniddry House and Longniddry Gardens quickly filled with mass-produced 'identikit' housing - detached, harled, tile-roofed, cottage-type homes with small gardens – which swept over the site, at a substantially greater density than had originally been planned.

A third phase extended over the old Dean Road to Longniddry Dean. Meanwhile, Wimpey filled in the remaining vacant land with similar private building, forming an extension to Douglas Road. At around the same time the ground that had belonged to Elcho Nurseries was also built over behind Church Way.

By 1970, all the available farmland had been filled between Longniddry Dean to the west, Gosford estate to the east, the golf course to the north, and the railway to the south. This more than quadrupled the size of the village, and radically altered its social composition.

The village is now virtually a dormitory suburb of Edinburgh for the clerical, professional, and executive middle classes.

During the 1990s, proposals emerged to build a 'new town' on farmland stretching from Longniddry up to Hoprig. This caused outrage among most Longniddry residents, and was eventually refused planning permission. A suspicion remains, however, that the threat has not entirely gone away, and that the building firms will be back in the future, perhaps with a succession of smaller-scale plans which will gradually nibble away Longniddry's rural setting.

Homes (cont)

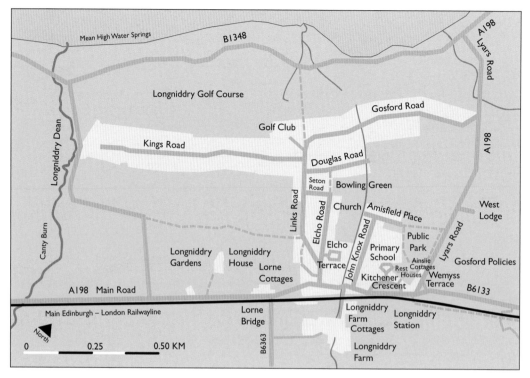

Housing Expansion: Longniddry c.1945 (above)

Housing Expansion: Longniddry late 1950s (below)

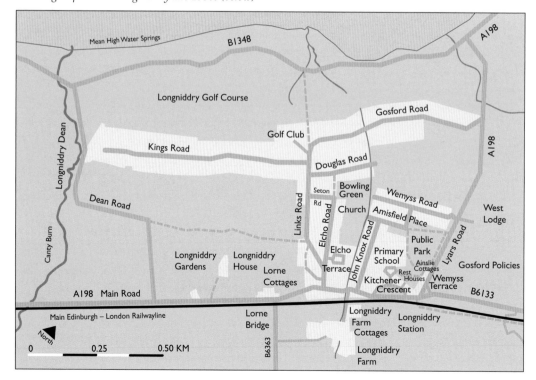

Homes (cont)

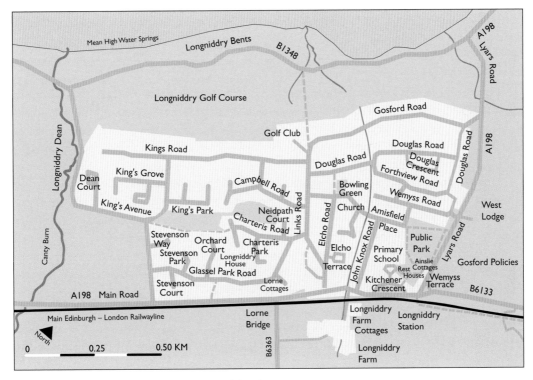

Housing Expansion: Longniddry early 1970s (above)

Housing Expansion: Longniddry late 1990s (below)

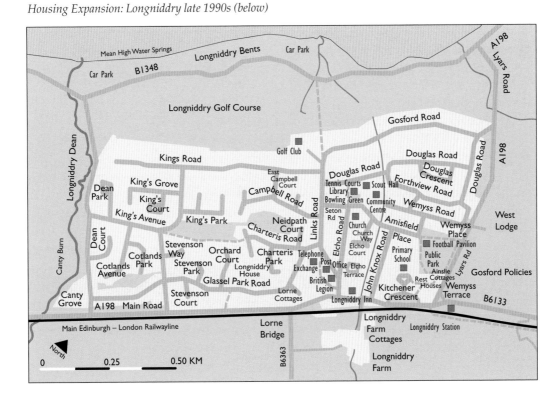

Utilities

Raw sewage was discharged into the sea until the late 1950s when a sewage treatment plant was built on the coast road. Treatment was only partial, however, and effluent continued to be discharged into the sea through a new outlet at Ferny Ness.

Longniddry beach suffered greatly from sewage pollution in the period 1945-2000, and became so notorious for this that nowadays, in spite of fine stretches of sand, few people would venture into the water. In 1999 the water here was found to contain 100 times the level of sewage-derived bacteria recommended by the EU; East Lothian Council posted notices warning against bathing.

A new sewage system taking waste to Seafield from Port Seton, Prestonpans and Musselburgh was completed in 2000, and improvements have also been made to the Ferny Ness treatment plant, so the situation should improve. In 2000, Longniddry beach was still not fit to be classified as a bathing beach.

Longniddry has long been connected to the public water supply and, apart from certain Main Street cottages, which were not connected until c1950, all homes had been connected to mains electricity. Mains gas became available in the 1980s.

There has been a rubbish collection throughout the period; the council has recently started a waste paper collection. There was a bottle bank for several years outside the Links Road shop and one beside the tennis courts off Douglas Road. There are now no bottle banks in the village.

Shops & Services

Longniddry's main role throughout the period 1945-2000 has been as a dormitory settlement, rather than as a centre of employment; until the 1960s and 1970s some local employment was available on the land and the railway.

Until the 1950s, residents shopped for food and other domestic necessities in the village. In the final decades of the 20th century, car owners began to buy in bulk from superstores within easy driving distance.

The commercial centre of Longniddry became more concentrated on the south end of Links Road in the 1970s, with the building of a row of new shops near the already existing Stuart's grocer's shop and the Co-operative store. By this time, some other retail businesses elsewhere in the village had given up or moved, and several cottages, a shop, and a smiddy on the Main Street were being developed as the Longniddry Inn (a pub/restaurant).

In the 1940s and 1950s there were grocers' shops, a baker, and a butcher in Longniddry, and several vans also served the village.

Clothes could be bought new in Musselburgh or Edinburgh, or in the drapery departments of the East Lothian Co-operative Society in Tranent or Haddington. Many children's clothes however were 'made down' from garments outgrown by elder brothers or sisters. Most housewives knitted and sewed to some extent. Everyone could darn and mend.

'I used to knit an awful lot. Knitted all the jerseys and things. My aunt used to make things for the children. She was a sewer. I wasn't so good at the sewing.'
Anon

Shops & Services (cont)

*Links Road, 1960s.
Stuart's grocer's shop
(once Bruce's bakery),
now a vet's surgery.
Further along is the
East Lothian
Co-operative Society.
'The Store' nowadays
has a pitched,
pantiled roof.*
(A&J Gordon)

*Links Road, 1950s.
Gordons' photography
business with
Gardner's butcher's
shop on left.*
(A&J Gordon)

*Links Road 1960s.
Douglas Welsh's
optician's premises
have long gone.
Note Chirnside's
lorry loaded with
coal.*
(A&J Gordon)

Shops and Services (cont)

'I used to make my own clothes ... and for the children. I used to go to - was it, Parkers? Up in Edinburgh. I used to get material - was it Bristo? Near the Infirmary. But often they were made down from other clothes ... I loved my fair isle. The boys had fair isle tammies.'
Mrs J Robertson

In the late 1940s and early 1950s, the retail outlets were as follows:
Links Road
> East Lothian Co-operative Society store;
> bakery (William Wallace Bruce);
> hairdresser (Margaret Thomson Murray) in a small wooden shop.

Links Road, *on the opposite side facing the above*
> butcher (Andrew Stevenson Gardner);
> photographer (A. & J. Gordon) - shop and studio.

Main Street *north side*
> blacksmith (Andrew & George Chirnside);
> grocer (Claude H McDougall);
> post office (postmaster Robert Smith)

Main Street *south side*
> grocer (Alexander & James G Stuart);
> chemist (Douglas Alexander Welsh);
> bank (Royal Bank of Scotland);
> garage (Longniddry Engineering Coy.)

Garden City
> confectioner and tobacconist (Mrs Margaret Thomson Murray);
> cobbler (Donald Fraser);
> confectioner and newsagent (William J Watt) - wooden shop;
> chip shop (Matthew Y Hardy) - wooden shop.

Elcho Road
> vegetable shop and market garden (Alexander Campbell).

(The subsequent history of these premises can be found on the CD ROM).

Anecdotes about a few of these follow.

East Lothian Co-operative Society had an important part to play in the community. Universally known as 'the Store', in the years after the second world war it was still run on a genuinely co-operative basis. The customers were shareholders, and a careful account was kept of their purchases so that a dividend could be paid to them. This dividend was eagerly anticipated in an era when customers were by no means as affluent as they are now. In the 1940s and 1950s, customers at the Store were served at two counters, one for foodstuffs, and one for firelighters, bundles of kindling, Zebo, Vim, and other household goods. Payment was made at a little glass-fronted office at the far end of the shop. Cooked meat was sliced and weighed according to the customer's request. Cheese was also cut and weighed to requirements, and sugar and salt scooped into thick paper bags. Nowadays only pre-packed goods are sold. Customers serve themselves from shelves and display cabinets, and pay at a checkout by the door.

McDougall's grocer's shop in Main Street did brisk business early in the morning with the squads of female agricultural workers stopping to buy their 'pieces'. The shop had a distinctive smell of coffee beans

Shops and Services (cont)

McDougall's grocer's shop, Main Street, 1950s, now part of the Longniddry Inn
(A&J Gordon)

and paraffin, canvas sunshades above the windows and, for a time, the village's only chewing-gum vending machine.

When McDougall's closed c1960, J. G. Stuart & Sons was left as the Co-op's only rival. Stuart's was thought of as being rather more up-market than The Store. Customers could run up hefty accounts, and could have their purchases delivered to their door. Alec Stuart, who took over from his father, was a church elder and session clerk, had a dry sense of humour, and was something of a village character. Small gatherings of favoured friends were allowed discreet evening refreshments in the back shop. Customer loyalty, however, did not survive the wider choice and cheaper prices offered by the superstores that sprang up within easy driving distance from the 1970s onwards, and credit cards soon made the whole business of a grocer's account an anachronism.

A. & J. Gordon, photographers, operated in the village from the 1930s until the 1980s, and recorded most of the significant events in the life of the community and the lives of the villagers. A large selection of the Gordons' photographic negatives is now with East Lothian's Local History Library.

Douglas Welsh, the chemist and optician, was well known in his day as a radio singer, and the inventor and manufacturer of Welsh's Pink Hand Lotion. His wife, Catherine Meston, was a pianist, and his son, Moray, became a noted cellist (see Miscellany).

Mr Watt, the newsagent, had lost both hands and an arm in the first world war, but could measure out quarters of sweeties from jars with practised ease, and would write up accounts with a pencil held in an elastic band round his wrist. He also painted pottery, which is now quite sought after, and signed his finished pieces with grim irony – 'Stump'.

In the 1950s and early 1960s there were several vans and mobile shops serving Longniddry. East Lothian Co-operative Society sent round a 'Store' butcher's van, a baker's van, and even for a time a draper's van. There was also a Dickson's butcher's van, a Gardner's butcher's van, and a Greig's fish van from Port Seton. A Mr Forsyth also served Longniddry with a baker's van in the 1950s, and a fruit and vegetable merchant sold his goods from a lorry. From the 1950s until at least the 1970s a Tranent barber, James McCran, came to Longniddry first on a bike, then a moped, and latterly by car, to cut customers' hair in their own homes.
(This list may well be incomplete).

Shops and Services (cont)

As people began to shop at superstores, the number of vans and mobile shops declined, and there now appear to be only James Dickson and J.K. Thomson's fish vans, and a fruit and vegetable van.

Milk was delivered in the early 1950s by the Dumfriesshire Dairy and by East Lothian Co-op, and from then until the 1970s by the Co-op alone. Sometime around the 1980s, East Lothian Co-op discontinued milk deliveries and their customers were taken over by Robert Wiseman Dairies, who still operate. Milk is now almost always delivered in disposable cartons.

Newspapers are delivered by Longniddry Village Shop and Nicolson's News.

In the 1950s, every household had a coal fire and required a weekly coal delivery. There were two main coal merchants delivering in the village at this time; McDonald, and 'Chirnside' (actually operated by Billy Lamb). Mr McDonald gave up coal deliveries in the late 1950s to become a haulage contractor. When Billy Lamb retired around the 1980s his customers were taken over by Watters of Port Seton. Other coal merchants from nearby communities also made coal deliveries in the last decades of the 20th century, but coal fires are now the exception rather than the rule. However, Mr Watters and Fortune of Macmerry still make coal deliveries in Longniddry.

Cafes & restaurants: in the 1940s and 1950s, Matt Hardy ran a chip shop in a wooden hut in his garden at the top end of Wemyss Terrace opposite the station. There were cramped and spartan facilities for a few customers to sit-in. Matt's was a popular meeting place for village youths in the late 1940s and early 1950s. When Matt gave up the chip shop and took over what had been Watt's shop next door, he had one or two tables and chairs set out where it was possible to drink a bottle of juice or eat a packet of crisps. This hardly constituted a cafe, however.

The Longniddry Inn has had restaurant facilities since it was built in the early 1970s. It is fair to say that until recently these never realised their full potential, nor were very popular. Standards indeed latterly became so abysmal as to attract the attention of health and safety inspectors. However, the Inn is now in new hands and is currently packed with satisfied diners every weekend.

Building services and tradesmen: George Taylor was a well-known local builder of the 1950s and 1960s, with a yard at 'Lornlea', on the main road on the western approach to the old village. Around the same time Eric Robertson ran a flourishing painter's business from premises in Links Road. In the immediate post-war years, a yard belonging to famous East Lothian builder Richard Baillie was situated behind the west end of the Main Street. Baillie's plumber, Mr David Hunter, was based in the old school building nearby which now houses the Royal British Legion.

Boarding kennels have been operating for some years in premises behind the railway, near Longniddry Station. There are several gardeners and landscape gardeners in Longniddry, but the only one with business premises in the village is Hard Graft on the Main Street.

At the present time there are several businessmen and self-employed tradesmen who live in Longniddry, but none as far as I am aware who have commercial premises in the village.

Outwith the village, E. L. Shopfitters is based at Seton Mains to the west of the village, and a civil engineering contractor at St Germains Level Crossing nearby. Just to the east of the village, the premises of J. McDonald (haulage contractor) were acquired in the 1970s by Iain Tait, and run as the Kiln Garage. The present proprietor is Eamonn Keiller, who undertakes most kinds of car repairs, but recently stopped selling petrol as it had become uneconomical.

An auto-electrician (Autolink Garage) operated until recently in the former premises of Robertson the painter in Links Road.

Seton Engineering recently set up business at Seton Gardens, at the west end of the dual carriageway. They specialise in converting cars to run on liquid petroleum gas, for which they are the only outlet in the area.

There is a well-camouflaged scrapyard (Glencairn Autobreaks) on the site of the former Glencairn colliery, just to the west of the village, where second-hand car parts can be bought, and scrap cars disposed of.

Healthcare

In the post-war years there was a district nurse resident in Longniddry and responsible for the village. Thereafter, the village was served for a while by the district nurse based in Aberlady. For some time now Longniddry has had the services of the district nurse based at Cockenzie Health Centre.

By the late 1940s and 1950s most children in the Longniddry area were born in hospital, sometimes in Edinburgh, but more usually in the Vert Memorial Hospital in Haddington. By the 1960s, home births had become most unusual. After the Vert was closed c1970 it became the norm for babies to be born in Edinburgh. Until the early 1970s it was unheard of for fathers to be present at the birth, but over the ensuing three decades this has become 'the done thing'.

At the end of the war Longniddry's GP was Dr Oswald Jarvis, whose surgery was in his house in Elcho Road. Not all Longniddry people were on his list however, and quite a few people were patients of the Gullane or Port Seton practices.

'(Dr Jarvis) was a wonderful person. He used to get the books out and draw out all what was wrong with you, and all the rest of it. But no time for scroungers! He was an army doctor. He came back here from India.'
Mrs J Robertson

Dr Jarvis looked very much the gentleman, with his tweed jacket and monocle. Following his death in a car accident c1950, the practice was taken over by his daughter, Dr Isobel Jarvis. She was assisted in the 1960s by Dr Beattie; Dr Jarvis retired in 1986. 'Doctor Isobel' could be just a little impatient with time-wasters and hypochondriacs. It was something of a joke in the village that her advice for a wide range of ailments was, 'I think you might just take an aspirin'.

On the other hand:
'She could be very kind. I found that very much. She was very good to us.'
Mrs J. Robertson

In 1980, the Cockenzie Group Practice moved into a purpose-built health centre in Cockenzie, by which time the practice already had over 400 patients in Longniddry. Soon the practice opened a Longniddry surgery in temporary premises beside the tennis courts off Douglas Road. When Dr Jarvis retired in 1986, the group practice took on most of her patients. Also in 1986 the former post office premises in Forthview Road became vacant, and were taken over by the group practice. Surgeries are held there Monday to Friday. In 2000 there were five doctors in the practice – Dr Susan Cramond, Dr Donald Bremner, Dr Peter Wood, Dr Susan Menzies and Dr John Turvill.

Healthcare (cont)

Children: by the 1950s, the days of childhood death from diphtheria and scarlet fever were gone, but epidemics of mumps, measles, and chicken pox regularly thinned the ranks in the classrooms temporarily. Another regular visitor was impetigo, a skin infection that necessitated the lurid painting of the areas with purple gentian violet.

In the post-war years there was a clinic where mothers collected the newly-introduced free orange juice and cod liver oil for their children. Other than this, there does not seem to have been a great deal of ante-natal or post-natal care then, apart from a visit or two from the district nurse. A baby clinic is now held once a week in the doctors' surgery in Forthview Road.

In earlier years, mothers still resorted to home-made remedies for various ailments
'If you had toothache you put a clove in your tooth.'
Anon

And

'Salt, heated up, if you had swollen glands, and it was put into a sock and put round your neck ... And then of course sulphur and black treacle was mixed up, and if they thought you were going to have measles, shall we say - you know, childish ailments - you got a great big spoonful of this shoved in your mouth'
Mrs J. Robertson

A dental surgery was opened in the Main Street in 1974, in what had been the chemist's shop, and has since expanded into the shop next door. In 2000 there were two dentists in the practice – Charles Simpson and Alan Whittet.

The village chemist, Douglas Welsh, also practised as an optician; he continued this role into the 1980s, long after he gave up the chemist's shop.

For the elderly: there are a few voluntary organisations operating in the village that provide some support for the older members of the community. The Wednesday Club for OAPs meets in the Church Hall on Wednesday afternoons in the winter. It provides pensioners with an opportunity to enjoy each other's company, and provides dominoes, tea, and entertainment. A Lunch Club for old folk is run by lady volunteers in the Longniddry Community Centre on Mondays.

Education

In the 1940s and 1950s there was no educational provision for the under-fives. In the 1970s some Longniddry children were allowed to enrol in Cockenzie Nursery School, and around the same time a private nursery school operated in Longniddry. There has been a nursery class at Longniddry Primary School since 1985.

Primary education has been available at Longniddry Primary School (formerly Longniddry Public School). The expansion of the village in the late 1960s and 1970s caused particular problems for the school; pupils were taught in temporary mobile classrooms in the school grounds. An extension was opened in 1978. In 2000 the school roll was 292. This compares with a school roll of around 120 in the mid 1950s.

I (David Robertson) was a pupil 1950-57: I contributed to the Longniddry Primary School's 50th anniversary booklet, and this is reproduced here with the permission of the head teacher, Mrs A McLanachan.

Education (cont)

I started school at Longniddry after Easter 1950… We learned to write on slates and had to take a rag and a bottle of water to school with us to clean them. … Sometimes Miss Campbell would use a big abacus while teaching us to count. It stood about five feet high and had large coloured wooden beads.

My next teacher was Miss Barret who must have been very young. …

I went into Miss Henry's class after that. She introduced us to 'cursive' writing and had a habit of grabbing evildoers by the chin to make them look her in the face as she gave them a row. I often wondered what she meant when she said someone's work was 'a troshus'. Later I realised it wasn't a noun, but an adjective.

Miss May Dunbar, the next teacher, taught us dancing for the school party, and thanks to her I can still make a not bad job of the 'Nips o' Brandy'. She was the first teacher to belt me. We were reading round the class in a nature-study textbook, and when she asked me to read the next paragraph I didn't know the place.

Mr William Allan took the 'Qualifying Class'. I was amazed that in his class you were allowed to put up your hand and ask questions on whatever he was teaching. That seemed a great innovation. Mr Allan had crepe-soled shoes and when he was out of the room, collecting dinner money or registers, he could creep up to the door unheard and suddenly spring in to catch anyone not working. We were regularly tested in every school subject and were seated in order of merit. The desks had hinged lids and seats, and heavy iron frames.

A less sophisticated generation: Longniddry school party, c1955. Kilts and hair ribbons are much in evidence (A&J Gordon)

Secondary education has been available throughout the period 1945-2000 at Preston Lodge School in Prestonpans. Until the early 1950s this was a senior secondary school, which accepted only those children who had passed the qualifying examination in Primary 7. Longniddry pupils who failed the exam were directed to the secondary department of Prestonpans Public School. Thereafter, Preston Lodge School (later Preston Lodge High School) became comprehensive and took pupils of all ability levels. In recent years some parents have preferred to send their children to North Berwick High School, which they perceive as being

Education (cont)

better than Preston Lodge. The reputation of Prestonpans as a rough working-class community may have not a little to do with this.

Some Longniddry parents sent their 12+ children to private schools in Edinburgh. In the 1950s and 1960s, parents in Gosford Road and King's Road did so almost without exception.

There are no facilities in Longniddry for adult education, other than night classes held in Longniddry Primary School, which are more hobby- or interest-based than academic.

University and college education has always been available close at hand in Edinburgh. Generous government grants in the 1950s, 1960s, and 1970s made it possible for young Longniddry people from humble backgrounds to achieve a university or college education without undue financial hardship, and it was usually taken for granted that those who had the inclination and ability would take advantage of the opportunity.

Transport

Throughout the period there has been a regular rail service between Edinburgh and North Berwick, stopping at Longniddry. This has become increasingly important, as Longniddry's population of commuters has grown. A branch line to Haddington was closed to passenger traffic on 3 December 1949. Goods trains continued to run on the Haddington line till 1968 when the line was closed and the track removed.

From 1945-2000 there has been a bus service between North Berwick and Edinburgh, stopping at Longniddry.

Since many commuters living along the East Lothian coast travel by car, the A198 through Longniddry is very busy at certain times of the day. A 40mph speed limit was recently imposed on the stretch of the A198 from Longniddry Main Street to the east end of the dual carriageway.

A massive extension of parking facilities at Longniddry Station has made the concept of 'park and ride' more attractive. On the other hand, the opening of the Tranent/Musselburgh bypass has substantially cut driving time to Edinburgh.

There are a number of footpaths and rights of way through the area. East Lothian Council has created a railway walk from Longniddry to Haddington along the track bed of the old Haddington branch line (purchased 1978). This is an important wildlife corridor and nature reserve (admittedly of a fairly unspectacular kind), and is carefully maintained. It is open to walkers, cyclists, and horse-riders, and leads through some very pleasant countryside. There are parking facilities at each end, and at Cottyburn to the south-east of Longniddry, where there are also picnic tables.

Police

Until the 1960s there was a policeman stationed in the village, initially in John Knox Road, and from the mid 1950s in Wemyss Road. The policeman's house was known to everyone as the 'Police Station', and it was taken for granted that he was Longniddry's own policeman, responsible for law and order in the village in much the same way as the minister was responsible for religion, and the headmaster for education.

Since then, concepts of policing have changed and Longniddry relies almost entirely on motorised police patrols based elsewhere. Phone calls to the nearest manned police station at Prestonpans will frequently find no-one present, and calls will have to be directed to Dalkeith, or even police headquarters in Edinburgh. There is currently a community constable resident in Longniddry, but his identity is probably unknown to the vast majority of villagers, and he is certainly not the high profile authority figure that the village policeman was in the post-war years.

There has been little in the way of serious crime in Longniddry during the period in question. However, the bodies of the victims of the 'World's End murders' of 1977 were dumped near Longniddry, one at Gosford Bay, and one between the Coates and Huntington. Crime in the village amounts to occasional outbreaks of burglary or shop breaking, but this is not the constant problem that it is in less fortunate communities.

It was well known in the 1950s and 1960s that one or two characters haunted the beach as peeping Toms (or 'pantwatchers' as the local youths jocularly termed them). Occasional 'flashers' also popped up along the beach from time to time, and there was at least one case of sexual assault of a young girl.

All in all, however, the 1950s and 1960s were an age when women and children were assumed to be safe in the village and its surroundings. Farm children walked long distances to school, young mothers with children regularly walked along the shore or in the countryside, older children roamed the countryside on bicycles or on foot, and rapists and paedophiles were the last thing on their minds. Perhaps the best illustration of this is the readiness with which mothers would allow their children to go for 'hurls' with the drivers of milk lorries and bread vans. Nowadays the street outside Longniddry Primary School is choked with cars as mothers drive their offspring to school from half-a-mile away, and the thought of their child being driven off on his rounds by the 'store baker' would probably induce a state of nervous collapse.

Rowdy teenagers, and the associated unpleasantness of litter, graffiti, drunkenness, loud public swearing and vandalism are felt to be more obvious than they used to be. However, although such behaviour does raise its head more often than it used to, the scale and frequency are negligible compared to what is endured by neighbouring communities. It should be said, too, that often the perpetrators are visitors from these communities – although not as often as Longniddry parents would like to think!

Leisure

Facilities in Longniddry varied over the years. There had been no pub in Longniddry since the late 19th century but, shortly after the second world war, a hut was obtained from the disused airfield at Macmerry, erected on to the former tennis pavilion and a local branch of the British Legion was set up - with a bar.

'I can remember Geordie Mitchell giving Billy the lorry to go up to Macmerry and bring down that big hut, and that was the start of the British Legion ... It was down at the tennis court.'
Anon

In 1961, the Legion moved into the old school building off Links Road, which was gutted and renovated. The Royal British Legion hall can be booked by members for private functions such as birthday parties and anniversary celebrations.

During and before the war the recreation room at the top of the main street was used for whist drives and dances. Whist drives continued to be held there in the years after the war.

Leisure (cont)

Longniddry OAPs setting off on their annual outing, early 1960s (A&J Gordon)

In the 1950s and early 1960s, the school hall was regularly used for whist drives and 'socials' (dances with a break for tea and sandwiches). These ceased in the mid 1960s.

Several other organisations met in the school hall at that time, including scouts, guides, and a Scottish country dancing club. Night classes have been held in the school throughout the period 1945-2000. Political meetings were also common in the school hall in the 1950s and 1960s.

When in 1961 the British Legion moved out of their hall next to the tennis courts, the scouts took it over. Regular rock and roll dances were held here in the early 1960s, with Dan Gillan's band, The Heartbeats. This hall was demolished around the late 1960s, and the scouts moved into a new hall nearby.

The church hall was also used by many organisations in the 1950s and 1960s - the SWRI, brownies, youth clubs, and of course church-based groups such as the guild and the youth fellowship.

Since the community centre opened in 1979, it has become available for all sorts of organisations and all sorts of functions. Not as much use is made of it as might have been thought, however.

Facilities are available in the Longniddry Inn for weddings, dinners, discos, and parties. Before the Longniddry Inn was built in the early 1970s, there was nowhere in the village to hold a wedding reception.

Organisations & clubs: the immediate post-war years were not an age when women were expected to have many interests outside the home. Women's organisations were typified by the WRI:

'There was baking and making rugs. There were classes for that sort of thing. The Rural used to have shows, you know, for the county, showing the different handicrafts that were made. And they still do to this day ... knitting, or sewing again, making toys now, all these kinds of things. And baking.'
Mrs J. Robertson

Longniddry bears the distinction of having started the first branch of the WRI in Scotland in June 1917; the group's 70th and 80th birthdays were celebrated with a craft exhibition (1987), and a craft and history exhibition (1997) in the church hall. The group was also active in the local community. For example, in 1967, Longniddry WRI sent a complaint to their MP regarding the proposed closure of the railway stations at North Berwick, Drem, Longniddry and Prestonpans.

Formally organised clubs and associations in Longniddry are as follows: bowling club; National Women's Register; bridge clubs (two); tennis club; biodiversity group; SNP; Longniddry Golf Club; Probus club; Artisans' Golf Club; Longniddry Stick Makers; Scottish country dance club; Garleton Singers; Phoenix Ladies' Club; Rotary club; Royal British Legion; and the Women's Rural Institute.

The woman's guild, the Scottish country dance club, the British Legion, the golf club, and the bowling club have all operated throughout the period 1945-2000, or near enough it. Scouts, guides and brownies have also operated since at least the 1950s. There have been drama groups from time to time but there is not one at present. A lapidary (stone polishing) club operated from at least the early 1970s but was finally wound up in 1999 due to lack of support.

Church organisations include: woman's guild; young women's group; TYC (Today's Young Christians); and the theatre bus.

British Legion
Until the creation of the Longniddry Inn in the early 1970s, the Legion had the only bar in the village (apart from the rather more up-market golf club), and in the 1960s many young people waited impatiently for their 18th birthday to be able to apply for associate membership of the Legion. At that time, and in the 1970s, the Legion ran regular Saturday night dances, an annual dinner dance, and an annual Burns supper, and fulfilled to some extent the dual function of pub and village hall. For a few years in the late 1950s and early 1960s the Legion had public film shows in their old hall at the tennis court once a month in the winter months. There was occasional confusion with the changing of reels, but such films as *Rob Roy, Reach for the Sky, A Town like Alice, The Thief of Baghdad,* and many others were all much appreciated. At the present time, the Legion still has a programme of entertainment but it tends to be more on the lines of discos and country-and-western evenings.

Children/teenagers
There is no support to Longniddry children in general through the Youth and Community Service, and no paid youth leaders. There is a wide range of clubs and organisations for children in the village, a community centre and sports facilities, and both Longniddry Primary School and Preston Lodge High School offer a wide range of extra-curricular activities. These include: 1st Longniddry Guides; beavers; brownies (three packs); baby & toddler group; rainbows (two groups); youth clubs (S1-6), (P5-7), (P2-4) at the community centre; Longniddry & Aberlady rangers; guide unit; scouts; cubs.

Gala
The annual gala has been running since 1970. Events during Gala Day and Gala Week have taken different forms over the years, but Gala Day itself always includes a parade in the early afternoon and a dance at night. The gala committee resolved from the beginning to have no

Leisure (cont)

Gala Day parade, Longniddry – note prefabs on the right (A&J Gordon)

truck with the business of gala queens and courts, which is the norm in neighbouring communities.

Dances: in the 1940s and 1950s Scottish dance music was still very popular. Andrew Bathgate who lived in the village played with and eventually ran Tim Wright's Band based in the Cavendish ballroom in Edinburgh. Andrew was a highly respected musician in his day, and his compositions are still part of the Scottish dance band repertoire. Andrew's main instrument was the clarinet, but the favourite instrument for local musicians was the accordion.

'My brother brought my first accordion from Germany during the war ... I loved it, you know, loved the sort of music it produced.

We went to a man in Prestonpans by the name of Jimmy Dowther ... We jumped on the bus and went along to Jimmy Dowther to see if he'd give us lessons, and I think he lived in Gardiner Crescent. And he says "Aye, come in boys, come in". He took us up the stair into the bedroom and he put his hand underneath the bed and he drew out his accordion. And it was the most beautiful accordion I ever saw. It was a 'Ranco', lovely black accordion ... And oh, he could play! Some beautiful stuff! It just about sickened us completely listening to this man.'
Morris Glen

Farm kirns - harvest home celebrations - had been very much part of the rural East Lothian scene, and continued at Longniddry Farm until around 1950. The farmer recalls

'Oh yes, we used to have the Johnstons, Alec and Nicol. The Johnstons used to come. Or Chrissie Letham. Remember the Lethams' band? The women used to scrub the place. We used to have kirns regularly, and then during the war we ran them for the Red Cross ... It was in the granary. We used to put props underneath it. The floor used to rise and fall like that; and we used to prop it all up underneath'.
Gordon Morrison

'I went to the kirns but I never played at a kirn. Andrew Honeysett always ran the Longniddry Farm kirn. Longniddry Farm always had a kirn, you know. It was always after the harvest. Once the harvest was in you had your kirn. And you had the kirn on the Friday night. And the dance after the kirn was on the Saturday night. It was always a two-night thing. Now, I went to a kirn at Longniddry, I went to two or three at Longniddry. Andrew Honeysett, I can always remember, he was the man that ran them ... They always started with a Grand March. And the farmer and his wife always led the Grand March down the middle of the hall. Then they split at the bottom of the hall and they marched right round the hall. And when the Grand March was finished it went on to the Circassian Circle. Everybody stayed in the hall for the Circassian Circle. And that was how the kirns always started off on the ferm ... It was the grainary! And a' that was roond aboot for seats wis bales. Everyone sat on bales ... the fermer's wife and the ploomens' wives and whatnot, they made all the baking, scones and cookies and biscuits and everything, and sandwiches. They did all that for the kirn, and if there was food left over they brought it to the dance on the Saturday night. There was always two nights at a kirn ... The floor on the grainary, it used to go up and doon when they were dancin. An Eightsome Reel, an the bluidy flair wis gaun up an doon! Bouncin!'
Morris Glen

Although the farm kirns petered out around 1950, several of the village organisations would hold a 'whist drive and dance' in the school hall to raise funds. These 'socials', as they were often called, tended to be held in the spring and the autumn, and the dances in some ways were not unlike the farm kirns. By the mid-1960s many people had begun to feel that accordion bands and whist drives were a bit old fashioned.

Many of us remember the 'socials' fondly however.

'They would advertise it, and go round the village selling tickets, and they would hire a band. Well, we got the chance to play at one or two of these. They had Johnny Johnston's Scottish Dance Band. He came and played at them. Chrissie Letham and her band. Her father was Peter Letham. They came and played. You had all different bands round about the Lothians; came and played. Anyway, we got our turn as well, and played at these dances. And the whist drive was always first. They had the whist drive and it was followed by a dance. And the whist drive would start, say seven o' clockish, and the whist drive would go on till maybe half past eight, nine o'clock. Then the hall would be cleared, then the band would come in and the dancing would start, maybe about half past nine, towards ten o' clock, and they danced right through to two o' clock in the morning. In those days it was a selection of Circle Waltz, St Bernard's Waltz, Dashing White Sergeant, Slow Foxtrot, Military Two Step, Gay Gordons. These were all the dances that we had then. Eightsome Reel, Nips o' Brandy. There was always somebody from the village would do what we called MC. Maybe somebody like Jim Maule he was a guid singer. Or Jock Rowberry, Billy Gillan ... Billy Gillan was a great M.C. Billy Gillan used to sing. I can always remember what he sang. He used to always sing 'Nicky Tams'. 'Roll out the Barrel'! And I used to play along with him when he was singing 'Roll out the Barrel'. He used to say to me, 'Come on Morris, play Roll out the Barrel, and we'll give them a song!'
Morris Glen

Some village organisations still organise fundraising dances in the community centre. These however, do not occupy the important place in village life that the 'whist drive and social' did in the 1950s. Whist drives have long since disappeared from the scene.

Leisure (cont)

By the early 1960s the age of rock and roll had arrived in Longniddry:

'Jim Marshall played bass because he had money. He could buy a bass and a bass amp. But Ronnie Noon played bass at one time. Derek played the drum ... My brother played rhythm guitar. I tried to play a wee bit of lead guitar. We were playing sort of Buddy Holly stuff, Roy Orbison stuff, because George was keen on Roy Orbison ... Used tae dae 'Love Hurts' and 'Running Scared' ... Bobby Beith used to play the piano occasionally.'
Danny Gillan

These dances with Dan Gillan's band The Heartbeats were held in the scout hut (the former Legion hall) and were very different from the school hall 'socials'. The era of the teenager had arrived:

'There were mair adults at a social in the school hall, so that it put certain restraints on the teenagers whose main aim was tae bag off wi a burd. And so there was a big difference. But it was fun. I enjoyed the socials in the school hall. We used tae dae mair sort of traditional dances. We used tae dae sort o Scottish dancin a well sometimes. The band would be a traditional band - accordions and a drum and that would be about yer lot. And locals would get up and sing, folk like Jim Maule and ma faither wid sing. Jock Stewart would sing, and two or three others. It wis braw. It was a right guid laugh. Did they no used tae have them efter the whist drives? ... Whereas, at the Scout Hut it was darker, more sort of, the leanings were towards females' bodies ... It was much more erotic, because ye were hotchin on a lassie.'
Danny Gillan

So were the 1960s indeed the decade of 'sex and drugs and rock 'n' roll' in Longniddry?

'Very little sex. I mean, well, maybe there was. Maybe it was a' doon the wuids and – I think there probably was in a sort of highly furtive sort o way - clandestine findins [1]. Drugs? No, just drink. I cannae mind any drugs. Rock and roll was definitely the thing. Music was the big thing, that's right, you could find solace in. And folk like Buddy Holly were talking our language. They put into music and words what we felt.'
Danny Gillan

The first few gala dances in the early 1970s used Scottish country dance bands, but for many years now the bands engaged have been pop groups, usually specialising in 1970s hits.

Eating out has become popular in recent years with the Green Craigs and the Old Aberlady Inn being currently very busy. The Longniddry Inn somehow never managed to fulfil its potential in this regard, but there are encouraging signs that the situation there has changed markedly for the better.

A fair number of young people are attracted to the Bottom Bar of the Longniddry Inn, or to the Legion, but most prefer to seek entertainment and adventure in Edinburgh as soon as they can afford it.

Gardening is very popular in Longniddry, although, perhaps surprisingly, there is no gardening club or horticultural association in the village.

There has been a public park in Longniddry, with a football pitch and swings, throughout the period. In the 1940s and 1950s, the swings were always kept chained up on Sundays. A dangerous 'sweezy-boat' was removed in the late 1950s after several accidents involving broken bones. Around the 1970s, children's swings, chute, and climbing frames were erected on the north side of the park, and the swings near the school fence taken away. A football pavilion

Longniddry Golf Course, 1950s, with a flock of resident sheep. The tank traps in the foreground were supposed to hinder any German invasion in the second world war. Almost all have now been removed (A&J Gordon)

was erected around the same time. In the late 1940s there were still several allotments in the park. The site of these is now a tar-covered car park.

In the 1950s, there was a library in Mr Watt's shop opposite the station, mostly of thrillers and crime fiction, from which books could be borrowed for a small fee. Also in the 1950s, the council supplied a public library cupboard in the school. After the British Legion vacated their hall by the tennis courts, part of the premises was partitioned off and opened as a small public library in June 1962. A larger, better-stocked library was opened in a temporary building nearby in June 1970. A long-promised new library is to be built next to the community centre.

Sport: obvious to anyone passing Longniddry along the coast road is the village's link to golf. Longniddry Golf Club[2] – a seaside links course – was established in 1921, and has always attracted large numbers of enthusiasts from all sections of the community. The Artisans' Golf Club also uses the course subject to certain restrictions. With such excellent facilities close at hand, golf has always been popular; most young people growing up in Longniddry will at least have a crack at golf at some time (see also Economy – Golf).

The park with its goal-posts and football pitch will also be obvious to anyone passing down the Lyars Road on Longniddry's east side. There have been boys' teams off and on throughout the period.

Rugby too has been played and followed; it was enthusiastically taken up by significant numbers of boys and young men in Longniddry in the 1960s and 1970s, as a result of the importance placed on the game at Preston Lodge High School. There was no rugby pitch or rugby club in Longniddry, but for many years Preston Lodge FP Rugby Club in Prestonpans played an important sporting and social role in the lives of a sizeable group of Longniddry men and their wives and girlfriends. The rugby club bar was not an altogether negligible factor in the club's popularity.

Leisure (cont)

'*Bill Petticrew was the games master at Preston Lodge (1960s), and he was a pretty - he wisnae very impressive visually, because he wisnae a big man, but he certainly put the fear o death in ye. He was an awfy strict severe boy. And I think he was one o thae ex-army blokes. I mean, he wisnae against lashin boys wi six o the belt an a' that for daein trivial things ... But anyway, apart fae that, apart fae his sort o sadistic side, he was a decent bloke when ye got tae ken him.*

It was only rugby. Rugby and athletics. He did play cricket but fitba wis just oot, oot the box. There wis plenty really good fitba players that played rugby wi me but wisnae allowed to play fitba. And Bill was the type o bloke if you said to him "No, you've given me the choice of playing rugby on Saturday morning or play football for the local club, and I'm going to play for the club" that was you condemned for the rest o your life as a scumbag!'
Danny Gillan

In spite of such uncompromising attitudes, many Longniddry boys were not deterred.

'*It was something that appealed to me about the game. There's a sort of heroic quality about it – 15 gadgies rushin aboot tryin tae win the game, ye ken. And I felt as if I was part of a team, and yet I wanted to be the star.*'
Danny Gillan

A good player might make it to the 'firsts' by the fourth year. As for the first team:

'*I think it was moderately successful (mid 1960s). We were quite good at playing the local schools like Musselburgh, North Berwick, and Haddington, and Dunbar.*'
Danny Gillan

Preston Lodge also played Loretto and Broughton:

'*We didnae often beat them, but it was great when we did beat them. And we certainly didnae play their firsts. I think our firsts played their seconds.*'
Danny Gillan

For an outstanding player there were proud moments:

'*Bill Maclaren was there and Bill Petticrew introduced me to him. And he wrote an article in the Scotsman, and I got a good mention.*'
Danny Gillan

Schoolboy rugby had its lighter moments:

'*I remember meeting at Waterloo Place at the Prancin Horse (early 1960s). And we used to walk up the Bridges and get a bus. We had to get this bus away up to Liberton. And I remember there was a' these Panners* [3], *for some reason they had this enormous box o condoms ... Ach, it was awfy! We were supposed to be representing Preston Lodge and here they were lettin them doon by blawin them up and - ken, it was awfy! I remember bein black affronted cause there was hockey on another pitch an a' these Panners were blawin them up an makin obscene gestures wi them an a' thin. It wis a rid neck!*'
Danny Gillan

When they left school, keen rugby players would automatically join the FP Rugby Club:

'*At one time when I started playing there were at least four teams (mid 1960s), and there was a fifths, and that's how popular rugby was then. I mean, the fifths obviously was more an amusing outing on a Saturday efternuin, but the firsts and seconds were pretty serious, and even the thirds to some extent ...*

We went right up the leagues, up the Junior Leagues, up the Senior Leagues until we were in Division Two, National Leagues of Scotland. And I packed in then (c1983). And then they got in to the First Division, and I actually played yin game against Gala, at the Penny Pit, in the First Division.'
Danny Gillan

The rugby club acquired premises in the old British Legion hall in Prestonpans, and a social side to the club flourished in the 1970s and 1980s, with dances, discos, and other social events.

'Captains' Suppers, aye. They were at the end of the season where they had a big dinner and prizes were presented to 'Player o the Year' and a' this business. And then they'd get guest speakers. Sometimes really amazing speakers. And then the rugby members, one or two would sing. That would be great ... There was very much a 'dose o drunkenness'. Amusing things would be like Dirty D - M -. He kent 56 verses o Eskimo Nell and he used tae spile the hail night by singin the hail lot o them. We'd hae tae drag him oot!'
Danny Gillan

Enthusiasm for the game however is not what it was:

'And then as the years wore on the fifths were abandoned. The fourths were abandoned after that. And I think even now at the present time they've got a firsts and seconds, and the thirds are there but jist hingin by a shoogly nail.'
Danny Gillan

The social side seems to be similarly failing away. Young club members are keen enough to play, but prefer mostly to socialise elsewhere. There may be many reasons for the club's lack of success and the decline of enthusiasm for the game, but the finger of blame is pointed at one cause in particular.

'The professional thing came in seven years ago, and I think that's knackered it. Scottish rugby's in a dire way ... I think the sheer playing for the enthusiasm for the game, for the love of the game, has definitely gone out of it I think, to some extent. It seems to be awfy hard-nosed nowadays. It seems to be awfy 'winning at all costs".
Danny Gillan

The magic may now be waning, but for several decades rugby was a powerful force in the lives of not a few Longniddry folk.

'I mean, when I played rugby it really took masel oot o ma normal life, and for the 80 minutes, 40 minutes a half, I was like a different person.'
Danny Gillan

Bowling, tennis and sailboarding all have their supporters.

In the 1940s, 1950s and 1960s, families would spend much of the summer on the beach, and youths would swim from the diving board rocks at every opportunity. Now, the level of pollution has put folk off. Riders from the equestrian centre at Harelaw take regular advantage of the railway walk and the tracks and estate roads around Longniddry.

There are pheasant shoots in Gosford estate in winter, and farmers and their friends try gamely to keep down the populations of wood pigeons and rabbits in the fields around the village.

Leisure (cont)

Traditional crafts are represented by the flourishing stick-making club in Longniddry, devoted to the traditional craft of shaping walking sticks and shepherds' crooks from wood and horn. Surprisingly, this essentially rural craft is very popular in suburban Longniddry. The 14-15 members meet in a garage in Wemyss Road.

David Robertson talked with stick-maker Alan Hay

'The type of sticks that I like making are crooks and market sticks … They go from your toe to your chest, that's the ideal length for a market stick. But a crook goes from the floor to your shoulder. But you also get sticks called 'ordinary walkers' or 'crutch sticks'. They go from the floor to your hip…

You also get 'leg cleeks' too. They're smaller in gape. The leg cleek's used for catching up lambs' legs. The inside curve is the same diameter as an old penny, and the gap is the same as an old ha'penny. And that's how they measure them …

I also make 'thumb sticks' too. A thumb stick is when you've got a stick wi a natural vee in it … If ye get that maybe nigh on shoulder height you can get your thumb over the top of the vee and then plant the stick in the ground and you can stand there like that and it takes a guid lot o the weight off your legs.'

Hazel is mostly used.

'Usually in the show programmes it says, "Plain horn head or a fancy horn head on a hazel stick" … We usually get our hazels up at a secret location on the shores of Loch Ness.'

However blackthorn, holly, ash, and fruit-bearing trees are all satisfactory. *'Once you start making sticks every wood and copse becomes an interest. You see sticks in a different light.'*

The horn head is usually made from tups' horn or buffalo horn. As far as rams' horn is concerned, horn from older beasts is superior to horn from a young ram. Even so, horn has to be matured for about a year.

'It's classified as a 'green horn' until it matures. It won't polish or it won't shape right until its matured.'

With rams' horn it has to be heated to take out the curl, usually by boiling. The hollow in the 'neck' of the horn has to be greatly reduced. The horn in cross-section is roughly triangular and has to be coaxed into a more rounded shape. All this is done by applying heat and pressure. Heat, usually from a hot-air gun, is then used to bend the horn into the shape required for the head of the stick.

'Once you get the shape that you want, then you'd get a shank about the same diameter as the neck. And then you'd cut a peg on the shank, and then you'd drill the neck of the horn out to the same size as the peg, and set it on, and Araldite it in place. And after that it comes down to the filing and polishing. All the filing's done from the shank over the crown, down the nose. That's how it's worked. And after that the stick would be polished using different emery cloths.'

Some stick-makers prefer fancy heads, thistles for example, or trout, or pheasants. As far as carving is concerned

'You've got to draw it out on the horn, but you've got to think three-dimensional … I use carving chisels. I've got a box of carving chisels that I use.'

Some of the work is very intricate

'It would maybe take about 40-odd hours, a trout … I use a pyrograph to cut the fins into it. It's like a soldering iron with a very hot tip on it, and you can burn into the horn … I've got a wee chisel that I

ground at my work I can use. I can push into the horn and bring it up, and it's like scales on the fish. And that's a long drawn-out job, pushing the scales into the fish.'

Some Longniddry stick-makers sell their sticks, others don't.

'A good wooden handled stick will go for about 70-80 quid. A good horn walker, a good plain horn stick will go for about a hundred pounds. And a fancy stick will go for anything from £130 to £200, maybe more…. We show our sticks at the horticultural shows in East Lothian … We run our own show at the gala at Longniddry; an open show, everybody's welcome … The stock shows in the Borders such as Ellemford, Duns, Peebles, and Kelso also have stick sections. If you get a 'Best in Show' at these shows your stick goes into the 'Champion of Champions' at Yetholm and that is the show to be in … just to get in it is a feat in itself.'

Alan modestly says,

'We're just a bunch of boys that have a wee bit banter in the workshop and do a bit of work and things like that.'

He personally however has a room full of rosettes, has had nine 'Best in Shows' since he started, and has had sticks in the coveted 'Champion of Champions' stand at Yetholm for the past four years. In 2000 he had two! He says,

'I just enjoy it! When I'm standing welding at my work I'm thinking of the next project for the sticks.'

There is no doubt that golfing and gardening are vastly more popular pastimes in Longniddry than stickmaking, but as Longniddry becomes progressively more middle-class and suburban, and the old rural ways are left ever further behind, it does the heart good to see 'a bunch of boys' taking pride in such a fine old traditional craft.

Economy

Longniddry people worked in a wide range of occupations in the years between 1945 and the rapid expansion of the village around 1970. Immediately after the war there were quite a number of civilian employees at the army base in Gosford estate. Several of them were allocated council houses in Wemyss Road, and most of them left when Gosford PoW Camp was closed down. Quite a few Longniddry men in the 1950s and 1960s were also employed at Calum Grant's (later Lothian Structural Developments), a galvanising plant near Gladsmuir, which closed in the 1970s.

However, the importance of Longniddry as a busy railway junction ensured that a significant number of men in the village were railway workers. Also, Longniddry was surrounded by farmland, and indeed until around 1970 several of the community's streets were separated from each other by cultivated fields. Agriculture was still a fairly labour-intensive operation, and employed a number of village residents, and of course everyone who lived on the farms round about. There were no computer programmers living in renovated farm cottages in 1950! Even the majority of villagers who had no connection with farming could not but be aware of the work of the farming year as it unfolded around them and in their midst.

Thus, the two sources of employment that convey the essence of Longniddry in the period 1945-65, were above all, agriculture and the railway.

The seaside car parks are very popular with day-trippers. Apart from that, Longniddry could not be said to be a tourist destination, and there is next to nothing in the village in the

Economy (cont)

way of tourist accommodation. It is perhaps strange that, in spite of its excellent beach and golf course, and easy access to Edinburgh, Longniddry has made no attempt to attract tourists, but this is indeed the case. In recent years three or four private houses have begun to offer bed and breakfast accommodation, but there are no hotels, guesthouses, or campsites. The Longniddry Inn is something of a misnomer, as it has no bedrooms and cannot provide overnight accommodation. A proposal for a golf course and hotel at Seton Mains, to the west of the village, was recently turned down by East Lothian Council.

Economy - Industry

The railway

Nowadays, Longniddry is an unmanned station. Not a single employee works there, and the two bare platforms are graced only by three graffiti-bedaubed basic shelters. However, in the 1940s and early 1950s, Longniddry was a busy railway junction with goods trains running on one branch line to Aberlady and Gullane, and on another to Haddington. Until 1949 there was also a passenger service to Haddington. At Longniddry station there was a ticket office, waiting rooms, bookstall, a towering three-storey signal box, and a large goods yard.

'The way the old station was set, there was four houses over - the Station Cottages - then when you came into the goods yard the first building you came to was Tom Dickson's who was the signal engineer, telegraph and signal engineer. The next one was Owen Traynor's, he was the stores manager, and then the next one was the surfaceman's, and the next one was the lamp room for the paraffin for the lamp room, and then down to the station.'
Bob Porteous

The numbers of men employed at the station in the late 1940s are surprising to say the least. Almost all of them lived locally. The station was manned by two shifts.

Booking Office	1st shift	Greta Grierson
	2nd shift	Andrew Scott
Foreman porter	1st shift	Donald Hutcheson
	2nd shift	Charlie Bruce
Porter	1st shift	Jimmy Glen
	2nd shift	Bob Melrose

Three shifts were worked in the signal box	1	John Aitchieson
	2	Charlie McNeill
	3	Harry Reid

Relief signalman	John Grierson
Signalman/Telegraphic engineer	Tom Dickson
Signal fitter	Willie Small
Storeman	Owen Traynor
Station Master	Willie Kerr
Ganger	Hugh Reynolds
Surfacemen	Archie Porteous, Wull Henry, Bob Samuel,
	Eck Wilson (Known as 'Stabs' Wilson because of

Economy – Industry (cont)

the amount of fencing he did), Jimmie Ramsey, Jimmie Lugton, 'Auld Telfer' (William).

Engine shed	Willie Griffin, driver
	Willie Nicholson, driver
Night watchman	'Auld Cruikshanks' (William)
Bookstall	Mr William McAdam
Porter/signalman	Archie Samuel (His work in the Aberlady Junction signal box at the Spittal was only part-time. The rest of his day was put in helping around the station.)

The station was always a magnet for boys, who were encouraged by some railway staff who enjoyed their company.

'I used to run away from the school when it closed in the afternoon (c1937) and I used to get on the engine and go to Haddington. The driver was old Charlie Cruikshank ... the fireman was Willie Nicholson ... and we used to go to Haddington. They had a special box for me to stand on to drive the engine.'
Bob Porteous

In the 1940s and 1950s, Longniddry station was a hive of activity:
'We had a lorry at Longniddry that delivered Longniddry, Aberlady, and Gullane ... There was two loading banks and one other road where you could load putting the lorries right up to the wagon.'
Bob Porteous

The variety of goods transported in and out of the station is fascinating;
'They had a train at night that started from Dunbar they called the 'Drem and High Street' - vegetables to be on the market in Glasgow the next morning. And it went Dunbar, Drem, Longniddry, Prestonpans, and then that was it.... All the cabbage plants came by train ... and the farmer came and collected his cabbage plants'
Bob Porteous

'They loaded tatties and everything at Longniddry ... sugar beet.'
Albert Ogg

Crates of dead rabbits came down from Haddington, and baskets of racing pigeons were off-loaded at Longniddry to be released from the station platform. There would be fowls in boxes, calves in bags, grain and cattle to load or unload.
'They used to put calves, a young calf, in a sack, and tie the neck round the neck of the calf. The poor calf couldn't walk. It just, when it was put down, that was it till it arrived at its destination.'
Bob Porteous

Perhaps strangest of all
'They used to send away bag-loads of crows to make crow pie. They went to England.'
Bob Porteous

The Haddington branch line carried a passenger service until 1949, and a goods service until 1968. The engine was based at Longniddry, and after the last passenger train arrived in

Economy – Industry (cont)

Haddington in the evening, the engine returned without the coaches to Longniddry. Early next morning it would pull a goods train to Haddington, then bring down the first passenger train of the day. The engine returning from Haddington at night was often crowded with youths returning from dances or the pictures – *'as many as you could get in.'* (Albert Ogg) - a blatantly illegal practice which was nevertheless taken for granted.

'Ye mind old Mr Welsh the chemist? (Willie Griffin was the driver I fired tae.) His young family were all born in the Vert in Haddington, and Welsh, he used to get down on the engine when he was visiting his wife ... anyway, he was aye on the engine.'
Albert Ogg

As for working on the Haddington line,

'That was in 1945, and I was only a year on the Haddington branch, David, and I went into the air force ... We started at 4.40 all week, like, ye ken. But on the Monday morning we turned out two 'oors earlier to light the engine fire ... the fireman got a couple of hours overtime tae dae it ... And ye got oot and ye met the goods from Edinburgh in the morning, 4.40 in the morning ... and ye left for Haddington wi the goods ... quite a busy branch wi the goods traffic, you know, Haddington ... coal, various things, cattle ... Anyway, at Haddington ye shunted them off, and when ye were feenished ye cam doon wi the train, first passenger.

Then ye did that till ye got a connection wi the Berwick slow in the mornin aboot twenty minutes to nine. Ye met it, and efter that ye went and put some more coal on, coaled it up, you know ... and shunted all the traffic (ie wagons) that was left on the North Berwick goods. And ye had Aberlady and Gullane - ye went doon the Gullane branch. We did Aberlady and Gullane and came back up. And then ye started again wi the passenger, was it eleven o'clock? ... Ye came doon at denner time and got relieved at Longniddry station by the back shift'
Albert Ogg

The portering work was often hard

'The carts were coming one after the other with potatoes. And you had to load the wagons almost to the roof. You had grain to load, and you had 16 stone bags of grain to load on to wagons ... They went home tired, believe you me! And then there was a great deal of parcel traffic. I mean, Longniddry at that time ... the lorry I'm speaking about from Gullane, he had all of Longniddry to deliver, all the parcels. There was no vans came from Edinburgh; all the traffic came by train.'
Bob Porteous

Porters also had to wash out cattle wagons, and there were *'taps to clean, waiting rooms to clean, toilets to clean, windows to wash'.* As for carrying passengers' bags, *'That was his easy work!'*
Bob Porteous

The derailment of 17 December 1953 made a lasting impression on Longniddry's railwaymen. The train in question

'...was a relief train that they had put on with Christmas parcels for the south ... So when we came into the village, there was a policeman standing at the Bank, and he had his hand up, and he turned the bus into Links Road ... So I jumped up and I says to the conductor, "Just let me off here" I says "What's the diversion for" He says, "There's a rail smash up there"... So I jumped off the bus at the co-operative and walked down through the village, and I couldn't believe the mess that I could see as I was walking through the village.'
Morris Glen

'There was a set of miniature rails on a wagon. And instead of being tied by chains they were tied by rope. And due to the oscillation of the wagon the rope became severed and the rails parted company with the wagon, and wedged on the opposite line and derailed the train coming the other way. Unfortunately the ramp of the platform was where it was derailed, and the train mounted the platform, and it actually turned in the opposite direction within 90 yards of the way it was going. It was facing back to Edinburgh, and the tender was about 40 yards from it. The fireman was killed. The driver was still in the engine when it was down the banking. The driver fell about eight feet and broke his leg and that was all that was wrong. Unfortunately the fireman didn't be so lucky. ... I was in digs with Miss Wight when the station master, Willie Kerr, came round knocking at the windows, "Come on, come on! There's been a disaster!"'
Bob Porteous

'The whole train went forward and scattered all over the place. It was nothing but a bloody mess! The line was torn up, rails sticking up in the air. Just like matchsticks, sticking up in the air!'
Morris Glen

The hero of the hour was young Doctor Isobel Jarvis, who treated the driver and crawled under the wreckage to help to bring out the fireman's body. The dead man was
'... Donald McKenzie. The driver was Davie Drummond. I knew the fireman.'
Albert Ogg

Today, the Haddington line is a railway walk, and the Aberlady and Gullane branch has disappeared over most of its length. The station buildings have vanished without trace, the platforms have shifted some 50 yards or so eastwards, the goods yard has become a car park, and Longniddry station now gives employment to nobody whatsoever.

Economy – Agriculture

All the building expansion until the mid 1960s took place on land that had been part of Longniddry Farm. David Robertson talked with tenant Gordon Morrison:
'That's some of the best land in East Lothian that's been built over.'

Mr Morrison is a tenant of Wemyss & March Estates, and has farmed Longniddry Farm since he inherited it from his father in 1948. Much of the large original early 20th century farm of 700 acres has been swallowed up by the expansion of Longniddry, but to compensate for this other fields are rented in Gosford policies and at Craigielaw, near Aberlady. He now concentrates exclusively on growing wheat, barley and oilseed rape, and on breeding and raising beef cattle. Crops formerly grown on the farm included potatoes, oats, swedes, mangolds, and sugar beet. Around 1950, the farm employed eight or nine men, several women, and squads of seasonal workers. Every farm cottage on the farm housed a farm worker and his family. Now Mr Morrison employs only one man, who does not live on the farm.

In 1950, horses still pulled the plough, and most of the grain harvest was cut by the binder, stooked, stacked, and subsequently threshed. Nowadays Mr Morrison breeds cattle and grows only wheat, barley, and oilseed rape. In 1950 hay, swedes, mangolds, sugar beet, oats, and potatoes were also grown.

In the post-war years the labour force on Longniddry Farm was *'eight or nine men, and three or four women'*. There were *'four pairs of horses and an odd horse. And then mares breeding as well'*

71

Economy – Agriculture (cont)

Tam McDonald in his garden in Amisfield Place, 1940s. The field behind the garden contains stooks of corn, and the large villas of Gosford Road can be seen in the distance. These fields have all been built over (A&J Gordon)

The ploughman's day went as follows,

'The horses were fed at six in the morning and they started roughly half past seven, and then stop at quarter past eleven in these days, and lunch till one – that's to give the horses more rest! Ha ha! And then from one till five. And quarter past eleven on a Saturday.'

Women did such jobs as hoeing and singling turnips and sugar beet, and forking sheaves at harvest and threshing. *'They did everything. They worked like men'*.

Extra labour was hired for the potato lifting, local squads from Haddington or Dalkeith, or Irish squads whose macho amusements could sometimes seem a little extreme to the douce East Lothian farming community.

'They used to go up into the stackyard and just knock the stuffing out of each other for fun ... I've seen the men carrying 15/16 stone bags of grain round the back there, and one of the women used to sit on the top of it ... They were mad of course.'

In 1950 Mr Morrison's ploughmen earned (in modern money) around £1.50 to £1.60 a week. They had a free house, 16 bags of potatoes a year, and free milk from the farmer's cow when it was available.

The local farms kept the village blacksmith in business, not just for the shoeing of horses, but in the maintenance and repair of implements.

'Anything worn on machinery he would lay it, as we would say. Take the coulters down and he would lay them - reshape them. All the plough machinery got worn. Nowadays of course you would just buy new ones. It costs a fortune. You used to always take them down and get them laid.'

Several of the farms in the area specialised in vegetable growing until recently. Now, as at Longniddry Farm, agriculture is given over almost entirely to barley, wheat and oilseed rape.

George Mitchell, of Chesterhall and Archerfield, specialised in vegetable growing. Most of the fields between Links Road and the Dean were his, and several of his employees were given new council houses in Wemyss Road in the early 1950s. Apart from the actual ploughing and driving, most of the work in vegetable growing was considered women's work, and squads of women could be seen labouring in Mitchell's fields at all seasons of the year. Not many of them

Economy – Agriculture (cont)

were Longniddry women however. Field work was not popular among the women of the village most of whom by the 1950s considered themselves rather too good for such lowly toil.

One of Mr Mitchell's employees recalls

'[In the 1940s and 1950s] you used to walk down and cut the cauliflowers. And what else? Cabbage, cauliflower, leeks - dig leeks, and sometimes the ground was so hard with the frost it could be a terrible job, that. It was hard work but we survived ... What else? Well in the summer time it was lettuce, sybies; but it was mainly lettuce. He sold an awfy lettuce. Hoeing and weeding. Singling. Beetroot, he grew beetroot ... Weeding, on your knees, crawling along the ground all day'.

The women got their orders from a grieve; *'We started at seven. When there was orders, big orders, we used to go out at four o'clock in the morning.'*

Overtime was paid for such early starts but the squad worked on till 5pm irrespective of the starting time. Work continued in near darkness on Christmas Eve to finish a big order, pulling Brussels sprouts with the snow lying on top of the plants. *'I can't remember when Christmas Day became a holiday, for at one time you always worked. You got the New Year's Day off, but you didnae get Christmas'.* The farm grieve's diary makes it plain that it was also business as usual at Christmas on Longniddry Farm in 1950.

The women got an hour for lunch, and took a 'piece' to eat. There were short breaks morning and afternoon. As for toilet facilities, *'That was a bother. That was a bother! No, there were just woods! You were lucky if you got to a toilet.'* Many of the women wore the distinctive 'uglies'. *'It was a bonnet. And it had canes so that you could pull it right out. And there was a wee bit at the back for your neck. To keep the sun off you, or the weather.'* It may seem fantastic to compare East Lothian with America's Deep South, but as far as working conditions went, my informant was of the opinion that *'It was like the black people. It was the very same.'*
Anon

Mitchell's fields, of course, are now just a memory. This rich market gardening land was all built over between 1965-75.

It is not beyond the bounds of possibility that Longniddry Farm may go the same way in the not too distant future. Quite apart from the severe crises which have rocked agriculture in recent years, there is a feeling that the big building firms have not entirely given up hope of exploiting Longniddry's fertile acres, and that the council might not be entirely unsympathetic to their ambitions.

'Well, I'm quite glad that I'm getting to the finish of farming really. I don't know what's going to be in the future, because there's still talk of building a new town here. That's still being talked about.'
Gordon Morrison

As well as Longniddry Farm, there were a number of smallholdings and market gardens – almost all gone now. One of the schemes associated with the Garden City war veterans' homes was a sort of agricultural co-operative around the former limeworks; when the scheme was eventually wound up, the ground was rented out as a smallholding, and continued as such into the 1970s. The fields were taken in by Longniddry Farm and the outbuildings allowed to become ruinous.

Economy – Agriculture (cont)

Ben Mackintosh's smallholding at the Dean c1950; the house still stands, much extended, but the adjacent ground has all been built over (A&J Gordon)

Another smallholding at the Dean was cultivated well into the 1960s. The house still stands, much extended, and the land has been built over. In the 1940s, 1950s and 1960s, there was a market garden in Elcho Road; this, too, was built over in the 1970s. There is a market garden at Redhouse, a mile-and-a-half to the east of the village. The present proprietor now specialises in garden plants and cut flowers.

Forestry: Gosford Estate, bordering on Longniddry, is well wooded, although commercial exploitation of the timber has been minimal. Maintenance of the woodlands over much of the period 1945-2000 was fairly haphazard, but has improved greatly in recent years.

Economy - Golf

Golf plays an important role in the economy of Longniddry. In the 1920s, the 18-hole Longniddry course took in land on both sides of the coast road. During the war, much of the course was ploughed up for agriculture, but was returned to the golf club at the end of hostilities. The course was reopened in 1947, now lying entirely south of the coast road.

In 1996, the year of the club's 75th anniversary, there were 1122 members. The club employed a head greenkeeper, an assistant head greenkeeper, and four other greens staff. There was a resident clubmaster (club steward), and kitchen, bar, and cleaning staff. There was also a golf professional with two young assistants.

Wemyss & March Estates have just completed a new golf course at Craigielaw adjoining Aberlady village. The estate also has planning permission for another golf course in Gosford policies, coming close to Longniddry. East Lothian Council recently turned down a planning application for a golf course at Seton Mains to the west of Longniddry. Landowners now see golf courses as an attractive alternative to agriculture, especially if the courses can be constructed in conjunction with lucrative executive housing developments. This is a prospect that is not going to disappear from the Longniddry area. The demand for building land in Edinburgh's commuter belt seems insatiable, and one suspects that planning authorities may not be able to resist the pressure forever. At least turning the land over to golf would stop the open countryside around Longniddry being completely swamped by a tide of housing.

Local Government

In the 1950s, Longniddry's county councillor was John Bruce (Conservative), a member of a prominent local farming and business family. He was followed by Ronnie Smith (Independent) the village postmaster. He in turn was followed in the late 1960s by George Pollock (SNP). In 1971, Mr Pollock was succeeded by Bob Cunningham (Labour). In those days, the Longniddry ward was styled 'Gladsmuir North'. The county councillor also automatically had a seat on Prestonpans District Council.

Also representing Longniddry on this landward district council in the 1960s was Longniddry's minister, the Rev R.I. Johnstone, followed in the early 1970s by Morris Lee. Mr Johnstone was also a member of East Lothian education committee. Some of his parishioners were not too happy that their minister should be 'meddling in politics'.

The county councillor Mr Cunningham resigned from the Labour party after a disagreement over local party policy, and sat thereafter as an Independent. Around this time, Longniddry and Macmerry were put together to form 'Gladsmuir' ward. In the next election, Bob Cunningham was voted out, and Tommy Wilson took his place. Mr Wilson was a Macmerry man who had previously represented Macmerry as an SNP councillor, but subsequently changed his allegiance to the Labour party. It was probably the combination of Mr Wilson's personal following in Macmerry, with committed Labour supporters in both communities, that ensured Bob Cunningham's defeat.

In 1975, Scottish local government was reorganised. Longniddry was now represented by a regional councillor on Lothian Regional Council meeting in Edinburgh, and by a district councillor on East Lothian District Council meeting in Haddington. Tommy Wilson was succeeded on the district council by Cathy Gray (Labour), then Pat Burton (Conservative). The first regional councillor was Rev Colin Morton of Prestonpans (Labour), followed by Jimmie Nisbet (Labour).

Also in 1975, the old landward district councils were abolished and local communities were encouraged to form community councils. Bob Cunningham helped to set up Longniddry Community Council, and acted as its chairman for the next 20 years.

In 1996, local government was revamped yet again. The 'regions' and 'districts', with their confusing division of responsibilities, were abolished and replaced by 'unitary authorities'. Haddington was once more the hub of local government and Longniddry was represented there first by Ian Stewart (Labour), and currently by Peter Ford (Conservative), a retired businessman newly resident in the village.

At the last local government election, the boundaries of several of the wards were redrawn. Longniddry now lost all connection with Gladsmuir and instead was lumped together with a substantial slice of the east end of Port Seton. The boundary changes had not been well publicised, and caused considerable confusion in Port Seton. Bewilderment was not confined to Port Seton, however. The farmer at Lochhill (postal address Longniddry, school catchment area Longniddry, 'parish' Aberlady) went down to vote in Aberlady as he had always done, only to told that he was now required to vote in distant Athelstaneford! He didn't bother.

Longniddry Community Council issues a regular newsletter, and plays a useful role in bringing community issues to the attention of the village, and in lobbying higher authorities. Over the years it has been instrumental in such things as improving road markings, street signs,

Local Government (cont)

and street lighting; in having a switchbox and cables provided for Christmas lights, in getting a community constable provided, in dedicating a memorial in the village to the victims of the Ferny Ness disaster during the war, and in installing the Millennium window in the church.

Without doubt, however, the community council's greatest achievement was in leading the successful fight against plans in the 1990s to build a 'settlement' or 'new town' stretching from Longniddry almost to Gladsmuir, which would have radically altered the character of the village and wrecked its rural setting.

Revisiting the Past

At least one Iron Age grave was excavated in the 1950s in the garden of Thrushes Mead near the foot of the Lyars Road.

Tradition points to a fragmentary ruin in the grounds of Longniddry House as John Knox's Kirk, a chapel where the reformer publicly catechised his pupils when acting as tutor to the sons of the laird of Longniddry.

Longniddry's war memorial is a plaque inside Longniddry Parish Church commemorating those who died in the second world war. Those who fell in the first world war are included in the war memorial in Gladsmuir Parish Church.

A plaque was placed in front of the British Legion in Links Road in 1993 to commemorate those who died at Ferny Ness in 1943, when a target-towing plane crashed on to a bus carrying naval personnel.

The recent past

Most of the concrete blocks used as shore defences during the war were removed and used during the construction of Cockenzie Power Station. Several still remain on the east side of Ferny Ness, along with a scattered few elsewhere.

Miscellany

Longniddry Parish Church holds an annual art exhibition in the community centre, where works by local amateur artists are sold to raise money for Christian Aid. Morris Lee, a retired art and guidance teacher, holds occasional exhibitions and has no difficulty in selling his pictures.

The public library has occasional exhibitions by art groups and individuals. The church has a prominently placed stained glass window, designed in 1945 by W. Paterson of Edinburgh, depicting the archangel Michael and commemorating the contribution of the RAF to victory in the second world war. There is also a stained glass Millennium window in the church hall, designed by Longniddry native Kate Kennedy, and based on drawings by pupils of Longniddry Primary School.

People

Michael Turnbull is a Longniddry writer with several publications to his credit; he has contributed material on the Roman Catholic church to the county volume of the statistical account.

Moray Welsh (1947-) is one of the sons of Longniddry's longtime chemist Douglas Welsh, Moray is joint principal cellist with the London Symphony Orchestra (1992-date). He is a regular soloist and chamber musician, performing all over the world; he has made a lot of recordings and gained many accolades.

There is no doubt that the outstanding figure in local politics in Longniddry in the last three decades of the 20th century was Bob Cunningham. He was a county councillor, then chairman of the community council; he was also chairman of the gala committee, chairman of the British Legion, chairman of East Lothian Association for the Mentally Handicapped, a kirk elder for a time and, before his retirement, convener of the works committee at Cockenzie Power Station. As a county councillor and community councillor, his priority was not what was politically expedient but what he felt was for the good of the village. In 1995 he was awarded the MBE for his services to the community.

This account of Longniddry was written & researched by David M. Robertson. Additional information, research and essays were provided by the following:

George Millar   Belief - Longniddry Parish Church

Thanks are also due to the following interviewees (all interviews conducted and transcribed by David Robertson)

Danny Gillan (LN tape 3, 16 July 2001); rugby, music
Morris Glen (LN tape 4, 20 August 2001); Longniddry in the 1940s, the railway, music
Alan Hay (LN tape 8, 2001); stick-makers
Archie Mathieson (LN tape 1, 11 June 2001); wildlife
Gordon Morrison (LN tape 2, 18 June 2001); farming and life on the farm to the 1960s
Albert Ogg (LN tape 7, 3 September 2001); Longniddry railway station to the 1950s
Bob Porteous (LN tape 7, 3 September 2001); Longniddry railway station to the 1950s
Mrs J Robertson, nee Ima McDonald (LN tape 5, 2001); domestic life in the 1940s and 1950s
Anon (LN tape 6, 27 August 2001); domestic life during the 1940s and 1950s

FURTHER READING & REFERENCES
Allan, W. (1961) *A Short History of Education in Longniddry* Longniddry Primary School
Johnstone, R. I. (1965) *Longniddry Church and its Parish 1925-1965* (50th anniversary booklet) Longniddry Parish Church
McLanachan, A. (1981) *Longniddry Primary School 1931-1981* Longniddry Primary School
McVeigh, Patrick (1999) *Look After the Bairns* Tuckwell Press
Millar, George (2000) *Longniddry Parish Church - The First Seventy Years* Longniddry Parish Church
Robertson, D. M. (1993) *Longniddry* East Lothian District Library (earlier editions 1975, 1977 published by Longniddry Parish Church)
Tindall, F. P. (1998) *Memoirs and Confessions of a County Planning Officer,* Pantile Press
NB Reference copies of Allan and Johnstone are held at the Local History Centre, Haddington Library

Photographic records
The East Lothian Council Library Service in Haddington has a large selection of photographic negatives produced by A. & J. Gordon, professional photographers in Longniddry from the 1930s to the 1980s. 1000 of these have been printed and can be viewed at the Local History Centre, Haddington Library.

Notes

[1] Find (pron. 'i' as in inn): 'feel with the fingers, grope (in an indecent sense)'. *The Concise Scots Dictionary*

[2] See Mackechnie, Alastair *et al* (1998) *Longniddry Legacy: A History of Longniddry Golf Club* Longniddry Golf Club Ltd Published to celebrate the club's 75th anniversary

[3] Boys from Prestonpans

Humbie

Parish Representative: *John P. Bolton*

Introduction

This social history records changes to life in the parish of Humbie, during the period 1945-2000, more specifically changes in the period since the publication of the Third Statistical Account for East Lothian in 1953 (hereafter referred to as the '1953 account'). Although it is intended to form an update of the information in that account, it is written not from the perspective of a minister of the church, but from that of a retired civil engineer, a Humbie resident from 1970. The Reverend Bain's contribution to the 1953 account, together with East Lothian County Council's 1953 *East Lothian Survey: The Hillside Area* (the '1953 survey'), has been used throughout to provide information relating to the state of the parish in the early 1950s. Other information has been obtained from a number of published sources (see references), in particular local authority studies, and histories produced by the Humbie WRI in 1966 and 1989, and from discussions with present and former members of the community.

The parish is situated in the extreme south-west corner of East Lothian, bordering onto Midlothian to the west, and the Scottish Borders to the south. It covers some 3448 ha (8520 acres), having 'lost' about 150ha at Whitburgh, which was transferred to Midlothian in 1987. The village of Humbie is now identified as the area, which, until the 1960s, was signposted as Upper Keith (after the farm of that name). It contains the post office and shop, the school and the village hall; but not the church, or Humbie House!

Humbie is situated on the former A6137 road from the A68 at Soutra to Haddington. This road carries a certain amount of through traffic into East Lothian. The road has a number of sharp bends both within and to the west of the parish and is narrow in places, which makes it unsuitable for modern heavy traffic. In the early 1970s the road through 'the village' was

Humbie Water from Saltoun viaduct

Introduction (cont)

realigned to take it away from the school, and street lighting was installed. In the 1990s the road was downgraded to B road status (B6368) but this did not perceptibly change the amount of traffic passing through the village. A second B road northwards towards Ormiston and Tranent (B6371) joins at an awkward junction immediately to the east of the 'village', and at the west of the parish a B road links Humbie to Fala in Midlothian (B6457).

Environment

The land in the parish mainly comprises fertile farmland, rising to moorland on the northern slopes of the Lammermuir Hills. The 1953 survey (p63) noted that Humbie contained some of the best hill farms in the county. In the 1980s and 1990s there was a significant loss of trees, in particular hedgerow trees, due to Dutch elm disease and the felling of over-mature trees which endangered road traffic. There are still however many beautiful wooded areas. Since the 1950s a number of additional conifer plantations have been planted as shelterbelts and as a long-term cash crop. The parish therefore has a wide variety of habitats for wildlife.

A notable feature of the countryside for more than a century has been the beech hedging planted on the Humbie estate, in particular that planted in the 1860s adjacent to the main east-west road through the parish. The gardens of Humbie House and Stobshiel House have for many years been opened on occasion to the public as part of the Scotland's Gardens Scheme and for other charities.

A small area of exposed glacial material in a side valley of the Keith Water was designated as a Site of Special Scientific Interest (SSSI).

The landscape was visually changed in a number of ways. The majority of roadside telephone wires were rerouted underground from the 1970s, but in the 1980s the power lines and pylons carrying electricity from Torness power station to central Scotland were, despite local protests, carried through the east of the parish. Two other routes with even greater impact on the parish were successfully resisted. At the end of the 1990s Dun Law Wind Farm on the Lammermuirs outwith the parish was nevertheless visible and visually intrusive to some, although an interesting feature of the skyline to others. The community accepted in compensation a small annual ex-gratia payment from the power company for local projects.

Land Ownership

The 1945 East Lothian Yearbook identified seven 'mansion houses' and seventeen farm properties within the parish. Five of the farm properties were owner-occupied, and the remaining twelve were tenanted from larger estates. Only two of the properties (Duncrahill and Keith Marischal) were at that time farmed by the same tenant. During the 1960s and 1970s, most originally tenanted land was purchased by the sitting tenant or was owner-occupied when the tenancy was relinquished. In the 1980s and 1990s subsequent sales combined some of the land into larger more viable units, and some hill land was sold for forestry. By 2000, the 16 operational farms listed in 1945 had been reduced to eleven, of which Whitburgh was no longer part of the parish, and some farm work had been let out to contract. Six farms were still occupied by the families of the 1945 owners or tenants.

By the 1980s all of the 'mansion houses' had been separated from their lands by sale to professional and business people from Edinburgh.

Townscapes, Buildings & Landscapes of Distinction

The majority of substantial Humbie properties and steadings are stone-built and slate-roofed (from a variety of sources). A small number of cottages were built on farms and in the village area in the 1940s and 1950s and have mainly roughcast walls and dark red concrete tile roofs; there are also individual examples of 'system' built Orlit, Dorran and Colt houses. Also in the 1950s many pantiled cottages were re-roofed with concrete tiles or with second hand slates available from demolition works in Edinburgh. By 2000 only two or three originally pantiled dwelling houses in the parish were still pantiled, two other former outbuildings were converted to domestic use in the 1990s and were required by planning constraints to retain their pantiled roofs. Planning constraints also required that some recent new buildings be roofed with slates (imported from Spain!). Many originally pantiled (or slated) steading buildings were replaced with large, usually asbestos cement sheeted, buildings from the 1960s. By 2000, although small sections of pantile roofs existed in some steadings, only one had substantial pantiled areas remaining. No pantiled roofs have the slated lower courses typical of other parts of the Lothians.

Humbie Children's Village

The Children's Village (see also Education) has been a feature of Humbie since the early 1900s. The village was built over a period up to the 1920s in a colourful 'Arts and Crafts' style, on a conspicuous eleven-acre site, and after a change in use in 1967 it continued to be occupied until 1995. It subsequently remained unoccupied pending redevelopment. The Local Plan (1998) identified the children's village as 'a prominent feature in the landscape', several of the buildings themselves being 'listed', and hence subject to planning controls, for their special architectural or historic interest. In 1999 the Children's Village was sold to developers, but by 2000 no acceptable proposals for development had been submitted.

Historic Scotland listed many of the parish buildings (see CD-ROM). Keith Marischal home steading is the sole category A property.

Population

By parish, from the General Registrar's office

1931	556	268M	288F
1951	490	240M	250F
1961	399	196M	203F
1971	392	189M	203F
1981	332	165M	167F
1991	372	197M	175F
2001	342	169M	173F

By parish, from ELDC				By settlement, from ELDC
1991	297			--
1997 (est.)	389 (sic)	191M	197F	92
2001	NO DATA			NO DATA

Population figures are difficult to compare, as no two sources extract data in the same way.

The 1953 survey identified (p60) that of the 489 residents in the parish, only 376 lived within the Humbie 'sphere of influence'. The populations to the north of the Keith Water (whose children were directed to Crossroads school in Ormiston parish and subsequently to Ormiston school), and in particular those in the Duncrahill area which receives its postal and telephone services from Pencaitland, were not considered to be an integral part of the Humbie community. By 2000 all but the Duncrahill area could be considered to be part of the Humbie sphere of influence, although its significance was probably much reduced.

In the 1950s, the parish was almost entirely agriculture-based. Within the 'sphere of influence', 87% of the workforce was in local agriculture-related occupations, 3% were in non-agricultural occupations, and 10% travelled outwith the parish to work. With mechanisation of farming, the balance of occupations changed rapidly, to the extent that by the late 1990s, apart from the farmers and farm managers, only two or three full-time agricultural workers lived in the parish, the few others required preferring to commute from nearby towns. Also, although in the 1953 account the Rev Bain (pp254, 255) regretted the transient nature of a large part of the population, the majority were of relatively local origin. By the 1990s the transient agricultural population had been almost entirely replaced by a more permanent 'immigrant' population. The origins of many of this population are much further away, in other parts of Scotland, in England, and from several overseas countries. The local agricultural dialect has been lost from the area.

The Rev Bain also identified (p261) a shortage of accommodation for people retiring from farmwork, who were forced to move away 'sometimes to great loss to the community'. In the 1990s, with the same loss to the community, a number of older persons moved away from the parish into areas of the Lothians with more suitable accommodation and better facilities for the elderly, where dependence on private transport is not so great.

Belief

The Humbie Church of Scotland is picturesquely situated but in a relatively isolated location. In 1953 the average attendance was 60. Sunday buses ran to Haddington and Tranent but it is not known whether persons visiting other places of worship used these. By the late 1990s the

Belief (cont)

average attendance at Humbie church was under 30 and the church itself was full only for Christmas, Easter and Harvest Thanksgiving services. The cosmopolitan nature of the population and the availability of private transport, allowed attendance at churches some distance from the place of residence. Humbie attracted a number from outwith the parish, and some Humbie people attended the Catholic services at Nunraw Abbey, Garvald, and others the Episcopal churches at Dalkeith and Haddington. A number of Humbie churchgoers had Anglican religious backgrounds.

In 1977, Humbie and Yester (Gifford) parishes were linked, that is each kept its own Kirk Session, under a new minister based in Gifford, the manse having been sold off the previous year. In 1979, the parish was further linked with the joint parish of Bolton and Saltoun.

Ministers

1938-60   Robert Bain
1961-69   Norman Macpherson
1969-74   William Rogan
1974-77   Interim moderator - William Cowie Farquarson
1977 Humbie & Yester (Gifford) linked
1977-84   Alan Scott
1979 further link with combined parish of Bolton & Saltoun
1985-98   John Wilson
1999-date   Donald Pirie

Homes

The 1953 account noted (p261) that of a total of about 150 houses, only ten 'all large except one', were owner-occupied. Six cottages (two at the station and four at Upper Keith) were rented from the local authority, there were two station houses, a schoolhouse and a manse, and the rest were tied to a farm or an estate

The 1953 survey, looking to develop the hill villages, noted (pp59-64) that the railway station at the north-eastern edge of the parish had no passenger services, and could 'no longer' (could it ever?), be considered as an adequate centre. Also, that the situation of the church - which was not on a main route and, with limited space for development – meant that it had never acted as a nucleus for development. Upper Keith, however, was thought to be well situated and a good site for a village; five roads met, it already had the post office and shop, and a few houses, and also the Children's Village. However, with a population of 67 it was hardly as yet an adequate focus. It was noted that Humbie was the nearest (East Lothian) hill village to Edinburgh and that it could become an attractive dormitory village, and that building by private enterprise would result in advantage to the community and to the village facilities. This development did not take place, although two houses were built in the 1970s on the site of the old village hall, and the local authority built the Kippethill group of ten houses in the 1980s. The area around Upper Keith has nevertheless become recognised as the village of Humbie.

Until the late 1980s, and with the notable exception of Scadlaw House, Upper Keith (built 1969), very little new building took place in the parish unless to replace existing unfit properties or for an identified agricultural need. However, the majority of properties had by that time been renovated and/or extended. All of the non-agricultural 'tied' properties recorded in 1953 were sold to private buyers when they became surplus to the original requirements - the manse in 1976, the (by then) two school houses in the mid 1980s, and the station houses at Humbie and East Saltoun by 1990.

By 2000, development of cottage groups into larger units had been matched by the small amount of new housing that was built. The housing stock was again at about the 1953 figure of 150.

Utilities

The 1953 account noted (p258) that, although all houses had internal water supplies, only a small part of the parish was served by the county council supply. The rest received private water from springs which 'might be more reliable' in dry weather. Only 90 of the 150 houses had circulating hot and cold water and baths. Water supplies to some properties were, at that time, provided by hydraulic ram pumps in the local watercourses. In the 1953 survey (p64) it was considered that a new water main from Stobshiel treatment works (to allow development of the village) would not be economic. However, it appears that new pipes were laid in the 1950s from Stobshiel to Humbie and to Windymains via Crossroads, and that service tanks were installed at Bankhead and at Keith Hill.

The extensive private supply system for the various parts of the Humbie estate continued in use until 1978 when difficulties in maintaining the distribution pipework led to its closure. Increased demands for water led to the laying of new plastic mains in the 1980s, and Pogbie received its first public supply in 1986. In 2000 however, a few properties still depended, perhaps by choice, on private supplies.

The 1953 account made no mention of sewerage arrangements or the availability of internal toilets, perhaps because these were universally available following legislation and grant provision to farms in the 1930s. In 2000, the village area itself had a communal septic tank; all other properties had individual or joint septic tanks of various ages and effectiveness, discharging directly into local watercourses or to soakaways.

In 1935 Lord Polwarth the then owner of Humbie estate arranged for an electricity supply to Humbie House (and to the church) from the East Lothian Power Company. The route of this supply is still indicated by ELPC markers from the church by way of Kirk Bridge and Humbie woods. The 1953 account noted (p258) that although electricity, principally for lighting, had been installed in many houses, the oil lamp was still extensively used. In the 1950s, following nationalisation of electricity and other basic industries in the 1940s, electricity was brought to all parts of the parish, including the village area in 1953. However the supplies were often subject to disruption in bad weather conditions, and only in the 1990s was a start made in renewing and interconnecting the system to provide a more reliable supply.

In 1953 the switchboard at the post office - described in the East Lothian yearbooks as the Telegraph & Telephone Call Office - connected 30 telephones in Humbie and 20 outside the parish in Fala, which was still in 2000 connected to the Humbie exchange. By the 1990s connections were available in all parts of the parish from the automatic exchange built adjacent to the post office. The exchange was upgraded on several occasions, although usually a few years behind urban exchanges. During the 1990s, many households obtained mobile telephones, often initially purchased for emergency use in cars, and an increasing number were connected to the Internet.

Shops & Services

In the 1950s the parish had two shops - Mrs Agnes Hogg's grocery and the post office (and shop) run by Frederick Murray, tobacconist. Milk was available locally and was also delivered to individual properties by the vans of the Edinburgh & Dumfriesshire Dairy and of the East Lothian Co-operative Society. However housewives shopped (usually once a week) in Edinburgh, Haddington, Tranent and Dalkeith.

*Humbie
village shop*

The grocer's shop was a small establishment at Keith Bridge which had been run as a cartage business and shop by the Pendreigh family since the 1870s. The business traded until 1952. The post office and shop at Upper Keith has always had to compete with 'the weekly shop' in the towns and with visiting traders. From the 1970s it was let to a succession of tenants, all of whom struggled to make it viable, with an ever-reducing income from post-office activities. In the late 1990s to avoid closure, the tenancy was taken over by a company set up by a group of residents. In 2000 the shop continued to be at the heart of the village for the 50 or 60 regular users and was the distribution point for newspapers, milk supplies, groceries and some local produce.

In the 1980s the village was still served by travelling butchers, bakers, grocers and fishmongers, and to a limited extent by milk deliveries, although by 2000 only a weekly visit by a fishmonger and a greengrocer survived.

For many years coal has been delivered by a number of hauliers on a weekly basis, and from the 1970s fuel oil and later bulk tankers delivered gas supplies. Petrol was available at a pump at the post office from the 1920s to the 1980s. Although the supply to the public no longer existed, the Shell sign was, in 2000, still a feature visible in the adjacent beech hedge.

Humbie parish has supported a number of services over the years: the 1953 account noted (p257) that a joiner Andrew Grieve continued to work at the Leggate, and that a visiting blacksmith also worked there. By 1966 both businesses had been discontinued.

In 1953 there were two daily deliveries of letters from the post office at Upper Keith, and collections from eight boxes. Then (as now), the Duncrahill area was served from Pencaitland. By the 1960s, sorting and delivery was carried out from Pathhead, and by 2000 sorting and delivery, and collection from the four remaining boxes, including the inconveniently small-mouthed antique Victorian box at the post office, was by van once a day direct from Dalkeith.

In 1963 a mobile library service was introduced by East Lothian County Council, which originally visited and stood at a number of farms and other individual properties. By 2000 the lack of people at home during the day, had led to the service only visiting the school and standing at the village centre, and calling 'by request' at other properties.

Healthcare

Medical services in 1953 were provided from Ormiston, Haddington, and Pathhead, and this continued to be the case to 2000. However, for many years the Pathhead practice had served the majority of Humbie residents.

Education

In the 1953 account, the Rev Bain reported (p258) that some 40 primary age children attended Humbie Primary School, which then had two teachers. Children living north of Keith Water (Windymains and Duncrahill) went to Crossroads school, just beyond the parish boundary. Older children went by bus to Ormiston Junior Secondary School and Preston Lodge Senior Secondary School. There were seven children (age not stated) at boarding school.

In 1961, under pressure from central government (the Scottish Office) to cut costs, the East Lothian County Council education committee agreed that

'Ormiston Public School should be altered to bring it up to the required standards and that the primary schools at Humbie and Crossroads should be closed and the pupils therefrom transferred to Ormiston in 1962/63'.

Humbie residents successfully fought to keep their own (Humbie) school open, but Crossroads school closed in 1969. The Crossroads catchment was however not transferred to Humbie. The children were bussed to Ormiston, together with secondary school children from Humbie travelling to the new (comprehensive) Ross High School in Tranent.

In 1979 the Humbie school capacity was 60 but the roll was 18. By 1982 the roll had fallen to seven and the local authority announced its intention to close the school. A local campaign committee was formed and the school was again saved from closure, but became a single teacher school. In 1983, as the teacher now travelled from outside the parish, both schoolhouses were sold. During the period the school roll fluctuated between single figures and over 40 with often major changes from year to year as cohorts moved on to secondary education. In the 1990s, perhaps a quarter to a third of primary aged children went to schools outwith Humbie. Nevertheless, the school and the active interest of the parents of all the children in the parish in events in the parish remained a significant factor in the cohesion of the community.

Meanwhile in 1997 major extensions were made to Humbie Primary School in anticipation of its continuing use.

Education (cont)

The school at The Children's Village provided education for needy Edinburgh children 'on holiday' in Humbie from the early 1900s until 1967 when the village stopped functioning as a holiday home (having provided holidays for about 176,000 children) due to increasing costs and difficulty in getting appropriate staff, and also changes of need due to greater provision of care by the state. Also the Fund (which still existed in 2000), decided it was more appropriate to send children incognito on other holiday packages. In 1967 the village was leased and subsequently bought as a residential and day care facility for the mentally handicapped; in 1995 this was closed, and the remaining residents were transferred elsewhere.

Transport

The erstwhile Gifford and Garvald light railway (Hajducki, A. pp156-171) ran along the eastern edge of the parish, with two stations, Humbie and Saltoun, within the parish. Passenger services had been discontinued in 1933, and the line was terminated at Humbie following the destruction of the bridge over the Birns Water (the parish boundary) by the floods of August 1948. Both stations were considered viable in the early 1950s with traffic mainly in timber for the then flourishing East Lothian coal mining industry, coal imports to Humbie and in particular to Saltoun for the Glenkinchie distillery, and outgoing potatoes from Humbie and whisky from Saltoun. By 1956 coal imports to Humbie had ended and potato traffic had been reduced since 1953 due to one of the largest growers of seed potatoes now owning two heavy lorries. Duncrahill farm continued to use the railway to move cattle and grain through Saltoun station up to the 1960s.

Humbie station closed on 2 May 1960, and in 1965 the closure of the coalmines around Ormiston made the whole line unviable and Saltoun station was closed. The track bed between the stations quickly became overgrown, and the viaduct over the Humbie Water was

Humbie Station, 1956
(Crown Copyright: RCAHMS (Rokeby Collection))

eventually demolished in May 1986 (*East Lothian Courier* 1986 May 9). The local authority established a railway walk northwards from Saltoun station and intended to continue it southwards towards Gifford, but by 2000 this had not materialised.

In the 1953 account the Rev Bain described (p256) road and rail services as 'insufficient', with a bus to Edinburgh four times daily, with a late journey on Wednesday and Saturday, and to Haddington only on Saturday and Sunday. The 1983 plan noted that in addition to a main service to Edinburgh from the former station, a twice-daily 'shoppers' bus ran to Haddington. However by 2000 only a token service to Dalkeith remained, dependent on Midlothian subsidies, with a post-bus service to Haddington. The services were sparse, slow, inconvenient, and under utilised, but remained a vital link for the handful of users without alternative transport.

Leisure

Facilities

In the 1950s the Humbie village hall was a wooden ex-army hut erected in 1921. It was replaced in 1973 by a new hall on a larger site adjacent to the school. This was, and continued in 2000 to be, used for dances, concerts, whist drives, auctions, and exhibitions, and for private parties. During the 1980s and 1990s the hall was also regularly used for a playgroup for the village juniors and for a lunch club for the village seniors

Clubs and groups recorded in the East Lothian yearbooks 1945-60, as all being active post-war, but discontinued by 1960 were: the British Legion, the curling club, the pigeon club, and the Scottish League of Wives & Mothers. The Rev Bain in 1953 recorded (p260) that five 'clubs' were run by the church but that some, including the scouts and the guides were at that time in abeyance 'due to lack of leaders'.

Two groups, the Woman's Guild and the (Scottish) Women's Rural Institute (WRI) were in continuous existence throughout the period. The WRI produced the 1966 history of Humbie, and the 1989 addendum, which were together published as *Gleanings of Humbie Parish.*

The Fala, Soutra & District History & Heritage Society was formed in the 1980s, and has included a number of Humbie residents in its membership.

Humbie has never had an inn or public house. Although Johnstounburn House developed as a guesthouse and hotel from the 1940s, (seen as 'a sign of the times' by the Rev Bain) it always aimed at the upper end of the visitor market. Up to the 1970s, farm workers often cycled significant distances to inns at Juniper Lea, Ormiston, Pencaitland and Gifford. The changing nature and increased mobility of the Humbie population had by the 1980s led to a greater use of hotels and restaurants further afield, especially those in Gifford, Haddington and towards Edinburgh.

Economy

While the parish supported no large-scale industry, from the 1970s onwards, a number of non-agricultural local enterprises were set up to supply goods and services to Edinburgh & the Lothians, and further afield. Most of these were for the self-employed or employed one or two out-workers. However, in addition to Johnstounburn House Hotel, two had by 2000 developed into significant local employers: Mavis Hall Park, a corporate entertainment business with six full time and several part-time staff organising country pursuits events, and Windymains Sawmill, with approximately 30 employees.

The smaller businesses included a house extension business, a model maker, a civil engineering plant contractor, and a producer of specialised wool products. The local authority gave this movement encouragement by the construction in the late 1980s of two houses with workshops as part of the Kippethill development.

Economy – Agriculture

Humbie though, remained essentially an agricultural parish. In 1945, the hill farms continued to be stocked with mainly black-faced sheep and hill cattle. The lower farms were principally concerned with stock rearing, of both sheep and cattle, which together with the arable crops grown mainly to support them permitted a rotation of crops and little requirement for imported fertilisers. Additional cattle were bought in for fattening in cattle courts during the winter months. Stock was fed during the winter from home-grown sources. Some barley and potatoes both for seed and for stock feed were sold but the predominant source of income was the sale of livestock, usually on a weekly basis at local markets.

Turnips were thinned and potato crops were harvested by itinerant groups of predominantly Irish labourers who were temporarily accommodated in bothies provided on each farm. Mechanised potato picking and the increasing cost of itinerant labour led to the discontinuation of this practice during the 1950s. The bothies were generally cottages with basic furnishings, and were sold for conversion in the late 1960s, or refurbished and let by the individual farmers.

In 1966 the WRI recorded that the hill farms (still) carried Blackface and Cheviot ewes, there were no dairy herds, and that most farms carried suckler cows. By the 1970s a number of farms had specialist herds of cattle, including Luing cattle at Duncrahill, Charolais at Windymains, and Aberdeen Angus at Humbie Mains. In 1983 a small flock of Wensleydale sheep was established at Leaston, which by 2000 had grown to about 50 and formed the basis of the 'Pride of Lammermuir' wool products business.

Since 1947 farm prices were supported by 'deficiency payments' from the UK government and subsequently by the Common Agricultural Policy (CAP) of the EEC/EU. This changed the economics of UK (and Humbie) farming, making the growing of cereals as a cash crop more attractive than stock rearing. In particular, the lower farms reduced livestock and extended the production of barley especially for malting. Large grain drying and storage sheds were constructed in the 1970s, the previous crop rotations were no longer possible and greater reliance was placed on artificial fertilisers and pest control chemicals. The quantities of straw produced were sold, sometimes on the field, to stock farmers in the area and further afield for winter bedding. The introduction of the round bale, and the mechanical handling of these, further reduced the requirements for manpower on the farms. Straw bales and polythene-bagged silage bales stored in the fields became a feature of the landscape.

By 1989 significant changes in farming practice were recorded by the WRI: whereas in 1966 a high proportion of arable crops were fed on the farm, ewes and cows had now been moved to higher ground and replaced by intensive cash cropping, made possible by agro-chemicals and plant research, and encouraged by the EEC support system and intervention. In addition to

Economy – Agriculture (cont)

Old Windymains Corner, Humbie (The Scotsman Publications)

wheat, malting barley and potatoes, oil seed rape and new varieties of peas and beans for animal feeds were being grown. The growing of peas and beans proved unsatisfactory due to difficulties in harvesting and transporting to distant processors, and was soon discontinued.

At the end of the 1990s the price of lambs was such that the hill farms were largely dependent on cattle for income, few of the lower farms carried sheep, and some (eg Windymains) had become entirely arable. Potatoes were being grown on only four farms, two by contractors, and turnips for stock feeding on two. The Aberdeen Angus herd at Humbie Mains continued but on a reduced scale, and Duncrahill had to some extent diversified into horse-breeding activities. To support major investments in larger more productive machinery, farmers were working more land, for longer periods, and with less manpower. Upper Keith, for example, in 1970 had a manager and four full time workers on the farm; in 2000 a manager and one man farmed Upper Keith and was also contracted to farm another Humbie property of similar size.

Local Government

In the 1953 account the Rev Bain noted (p259) that even though the community was locally represented on both the district and county councils, parishioners felt that they had no 'say', and therefore very little interest in politics. He added that to attract an audience to political meetings it was necessary for the organisers to provide 2 $\frac{1}{2}$ hours of whist and tea to 10 or 15

Local Government (cont)

minutes of political address. By 2000 even this practice had been abandoned, although local councillors did attend occasional meetings in the village. Following regionalisation in 1974 the parishes of Saltoun, Bolton, and Humbie were encouraged to form a community council, which would be able to make representations to the local authority, and promote local activities. A core of members represented the parish from that time, and there was at no time much competition for membership; up to 2000 there had never been a contested election for the Humbie representatives on the community council.

Miscellany

In conclusion, significant changes in the fabric of Humbie life since the 1950s have been due to the changes in the occupations of the residents and in land use, and the traffic generated thereby. From the 1970s agricultural traffic increased significantly, in part due to the increased centralisation of farms and the move to intensive cash cropping, requiring movement of tractors, machinery and agricultural chemicals and harvested crops between distant fields and central depots, and the export of these crops. In addition there is a substantial heavy traffic of grain to Ormiston and Pencaitland, and to and from the sawmilling businesses at Windymains and Petersmuir.

During the period, the size and weight of vehicles permitted to use public roads has increased, in part to comply with European regulations. The roads of the parish with the exception of parts of the main east/west road through the village were in 2000 structurally inadequate for the traffic wishing, and entitled, to use them. In addition, the inadequate width of the roads had led to the destruction of verges and road drainage systems by passing vehicles, leading to further deterioration of the road pavement edges.

With the increase of commuting to, in particular, Edinburgh, and the availability of second cars in many households, there was from about 1970 an increasing amount of relatively high speed through traffic on many roads. As the only roadside pavements exist within the village itself, the combination of cars and motorcycles, farm traffic, and heavy lorries made walking, pram pushing, dog exercising, cycling and horse riding particularly hazardous in some areas.

The influx of affluent non-agricultural households has, in general produced few strains in the community, where incomers have been welcomed for their diverse talents and enthusiasm. However, in common with other parts of Scotland, some landowners and farmers have found it increasingly difficult to accommodate the aspirations of the non-agricultural for 'rights of access' for themselves, their dogs, their horses, their mountain bicycles, and their off-road vehicles!

Farmers may not in the future be willing or financially able to continue their socially responsible attitude to the 'stewardship of the countryside', and in particular to maintain the attractive hedges and hedgerow trees that are a major feature of the local environment, but which are no longer required to enclose stock and which do not in themselves generate an income.

In the past, fund-raising for village projects (such as the new hall, and the church organ) brought the community together for a common purpose. Latterly, the availability of, albeit limited, funds from grants and through the community council, had reduced the need for such activities, and the availability of 'the wind farm money' may prove less than wholly beneficial.

In the 1953 account the Rev Bain considered (p255) that the almost entirely agriculture-based, and locally mobile, working population had little allegiance to the parish. At the end of the century the population was of a similar size but was largely non-agriculture based, from a more diverse background, and was much more widely mobile.

The assets of the village - the church, the post office/shop, the bus service, the village hall, and the school - were much as they were in the 1950s; their continued existence was still largely taken for granted, and they continued to be insufficiently supported to be viable on a long-term basis. There was a serious possibility that some or all of these assets might disappear in the foreseeable future. However, a strong mutually supportive spirit existed in many of the old-established and more recently arrived residents, which gave confidence for the future of the community.

This account of Humbie parish was written by John P. Bolton

FURTHER READING & REFERENCES

Bain, R.J. 'South-western District – The Parish of Humbie' Snodgrass, CP (1953) *The Third Statistical Account: The County of East Lothian,* pp252-268

East Lothian County Council (1953) *East Lothian Survey: The Hillside Area*

East Lothian District Council (1983) *The Haddington Area Local Plan*

East Lothian District Council (1998) *The East Lothian Local Plan*

Haddingtonshire Courier Yearbooks (1945, 1950, 1960, 1969/70)

Hajducki, A. (1994) *The Haddington, Macmerry and Gifford Branch Lines* The Oakwood Press

Hardie, Alastair (March 1987) 'Humbie Children's Village' *The Scots Magazine*

Humbie WRI (1966) *A History of Humbie Parish* (locally circulated)

Humbie WRI (1989) *Gleanings of Humbie Parish* (an update of the 1966 history) Humbie WRI

ORMISTON
PARISH REPRESENTATIVE: *Denise Brydon*

Main Street, Ormiston, 1979

Introduction

Ormiston is one of the most westerly - and oddly-shaped - of the county's parishes. Bounded to the west by Midlothian, it covers some 1396 ha (3450 acres), with two 'arms' curling protectively round neighbouring Pencaitland. Historic Ormiston village is situated in the north of the parish, on one of the 'arms' of land, separated from the remaining part of the parish by the upper reaches of the river Tyne. It seems that most of the parish population was centred on the village throughout the period of this account; while there is a cluster of 16 homes now at Ormiston Hall, there are no other settlements of any size in the parish.

Located on the B6371 road, which leads from Tranent and out of the village to Pencaitland, entry to Ormiston is by the impressive tree-lined Main Street planned (as was the village) by John Cockburn, Lord Justice Clerk, in the early 18th century. The history of the village plays an important part in its character with it changing from an agricultural centre to a mining village and recently - in common with many East Lothian villages - to a commuter habitat for the city of Edinburgh

Environment

The village is situated above the carboniferous limestone formation; the Tranent Splint, Four Foot, and Diamond No1 seams all outcrop in the vicinity of Ormiston but there are many faults in the area, which make the winning of coal both difficult and expensive. Nevertheless, for many years the fortunes of the parish were closely linked to those of the mining industry; in

Environment (cont)

Aerial view of Ormiston, 1988   *(Crown Copyright: RCAHMS (All Scotland Survey Collection)*

more recent times, modern opencast methods make the parish ripe for planning applications for coal extraction. Thus far, environmental considerations have won the day, as East Lothian Council continues to refuse such applications.

Coal has been mined in Ormiston since the 17th century, and many traces of this activity are still to be seen around in the woods of Ormiston Hall. Most of these were bell pits, where a shaft was dug down to the coal and as much coal as possible was taken out before the pit became unsafe; it was then abandoned and another hole sunk. It is recorded that in 1734 John Clerk of Penicuik came to Ormiston to give Cockburn advice about his coalmine. In March 1938, miners

Environment (cont)

working the Four Foot seam broke through into old workings and found an old wooden shovel tipped with iron (now in the National Museum, Edinburgh); unfortunately, the workings collapsed and nothing further was recovered. Surveyor Mr White estimated the workings to be at least 200 years old (so c1738). Situated between the Howden and railway bridges on the north side of the village, it was perhaps the mine mentioned in the Statistical Account of 1790.

Years of shallow mining resulted in problems of subsidence and drainage problems, which limit where new buildings may be erected.

Other minerals also occur. Ironstone (70% pure iron) is also found in the parish but in very thin seams. Limestone is plentiful in the southern part of the parish. There is an abundance of freestone and several quarries have been used; the oldest was of brown sandstone that can be seen in the older buildings such as the Hopetoun Hotel and the Cross. A new quarry produced a much finer and harder stone, which can be seen on the third storey of the Hopetoun Hotel.

The famous Ormiston Yew Tree mentioned in the previous statistical accounts still stands; Ulrich and Francesca Loening have prepared the statistics below.

Ormiston Yew Tree (David Fleming)

Measurements of Ormiston Yew Tree *in feet and inches*

Year	Ground Level	1' height	2' height	3' height	4' height	5' height	Ground Area expressed as diameter	Height of Tree	Source of Measurements
1790					11' 0"		53' 1"	25'	*Sinclair, Statistical Account 1790*
1824	12 '8"		11' 9"		13' 10"	17' 0"	59' 0"	29'	*Statistical Account 1835*
1834		12' 9"		13' 6"	14' 9"	17' 8"	58'		*Quoted in The Yew Trees of Gt Britain and Ireland*
1864		11' 8"							
1879	13' 4"			15' 00"	16' 10"	19' 8"			
1890		13' 10"	15' 00"	19' 8"			69'	35'	*An Historical Tree Hutchison*
1975	16' 1"		16' 7"		17' 9"				*Ormiston Hall Group*
1994	16' 3"		16' 11"		17' 9"				*Ormiston Hall Group*
2002		16' 6"	17' 00"	18' 6"	19' 6"	22' 6"	50'	30'	*Ormiston Hall Group*
Increase in Girth									
	3' 7" in 170 years	2' 8" in 112 years	5' 3" in 178 years	5 ft in 168 years	8' 6" in 212 years	5' 6" in 178 years			*Increase data unreliable*
Increase per year in inches									
	0.25	0.29	0.35	0.36	0.48	0.37			

Ground level measurements are unreliable as roots protrude above the surface of the ground
Measurements at 4 and 5 ft are unreliable as branches are forming at these levels
Present day ground level may be different from that in the past

Townscapes, Buildings & Landscapes of Distinction
The village itself is a designated Conservation Area, reflecting the importance of Cockburn's original planned village. Main Street is flanked by a number of 18th century houses, and many of these are listed.

Ormiston Hall lies about a mile to the south of the village, off the B6371; the remains of the old hall – dating back to the 16th century – were incorporated into the new hall when it was built 1745-8. In 1970, it was a roofless ruin, the result of a fire in 1944, which occurred when occupied by the Polish Army. Ormiston Hall had been largely unoccupied since before the first world war, though a caretaker lived in a corner of the steading courtyard until 1972. By 1970, the buildings of the steading, of which the original hall forms one side, the surrounding walled gardens and woodlands had fallen into neglect. In 1970 the Hopetoun Estates Development Company applied, unsuccessfully, for planning permission to build five new houses, with the steading serving as outhouses and garages. There was also a proposal, which was abandoned, to turn the surrounding land into a golf course.

In 1970 a group of four families (later five) approached the Hopetoun Estates Development Company to buy jointly the ruined hall, the steading courtyard, walled gardens and some adjoining meadowland and woodland. After the planning setback earlier that year the Hopetoun Estates agreed to negotiate a sale. Planning permission was granted to renovate the steading as three houses, a flat and a studio, to build two new houses and to demolish the ruined hall. This was to be undertaken as a unified project, to be overseen by one architect.

In 1971 the five families formed the Ormiston Hall Group (OHG) and concluded the purchase. The Hopetoun Estates Development Company remains the Superior and still owns the drives through the area.

The Edinburgh firm of Iain Lindsey prepared architectural plans for the renovations and new houses, and the Ormiston builders Campbell & Smith undertook much of the building work.

The conversion of the coach house (cartshed) in the steading, renamed House with Arches, was undertaken by Ulrich and Francesca Loening and their children as self-build, in an innovative style using mainly reclaimed materials. Aubrey and Margaret Manning and their children renovated the old hall in the steading. The gamekeeper's house in the steading, renamed Courtyard House, was renovated (self-build in part) by Colin and Marion Campbell and their children. The Courtyard House was sold in 1996 to Patrick Scott who finished the renovation and added an extension. Two new houses were added in 1973/4; Murdoch and Rosalind Mitchison and their children built Great Yew to the south of the ruin; Easter Haining was built adjacent to the ruin by John and Joan Busby and their children.

The ruins of Ormiston Hall were demolished in 1973, leaving the 18th century walls standing as a memorial. Between 1979 and 1985, eleven new houses were built in two areas of the estate that had been scrubby woodland.

In 1978 the Ormiston Hall Group purchased the wooded Belsis (or Leckie's) Glen to the north east of the Steading and the woodland containing the ruined St Giles old parish church (abandoned late in the 17th century) to the west. Much timber had been extracted earlier and the woods allowed to become overgrown with scrub and sycamores. Three families (Busby, Manning, Loening) of the OHG are replanting the woodlands with trees native to East Lothian. In 1982 a small lake was dug in Belsis/Leckie's Glen to enhance biodiversity.

95

Townscapes, Buildings & Landscapes of Distinction (cont)

The Ormiston Hall Group have endeavoured to undertake the renovation of the buildings, gardens and woodland in the spirit of John Cockburn, the 18th century improving landlord of Ormiston, who introduced many innovative practices to forestry and agriculture. Fruit trees have been replanted and the walled garden has been cultivated organically since 1970. A meadow is being managed for wildflowers and around 1000 trees have been planted. It is the group's hope that this work will be continued by those who will live here in the future.

Population

By parish, from the General Registrar's office

1931	2132(sic)	1072M	960F	*By locality – census –*			
1951	2234	1129M	1105F	*ie Ormiston village itself*			
1961	2195	1095M	1100F				
1971	2233	1116M	1117F	2004	988M	1016F	
1981	2121	1044M	1077F	2058	1012M	1046F	
				By Small Area Statistics - census			
1991	2241	1109M	1132F	2018	992M	1026F	
2001	2326	1141M	1185F	--	--	--	
By parish, from ELDC				*By settlement, from ELDC*			
1991	2226			2078			
1997(est.)	2370	1167M	1203F	2139			
2001	NO DATA			2079 (ELC)			

Population figures are difficult to compare, as no two sources extract data in the same way.

Belief

Ormiston had to wait until 1936 before a church was built within the village. For the preceding 300 years, the people had a long walk to their place of worship. The earliest parish church of St Giles was located near Ormiston Hall, and the Ormiston Hall Group owns its ruined remains. The next church (built 1696) was equally remote from the main centre of population, located close to Byres Farm, near the A6093/B6371 junction. A third was erected here, on the same site, in 1856. Nothing now remains of the Byres Kirk, except the Old Ormiston burial ground, in use from at least 1699. In 1986, Conrad W. Nystrom listed the gravestones here, and a copy of his list is held at the Local History Centre, Haddington Library; S. Duffy's updated list is available to consult during normal opening hours at E. Hart, newsagents in Ormiston village.

Although previously there were other churches in the village including a Roman Catholic chapel, and the earlier United Free Church of St John's, the main church within the village is now the established Church of Scotland, a modern (1936) building on Main Street.

Over the years, the church has been variously linked with Prestonpans, and with Pencaitland; in common with churches elsewhere in the parish, it is becoming increasingly difficult for individual congregations to maintain their own minister. The linkage with Pencaitland (15 November 1981) has an historic background; Ormiston parish was linked to Pencaitland and Cranstoun in 1568 when the first post-Reformation minister, Rev Andrew Blackhall, was installed.

Belief (cont)

The number of church members has remained around 200 in the 13 years to 2000, and in the same period the village population remained steady at around 2000. Incidentally, an indication of how much the influence of the church has waned may be gleaned from the communicant numbers. In 1627, the number of church communicant members stood at 280 out of a parish population of 860; in 1940 the number of members of the newly built village church was 496, when the parish population was 2000+.

Ministers

1924-57	William Y. Whitehead (minister of St Giles, then of the united charge from 1936)
1958-66	Robert W. Matheson
1968-73	William G. Dunnet

1975-81 linked with Prestonpans, Grange under the Grange minister

1975-81	Arthur T. Hill

1981 linked with Pencaitland

1981-99	Colin V. Donaldson
1999-date	Mark Malcolm

A further indicator of necessary economies was the disposal of various properties over the period. The Manse within the village was sold following the 1974 linkage, and in 1999, a small piece of glebe land beside the Tranent Road was sold for the erection of a gas pipeline installation. In 1989, repairs were carried out on the church hall roof (located on Main Street, opposite the old manse).

Homes

The village has seen many changes over the period. Although only one house seems to have been demolished – at the Main Street/High Street junction, many more have been built. A brief overview is given below.

In 1954, Fawn's Park, in Main Street next to the church, was converted from a house to a joiner's workshop; it was converted back into a house in 1990. In the High Street, Duncan's shop (Aggie Harrower's), and the old Sydey's building were converted to houses. The Co-op chemist at Limeylands Road/George Street was converted back into a house in the 1980s; the Coal Board offices in the same area were converted to houses in the 1960s, their role over in the village.

Both Turnbull's House and Clydesdale's (now once again named Hillview) House were converted into flats by a private building firm. Three new houses were built in Clydesdale House grounds, with two more nearby in Hillview Road.

Infill development permitted the building of several new properties between existing ones. Moravia was built between Dalveen and Strathdon; new houses were built at the back of Marketgate; five new houses were built in the gardens of Adelphi and Moffat Houses, one in the lane off Main Street, Aviemore House, and one in Stanley Place. One house was built in the police house garden, and Dr Iron's house was built in the 1950s. On the High Street, one house became two when modernised, and another two cottages became a single home.

Three new houses – Cockburn Court – were built to the rear of Beech Cottages; Beech Cottages themselves were converted into new houses. In the 1960s, New House was built at the end of George Street. On Main Street, three new houses were built where the garage was Cotterwall Court, and Tyne Steading was built at back of the old library.

Homes (cont)

*Clark Buildings,
Ormiston, 1940s
(left)*

*Clark Buildings,
Ormiston, 1975 (below)*

On a larger scale, several estates of council houses appeared in Ormiston.

In the late 1940s, new houses were built at the top of George Crescent/Limeylands Road. The prefabs were built in 1946; in the 1960s they were replaced with traditional houses. Housing to the south-west of the main village expanded in the 1950s: Park Road, Tynemount Avenue, Cockburn Drive and Moffat Road all date from this time.

In the 1950s, a small cul-de-sac appeared in Hillview Road. The top end of Cockburn Drive was completed in the 1960s. Sprinty Drive and Sprinty Avenue followed in the 1970s, and an estate was built at The Orchard. In 1987, the Coal Board houses on the High Street were upgraded after they were taken over by the council. By the 1990s, new initiatives saw the building of Hawthorn Drive – under a shared ownership scheme.

Shops & Services

In the time between 1945 and 2000, the village had changed. In common with most of Britain, village shops had closed as customers favoured large out-of-town superstores.

In 2000, Main Street had: a large store (dating from 1914) owned by Lothian & Borders Co-operative Society, which included a pharmacy; a chip shop/pizza takeaway owned by Roberto and Margaret Grilli; a post office owned by Alastair Main; and a newsagents and video/card shop owned by Denise and Ivan Brydon. There was also a mini-market at Park Road.

There were two public houses, the Coalgate and the Hopetoun Arms. There were also two social clubs – the Miners' Welfare and the Bowling Club.

The period covered by this account has seen the following changes to the village shops:

The old Tranent Co-operative Society store on Main Street, complete with butcher, drapery and grocery was replaced by a new store (on the same site) in the late 1940s. The new Co-op store (Howden) was converted from the old ARP hall. A further new Co-op was built at Moffat Road/Main Street at the end of the 1960s.

In the 1950s, T. & A. Gordon, grocers, was built in Park Road, and James Pringle opened a new chip shop in Main Street at about the same time.

The following had all closed: Lizzie McIvor's sweet shop; Mrs Mackay's sweet shop in The Wynd; Neil Wise, barber; Hector Carr, barber; Laidlaw's, draper; Richard McNeil, grocer at

Main Street in 1975 with chip shop which was at one time James Pringle's then later Roberto Grilli's. The building on the farther side of the chip shop was once Hector Carr's Barber Shop, but by 2000 had become Ormiston Day Centre

Shops & Services (cont)

The Wynd, pictured 1975. The shop on the corner was run by the Misses Walkingshaw at one time.

Ingram House; Davidson, grocer; a ladies' hairdresser in The Wynd; Sydeys, chemist and library, and its successor – a ladies' hairdresser; J. Neil's chip shop (which had a sitting area where the Coalgate pub is); Aggie Harrower's was also known as Duncans on the High Street, and sold beer and so on; there was a hut at the back where men went for a drink. W. Neill took over from Duncans.

The following had all moved premises: Davidson's/post office to Moffat House; Fulton's Sunday papers to a wooden hut located between the post office and the Hopetoun, owned by Miss J. Noble in the 1960s.

Other successful ventures changed ownership: Adelphi House Building changed hands in 1958, and was renovated as a house; Scott's paper shop changed to H. & E. Hart in 1972 and still trades to date; Kate Thin's general store at Limeylands Road/George Street was taken over by the Co-op for their grocery, then as a pharmacy, and latterly became a house.

Elsewhere in the parish, since the school closed in 1969, the Crossroads school buildings had been leased to small firms, in accordance with planning officer Frank Tindall's wishes. Callan Electronics, and artist Kenny Munro were amongst the first tenants. Latterly Crossroads had become private housing.

At Peaston, Emil Kozok ran the smithy from c1945 to his retirement.

Ormiston struggled for many years with its library housed unsatisfactorily near The Wynd/ Tyneview area, in a temporary portacabin building. On 8 January 2001, the new Andrew Purves library at Meadowbank (within the park), is due to open; named after the late local councillor it will offer a permanent base for the library, internet facilities and a meeting room. It may well be the first library in the world to open in the third millennium.

Healthcare [1]

Where previously there were four doctors' practices – that is Dr Ireland, Dr Nisbet, Dr Milne and Dr Irons – the village is now served by a purpose-built surgery. Built in the 1980s, it is staffed by Dr Davies and Dr Halliday Pegg with cover from the Tranent practice and the East Lothian Medical Emergency and Clinic Service (ELMECS) for the out-of-hours service.

There is now a day centre in the village, on Main Street, in what was Hector Carr's barbers shop; it opened in September 1992.

Education

At the start of the period, there were two schools for primary pupils in the parish. Most children went to the school (built 1888, and much extended over the years) in Ormiston village that, until 1954, served both primary and junior secondary pupils. The older pupils came both from the village and from all over the parish. From 1954, secondary pupils went to Ross High, Tranent, leaving the Ormiston school to the primary sector.

By the 1990s, primary pupil numbers at Ormiston were relatively stable at around 200, with 198 pupils in 2000.

An outlying primary school was located near Peaston – the Crossroads school (built 1871). It was said that no one lived very near to the Crossroads school, but all the pupils had a similar distance to travel to it 'to spread the misery' (Tindall, F. 1998, p123). In the 1930s, Crossroads school had two teachers and 95 pupils. During the post-war period, pupil numbers averaged about 30+, and the school was finally closed after the summer term, 1969.

Transport

Ormistons' passenger rail service ceased in 1933. The goods service and the line itself were closed in the 1960s. The track now forms the Pencaitland Railway Walk, a nature trail and path running from Crossgatehall, near Cousland to West Saltoun.

Ormiston Railway Station, 1960

Police

There was a police station in the village on Main Street; it is now a private house called 'Auldnik'.

Leisure

In 1945 villagers had the church hall in the Main Street (still there in 2000), and the old Free Church hall (1840-50). This last was also known as the ARP hall, and was converted to the Co-op, Howden branch, in the 1940s. The rebuilt village hall was opened on this site (George Street /Limeylands Road) in 1973.

The Miners' Institute opposite (opened 1925) had a hall, billiards and a reading room. The nearby bowling club also has a hall.

Organisations & Clubs

In the early days the following were available in the village:

church guild; Co-op guild; SWRI; mother's group; youth club; Sunday school bible class; guides; brownies; boys' brigade (disbanded in the 1970s); junior boys' brigade; cubs; after school club; the Ormiston Pipe Band (disbanded in the mid 1950s) and the Ormiston Community Association.

By 2000, only the church guild, Sunday school, guides and brownies were still operating.

Also gone were the picture house - the Kinetone Kinema (1934-58), the dancing, the night school classes - shorthand, dress-making, woodwork, country dancing, keep-fit – and even the bingo, whist drives and choirs.

The children's gala - the Ormiston Gala - in its present format began in 1938. Each June, a week of sports and fun events culminates in the village parade, and the crowning of the new gala queen in the public park. The gala is a self-funding event steered by a small committee and other helpers. Numerous fund-raising events are held throughout the year. The Millennium crowning and Gala Day saw a reunion of many previous queens, including our first gala queen from 1938.

Economy - Industry

Previously the main employers in the parish were: the National Coal Board; Wm. Brown & Son, building contractors; John A.G. Anderson (Ormiston) Ltd., joiners; builders Campbell & Smith; the Co-op; local shops; and local farms that needed field workers to harvest the soft fruit crops. Armstrong's garage, later Dunsmuir's Ltd., and McNeill's garage in the former picture house also provided some work.

In 2000, Campbell & Smith; the (much diminished) Co-op; local shops (although fewer in number) and McNeill's Garage remained as local employers.

New employers include the biotechnology industry – P.P.L. Therapeutics (see Tranent parish) operating at two East Lothian sites - St Clements Wells Farm and East Mains, Ormiston, and Inveresk Research (see Inveresk parish). Philip Wilson, corn factors (grain storage and drying facility), was located in the village, although few villagers were employed here. The vast majority of the population found employment outwith the village.

Economy – Mining

The biggest change to the village between 1945 and 2000 was possibly brought by the national decline of the deep coal mining industry. By the end of the 1960s, there remained no working pits in Ormiston.

Prior to that, there were several mines in the parish:

White's Pit was located $^1/2$ mile due east of the Tyne Brig on the south side. It was a small but very profitable mine; it closed in the 1940s.

Tynemount Colliery was sunk in 1925 and produced about 35 tons per day in 1948. It closed in 1962.

Limeylands was the largest colliery in the parish (sunk 1894). At its peak it employed over 200 men producing 300 tons of coal per day. It closed in 1953 with the miners being transferred to the Bellyford, on the other side of the main road about 200 yards north of Limeylands, which itself then closed in 1962.

Winton Mine started in 1949 and was the last pit working in the village. It finally closed in the late sixties leaving miners to commute to the remaining pits in the Lothians.

Bellyford Bing, Ormiston, 1994

Working at Limeylands, 1940-50 - David Fleming shares his memories

'I started work as an apprentice engineer in November 1940. The manager of the pit was Jim McIvor, probably because the McIvors were large shareholders [in the Ormiston Coal Company]. He was a fine old man and very well liked – not suitable material for a mine manager but things went smoothly most of the time.

Economy – Mining (cont)

The shaft was only 360 feet to the coal seam and the coal even after 30 years was still relatively near to the pit bottom. It was therefore still a profitable enterprise. The pit was also self-sufficient. Coal from the mine was used to fire the three Cornish boilers, which produced steam at 100 pounds per square inch. This steam was used to drive a Howden steam reciprocating engine, which in turn produced the electrical power necessary to drive haulages, pumps, coal machines and air compressors. Steam was also led by pipe to the workshops 60 yards away and the steam engine there drove an overhead shaft fitted with belt pulleys, and these belts turned the lathes, drilling machines and fans which supplied air under pressure to the blacksmith's fires. They also provided power for woodworking machinery.

The workshops had three blacksmiths, John Gardner, Tom Hepburn and Andrew Nisbet. The engineers were A. Montgomery (Chief), J. Fergusson, J. Molloy, W. Gardner, P. Rintoul, A. Brown (turner). The joiners were J. Sibbald, W. Scott, and W. Sinclair. The storekeeper was P. Hook. Electricians were W. Webster (Chief), E. Waterson, W. McIvor, and R. Allan. All maintenance work was done by these tradesmen, they made the hutches for carrying the coal, switchgear for the rail tracks and they repaired and refurbished steam engines, pumps and all the mining machinery.

On the pithead, when a hutch full of coal was brought to the surface ($^{1}/_{2}$ ton) it ran on rails to a checkweigh hut where it was weighed by a worker for the company then it was checked by a man for the miner. A token taken from the hutch showed who had dug the coal. The hutch then ran into a tumbler, a boy pulled a lever and the coal was tipped onto a moving conveyor belt. Boys on either side of the belt picked out any stones ensuring that only coal went into the waiting wagon. The wagons were about 30 tons and the coal was weighed again before it went to the customer. Waste and stones from the mine were filled into a tipper and a steam engine pulled the tipper by a wire rope to the top of the bing where it was tipped over. Limeylands bing was huge.

The miners needed a constant supply of timber pit props and boys filled hutches with them and they were sent below to where they were required. The pit also had a sawmill to cut the props etc – Jimmy Wightman was in charge.

The cage held four men - there were two of them. As one cage came up the one next to it went down. A wire rope was attached to each cage and a steam-winding engine lifted and dropped them as necessary to a bell signal. Once you were aboard the cage, the gates were shut, you were dropped like a stone and when the cage slowed nearing the bottom, you felt as though you were floating. Once down the weather was always pleasant. On cold frosty days it was nice and warm and on hot summer days it was cool and comfortable.

On the east side of the shaft lay the cross-cut section and walking along was quite pleasant. The roof was about 6 feet high. After about quarter of a mile you came to the cross-cut pump house, which was in a huge cavern dug out of the rock/coal. Inside were three turbine pumps which pumped water from a sump, which was a large hole, again dug out to collect water from pumps further in. They pumped about 200 gallons of water a minute. Water was a great and costly problem in these collieries. Water was pumped from sump to sump until it reached the surface.

Going further in you passed groups of hutches (six); they were clipped to a moving wire rope, which took the coal to the pit bottom. About a mile from the bottom you came to the section where the coal was being won. At the face conditions were bad. There was a low roof with a constant flow of water coming from it, which was pumped away by a small pump driven by an electric motor. The coal was undercut to a depth of three feet over a distance of between 60 and 100 yards then holes were bored in the top of the coal, which was blown down by sticks of gelignite. Everybody had to get out when they fired – the reek

and coal dust was horrendous and took ages to clear. It was a dangerous business with many injuries and a few fatalities over the years.

After the coal was down, the face men filled the hutches brought up to them by the drawers. When the hutch was filled the drawer pushed them to a road head where the haulage took over. It was backbreaking work. If you worked hard you could make a good wage and most of the young lads worked like horses.

With the gelignite reek, stone and coal dust, and the effects of water and dampness – many men were finished at 40 – some lasted longer but eventually they too paid the price. As the money was good they made hay while the sun shone.

Farther to the east side of the pit lay Winton mine but before you got there, there was a very steep dook (brae). They called it a wheel brae – it was a horrendous affair- the full hutches coming down dragged the empty one up. It took a highly skilled boy to work the brae. Most boys in the mine were skilful – they had to be to survive.

Going to the west side of the pit was Glen's section. On this side conditions were awful - dooks all over the place. The roads to the face where the hutches had to be pushed were very narrow and low and every so often a large piece of newspaper would be inserted in a roof girder. When I asked what it was for the drawer said "Well, when ye see a paper take yer hands off the top o the hutch or ye'll get yer hands taken off!" The top of the hutch scraped the roof and many more awful things had to be put up with. I remember working with an engineer at the coalface "Take yer hands off the top o' the machine". "What fer?" says I. "Jist dae it" the engineer growled, so I removed them. Seconds later a big stone fell from the roof onto the machine.

In general, the day shift started at 7am. At 9.40am you had a 20 minute break for your piece. The " piece" was bread sandwiches with roast beef, cheese or dried egg, which came from the States. To drink, it was usually tea. There was not much coffee. You got the piece at the canteen – old Churchill wanted the miners fed well enough to produce coal for the war effort. You held your bread with a piece of newspaper for if your hands had been in water where rats had urinated, you were in danger of catching black jaundice. Between 1926 and 1946 black jaundice killed three Ormiston men and made many more ill. The dayshift finished at 2.30pm.

During the war, there were no pithead baths – they came in the early 1950s. The pit was producing 350 tons of coal a day in 1947. The new Labour government nationalised the mines. The colliery was never the same again as the tried and trusted men who ran the pit were gradually replaced (political appointments). The union delegates more or less took over. Nothing could be done without their approval. Stones instead of coal were put in the hutches by some miners since more weight meant more money. There were many more abuses and by 1948 the colliery was unprofitable. The coal was too far away and incurred extra transport costs.

In August 1948, very heavy rains over a few days flooded fields west of the pit to such an extent that the water burst through to the workings. I was down the mine with another engineer when we felt a rush of air on our faces. We knew something was wrong so we made for the pit bottom with the rest of the men and we just made it before the water started to come up the shaft. All the machinery was submerged including 37 electric motors. The pit was closed down and special submersible pumps were brought from Newtongrange. The water was eventually pumped out but it was a long time before things returned to normal. Production was resumed but on a smaller scale.

The colliery closed in 1953 after a life of nearly 60 years. The neighbouring pits, Bellyford and Oxenford, closed in 1962 thus ending nearly 400 years of coal extraction in the area'.

Economy - Agriculture

The big change in agriculture between 1945 and 2000 has been the change from stock to white crop, which is less labour intensive. White crop has taken over a good proportion of the land. Oil seed rape was farmed for a time but is no longer being grown in the parish. The smaller farms have been incorporated into the larger farms – such as Dodridge, which is now part of Whitburgh estates. Two market gardens, that run by Slight at Marketgate and that by Watson in Ormiston Hall, have also disappeared from the village in this timespan.

The number of people employed in agriculture has also greatly diminished with more machinery being utilised and thus farms becoming less labour-intensive. In the 1950s, Ormiston Mains employed five men; now this farm can be operated by two men, and casual labour at harvest time.

Sheep are not now farmed in the parish but merely wintered. The sheep at P.P.L. Therapeutics (see Economy – Industry) are bred for their antibodies and are not agricultural stock. There are dairy cows at the Murrays where there is also a production dairy for Fairfield Dairies. A piggery is in operation at House of Muir.

This account of Ormiston parish was initiated and collated by Denise Brydon. Additional information, research and essays were provided by the following:

Denise Brydon	Homes; Economy
Dr Andrew Davies	Health
David Fleming	Homes; Economy - mining
T. Gifford	Economy - agriculture
Francesca Loening	Townscapes, Buildings & Landscapes of Distinction - Ormiston Hall
J. Nichols	Belief
Mabel Smith	Homes; Shops & Services; Economy

FURTHER READING & REFERENCES

Lyell, Annie (2001) *Ye see it a': the Ormiston Story,* East Lothian Council Library Service

Tindall, F (1998) *Memoirs & Confessions of a County Planning Officer,* The Pantile Press, Midlothian

Notes

[1] See also Pencaitland parish – Healthcare for extracts, and the CD-ROM for the full transcripts, of essays by Drs Milne, Kennedy & Davies; their Tranent practice covered Ormiston and Pencaitland too. This material was collected by the Pencaitland team

PENCAITLAND
PARISH REPRESENTATIVE: *Ralph W. Barker*

Introduction

The general aspect of Pencaitland parish is pleasing, with a distant view of the Lammermuir hills. In 2000, the parish was much the same as it was just after the war; conditions then were not very different, except for rationing and the general relief that the war was over. Housing was difficult in some cases. Homes were required for returning servicemen, and some Polish men, ex-soldiers, remained in East Lothian and made their homes in the county, some in Pencaitland. They were soon absorbed in the local population. The fighting men who lost their lives caused a great deal of sadness, however, and these tragedies are recorded on the war memorial.

Pencaitland village

The parish covers some 2056ha (5080 acres), and is bisected by the upper reaches of the river Tyne, which enters the parish when it leaves the adjacent parish of Ormiston. Known as the Tyne Water, it becomes the river Tyne proper at its confluence with the Birns Water at Spilmersford, and shortly afterwards leaves the parish.

The main area of settlement is clustered in the twin villages of Easter and Wester Pencaitland, which are situated one on each side of the river and the A6093 road. This Haddington/A68 road crosses over an old bridge joining what were at one time separate communities. The two villages are situated at the tops of steep banks with the river flowing in between. The haughs are frequently flooded after heavy and prolonged rain, sometimes resulting in damage to crops. The hamlets of New Winton and Glenkinchie lie nearby. Scattered houses are a feature of Jerusalem (six) and the Boggs Holdings, where there is a fair sized population living on the former smallholdings, centred on the old (now privately owned) Boggs farmhouse (see Economy - Agriculture).

The parish is well wooded. Estate policies are partly responsible for this, and the shelterbelts and the policies of Woodhall, Fountainhall and Winton House play a large part in the amenity of the village. The parish is almost entirely arable, with only a small amount of permanent or ley grass.

Environment

Pencaitland parish has been the same size, roughly three miles square, from time immemorial, and the civil parish boundaries remained the same throughout. However, Glenkinchie was transferred to Pencaitland ecclesiastical parish during the 1960s.

The parish has rather clayey soil, with the exception of the haughs and along the streams. Boulder clay covers carboniferous rocks. There is, however, a band of lower limestone as evidenced by the abandoned kilns and old quarries at Spilmersford; these last were unfortunately filled in, as previously they had been full of water creating large ponds. An old quarry remained at Jerusalem, which became a haven for wildlife.

There were small mines in the parish for hundreds of years. The only pit of any consequence was Woodhall pit, which was closed in the late 1940s. The spoil heap there burned through the 1950s to about 1961; thereafter the then county council levelled the bing and, with great success, created a mixed woodland and picnic site, thereby encouraging much wildlife.

Wildlife: on a parish level, the collared dove appeared in Pencaitland in the 1950s. About the same time the green woodpecker colonised the Pencaitland woods and was not uncommon in the neighbourhood; during the cold winter at the beginning of the 1960s the population dropped and has never recovered, though a few still make infrequent visits to the parish.

The red squirrel left the parish but the grey squirrel moved in, in force. The decline in farmland birds is such that many of them are rarely, if ever, seen or heard now. Modern farming practices may be partly responsible. There has been a decline in butterflies but the orange tip has made a welcome return, which, in season, is now relatively common. The species had not been seen for 100 years in Lothian, but it has now recolonised, and is present in Pencaitland parish [1].

Dutch elm disease made great inroads to the local elm population, which consisted mainly of Wych elms, though in many cases the brushwood lingers when it is part of a hedge. Plants of various species are scarcer than formerly. There is no doubt that the overuse of sprays and herbicides is responsible, although the council co-operates with the Scottish Wildlife Trust when vulnerable plants are present on grass verges; grass cutting is then restricted.

Changes

Woodland at Woodhall, formerly a Forestry Commission property, is now in private ownership and has been sensitively dealt with, hard woods now mingling with the reduced number of conifers. Fountainhall's owners too, purchased Forestry Commission woodland, as did one other proprietor.

Hedges feature in the parish; only five hedges were removed during 1945-2000 but many of the older hedges are slowly deteriorating. None have been replanted.

There were three ponds in the parish, two of which have now silted up. The third was formed but was drained and then reverted to grass. In 2000, a large pond or lake was being created in the meadows in front of Winton House. There was a small refuse tip in the village, but it was filled in post-war.

The old railway line is now a vibrant wildlife corridor, known as the Pencaitland Railway Walk. Some 60 species have been identified along its length.

Dr R.R.B. Leakey describes Jerusalem, in the far north east of the parish, off the A6093

'Six houses on about nine acres of land constitute the hamlet of Jerusalem. This enclave is surrounded by Samuelston Mains and Jerusalem Farm; recently, until the 1960s, a smallholding was based on Jerusalem Croft. At about the time the area passed to private housing, shelterbelts were planted with Scots pine, larch and Norway spruce to protect the houses from the north winds. Further spruce plantings were made about 25 years ago on part of the area, while much of the remainder became a hawthorn thicket. Over the last ten years, we have slowly started to transform all but a small part of this thicket into mixed woodland, planting a wide assortment of plants, including about 25 species of broadleaved trees and a few conifers. The transition from thicket to woodland is almost complete. The proximity of this area to the adjoining spruce and pine stands has created an excellent habitat for wildlife, and we enjoy very diverse birdlife. In this era when international attention is focussing on the loss of biodiversity on a global scale as a result of man's mismanagement of natural resources, it is nice to think that at least small pockets with diverse flora and fauna can be created, and hopefully sustained, around Pencaitland'.

Stone walls are a feature of the village, particularly in the east village adjoining the churchyard, where the height of the walls on each side of the road creates a canyon-like effect. One building site caused the boundary wall to be lowered but it still remains as a sizeable wall.

The provision of a footpath led to the demolition of a dilapidated field boundary wall; it is hoped it will be replaced by a boundary hedge. Several stone walls were demolished entirely by vandalism, with a stone wall opposite Beech Terrace being used as a 'quarry', presumably because certain individuals wish to increase their rockeries. Pleasingly, the wall was rebuilt c1997-8.

In the village, a few gap sites were filled by housing development; any remaining such sites should not necessarily be developed. Part of Pencaitland's character is the intermittent nature of the housing interspersed with gardens and natural areas (see Homes).

Land Ownership

Pencaitland is a rural/agricultural village with an original core of houses provided by local landowners, with the addition in the 1880s of mainly work-associated terraced houses and amenity building for employees in the local coal industry. In the 1920s, a council housing estate was built and was added to through the years.

The largest estate in the parish is Winton. With the exception of land sold for housing at Spilsmersford, the estate is largely intact and is still owned by the same Ogilvy family as in 1945. In the first half of the review period, fringe areas of the village changed ownership: the sale of Spilsmersford land – occasioned by inheritance factors and the need to pay for repairs and maintenance of the principal property – changed the balance, population and employment locations of the village.

The change in land ownership was not so revolutionary as in some other places, but new owners came about because of the new houses in the parish, mostly in Easter Pencaitland. In fact, in the housing estate the new owners were almost, in their comparatively small area, numerically dominant over the bigger landowners. The estates of both Woodhall and Fountainhall changed hands over the period. The fourth large house, 19th century Tyneholm,

Land Ownership (cont)

Housing at Spilmersford, 1990s.

was privately owned in 1945, but went through a series of uses and owners – including as a Dr Barnardo's home and a nursing home – and by 2000, was for sale.

Landowners in the Boggs Holdings changed through time as the holdings were sold for a variety of purposes, and new owners moved in. Some farms changed hands, but continued as farms under their new ownership (see Economy – Agriculture).

Townscapes, Buildings & Landscapes of Distinction

There were no buildings of great note demolished, reinstated or built in Pencaitland parish over the 55 years.

Winton House came through the war relatively unscathed, but the landscape and gardens did not. The west park was ploughed, and woodlands cut down, being replanted in the 1950s and 1960s. The east park was ploughed in the 1950s. Landscape restoration is an ongoing process; its importance being as a setting for the A listed house and the other listed ancillary buildings (Land Use Consultants, 1987, pp247-52).

There are several attractive, but perhaps somewhat smaller, private houses in the parish, including Beech Terrace and Islay House. The former United Free Church and its associated manse were both sold, and the church was subsequently converted to a house.

Easter Pencaitland has quite a wealth of older properties, all of them with character such as Pencaitland House (now actually two separate buildings). Larger houses are interspersed with cottages, and a house with decorative chimneys (St Michael's Lodge) and three larger houses for many years marked the extent of the village. As is common in Scotland, the parish has some large and handsome farmhouses, such as the listed Wolfstar.

Population

By parish, from the General Registrar's office

1931	1398	727M	671F	*By locality – census –*		
1951	1413	742M	671F	*ie Pencaitland village itself*		
1961	1620	819M	801F			
1971	1542	767M	775F	828	407M	421F
1981	1906	934M	972F	978	474M	504F
				By Small Area Statistics - census		
1991	2163	1074M	1089F	1244	608M	636F
2001	2467	1205M	1262F	--	--	--

By parish, from ELDC   *By settlement, from ELDC*

1991	1969	--	--	1287	
1997 (est.)	2497 (sic)	1230M	1266F	1697	89 *New Winton*
2001	NO DATA			1566 (ELC)	

Population figures are difficult to compare, as no two sources extract data in the same way.

Population Census by Decade

Year	1951	1961	1971	1981	(1991)	2001
Population	1413	1620	1542	1906	2163	2467
Decade Change	20 yrs +15	+ 207	-78	+364	+257	+304
% rounded	+1%	+15%	-5%	+24%	+14%	+14%

The increase of 207 between 1951 and 1961 can be mainly attributed to post-war private and council building in Wester Pencaitland; the council supported the expansion of Pencaitland to encourage people to the county (this was at the same time as the Glasgow overspill initiatives at Haddington and Dunbar). The high percentage increases in the 1981 and 1991 figures reflect the substantial amount of new houses built on land acquired by a developer from the Winton estate, in Easter Pencaitland (Tindall, F.P. pp149-151).

In January 1985, the district council announced that they had reluctantly agreed with the developers on a compromise plan to develop the Easter Pencaitland site in phases, with a mixture of council and private housing. The council would have to pay compensation up to £2.5 million if they refused to grant planning permission (*East Lothian Courier,* 10 January 1986).

There is no categorisation of employment and location that would help future planning but it is largely a commuter population.

Prisoners of war remained in the parish for some time (both Italian and German, but not in great numbers); displaced people from Europe settled in small numbers in the parish and some foreign troops, particularly Polish ex-soldiers, elected to stay in Britain, some of them settling in Pencaitland.

Liz Strachan and Jan Bundy interviewed Janet Bassett (b1934) on a wide range of topics -

'After the war, five or six Polish soldiers stayed in the village. German POWs were invited to tea eventually. [There is] a bit of anti-English [feeling]. [There were] no coloured [people] except the Barnardo's children. [There was] prejudice there, but it was not put to the test.'
Janet Bassett

111

Population (cont)

*Glenkinchie,
looking south,
1940s*

Although it is unwise to compare figures drawn from different sources, it would seem that the result of large-scale new housing schemes in the east village is that the population of Pencaitland has doubled in the recent past.

The parish has three main centres of population - the combined villages of Easter and Wester Pencaitland, and the settlements of New Winton and Glenkinchie. The latest estimate (1997) of the population of New Winton was 89 and the Glenkinchie population, for which no settlement figure is available, was about the same. From East Lothian District Council's Small Area Population Estimates, the largest increase in population is in Pencaitland itself with a population of 981 (1981) rising to 1287 in 1991. In spite of estimated increases to 1347 in 1994 and 1697 in 1997, the 2001 figure was less at 1566.

Belief

There is only one church, the parish kirk of the Church of Scotland. Up to the mid 1960s, the church was generally attended by those of a Church of Scotland background. Those affiliated to other denominations travelled to Haddington or (until 1952) attended the chapel at Winton House (Episcopalians), Edinburgh or Dalkeith (Baptists) and Tranent (Catholics and Methodists). However, from the late 1960s, Christians from a number of denominational backgrounds, resident in the parish, chose the parish church as their local place of worship. Consequently, although the majority were still from Church of Scotland backgrounds, there were also Baptists, Catholics, Christian Brethren, Episcopalians, Methodists and Salvationists. There were still those who, as before, travelled from the village to worship elsewhere: the Jehovah's Witnesses went to Tranent. Over the years there were a number of attempts to establish other places of worship in the village, based in the village hall, but these survived for only short periods.

Pencaitland's ancient church has 12th century foundations with 16th and 17th century additions. It is a modified T-plan kirk, holding about 400 people, with two aisles and a gallery.

Belief (cont)

*Pencaitland
Parish Church*

The organ, by Connacher (c1885) is in need of repair; there are plans to replace it with a more modern instrument.

Following complete replacement of the ceilings and thorough redecoration in the mid 1970s, and replacement of the spire roof following storm damage in the mid 1990s, the church is in sound structural order, although work on the external stonework is urgently required. The layout is unchanged, apart from the removal of a few pews in the central area in front of the pulpit to increase the size of the worship area and to allow for greater congregational participation.

The manse is situated adjacent to, and to the rear of, the church. From 1981, when Pencaitland parish was linked with the neighbouring parish of Ormiston, the manse became the home of the minister of the linked parishes. In the mid 1970s the servants' quarters and nurseries to the rear of the manse were converted into a church centre, to provide accommodation for up to 60 people. The church centre was later converted to provide a self-contained flat for church use and a church office; it became redundant when the church's stable block, beadle's house and carriage house were restored as the Carriage House in 1992. This provided two large rooms, a kitchen and two smaller rooms, which are used extensively by church and community groups and have become a focal point of much village activity. The church raised the money, some donations coming from the villagers.

The manse garden, almost an acre in extent, was until the early 1980s, the minister's garden. It is now used for church events like tent missions, children's evangelism and fetes, and is maintained by the church and by the local authority. The associated glebeland was sold in the early 1970s to the local authority for the building of the primary school and for private housing. In 1998, the remaining glebeland skirting the river behind the manse was planted with mixed woodland to add to the public amenity walkways being laid out through the Winton estate and around the south and east of the village.

The churchyard adjacent to the church building is no longer in use. The village graveyard is situated to the east of the village and adjacent to it is a large private burial plot (c1900) for the

Belief (cont)

Ogilvy family of Winton House, which was originally intended for an Episcopalian church, to be dedicated to St Michael & All Angels.

Burials, however, have given way since the 1950s and 1960s to cremations, which are carried out in one of the Edinburgh crematoria.

The number of official Church of Scotland members in Pencaitland parish has fallen since 1945 from approximately 500 to 280, in spite of the near quadrupling of the village population. However, the membership roll held steady at about 280 throughout the 1990s. The number of adults attending worship on a regular basis rose from c40-50 in the 1940s and 1950s to 80-100 by the end of the period; this number had remained stable since c1985/90. The Sunday school however, had declined from a peak of 100 children in the 1960s to approximately 40-45.

The greatest change in church life was the growth in the number of activities during the week. After the war, apart from the Sunday services, a young people's drama club, social and fundraising events and the monthly meeting of the Woman's Guild (which still continues), very few activities took place under the church's auspices. The Sunday morning service continued in much the same pattern throughout the period, with the dominance of the traditional 'hymn sandwich', the hymns accompanied by the organ. Dress too changed from 'Sunday best' to informal wear. The Sunday school continues to meet at the same time as the morning service.

During the 1970s and 1980s a midweek service was held on a Wednesday to meet the needs of those who were working on Sundays. There was no Sunday evening service until the mid 1990s. Then a monthly service was instituted which alternated between a less traditional format, with the music supplied by a praise band, and a more contemplative healing service with communion. The healing service was discontinued in 1999 and the informal evening service became a fortnightly event. Four parish communions are held every year. Since the mid 1980s, early morning communion services and evening communion services are held once per quarter. From 1988 the church also provided a service on a monthly basis at the nursing homes in the village. In the early 1980s a prayer meeting and a bible study group were formed; since then, the number of bible study groups has risen to four and the weekly prayer meeting is supplemented by fortnightly breakfast prayer meetings for men and women. The church also runs a weekly coffee shop. Youth activities have come and gone during the period and have tended to last as long as there has been active leadership.

The church has adopted the quoad omnia system of governance, with the Kirk Session consisting of 24 members maximum. Women were granted membership of the Kirk Session in 1972. Reporting directly to the Kirk Session are a number of sub-committees made up of elders and other regular attenders (not necessarily members); the two committees report on Fabric and Finance, and Outreach and Fundraising.

Since the war, there have been five ministers. Pencaitland was linked with Ormiston on 15 November 1981, and since then the ministers have had charge of both parishes. Each operates independently. The character of worship, outreach and ethos of the church are heavily dependent upon the minister and tend to oscillate between a greater or lesser involvement of the congregation and a more or less flexible adherence to traditional Church of Scotland practice and tradition. This has produced tension in the congregation at each change of minister. The minister has throughout this period been chaplain of the local primary school, and has taken an assembly at the school on a weekly basis.

Belief (cont)

Ministers

1935-63	George Grandison Morgan
1964-67	John MacFarlane Wilson
1969-79	Leon David Levison
1981 Pencaitland linked with Ormiston	
1981-99	Colin V. Donaldson
1999-2000	Mark Malcolm

Here and throughout the text, Ralph Barker shares his experiences of living in the parish.

The Rev G. Morgan was much amused when an elderly lady fell asleep during one of his sermons in the 1950s; she then fell out of the pew and landed in the aisle.

Generally speaking, rites of passage centring on the church declined steadily from 1945. Baptism, which until the 1970s was open to any villager, is now restricted to the children of married couples, one of whom must be a member. Just after the war, nearly every child in the parish was baptised, with whole families being baptised together on occasion; the number of baptisms is currently about six to eight per year. The number of parish weddings held in the church has also declined to approximately five or six a year.

'Got married in church (vestry or manse if baby on way). No white dresses. Now some marry in hotels. Guests still get dressed up, but much less formally, eg Elvis gear or fancy dress; hats no longer de rigueur. Hire of kilts and dress suits now, used to be own best clothes – reception has not changed. "Pour-outs" went out as traffic increased and it became dangerous in 1960s; confetti was not allowed on the streets.'
Janet Bassett

Admission into membership is also much less common than it was immediately post-war, with, on average, only three or four new members per year being admitted. Most regular attenders in recent years forego church membership.

'[the] old hymns have gone, far fewer go to church now. [It is] no longer needed for help, [people] go to social services now. Many attended out of fear of hell. After the war, more people questioned. [Now] more special services eg for children, much more tolerant, less stern. [The] structure of church organisation much the same as ever; more people help with elders, these used to be all older people – age range widened now. Events – Christmas, Easter, Outreach, visiting ministers and concerts…
Belief - now much wider range – including Baptists, Salvation Army, Church of England, as well as Church of Scotland and Catholics; much more ecumenical'
Janet Bassett.

And on death
'[In the past, most] died at home; the body was left in house in a separate room. [We were] used to seeing a dead body, [and the] neighbours came in to pay their respects. Now, bodies are well presented and made up, the hair done. [This] helps families to see [their] loved ones looking good. On the whole people don't see the dead nowadays. Most wore black or grey. After the funeral, [there was] always a big spread with alcohol for family and friends. [The] Co-op in Tranent did all funerals. Now people shop around for different firms, [and some] plan their own funeral and make arrangements, paid in advance'.
Janet Bassett

Homes

Historically, the location of housing in Pencaitland was along the line of the road from Haddington to the end of Beech Terrace, with the road from the Cross to the White House (now Lempockwells Road) going off the east-west road at the Cross. These roads formed the nucleus of the village, which was very small; from 1920 on, expansion was limited to the gradual building of council houses. The conservation area includes this historical core.

New Winton is located south and east of Tranent; the 19th century Square, and the 1930s houses opposite are not spoiled by a group of six new houses and one on its own.

New Winton from east (left)

New Winton from north (below)

Glenkinchie is a hamlet of some 32 houses situated south of Pencaitland, with an estimated population of 100. The village's core is based around the Glenkinchie distillery with further development extending towards Peaston Bank (see Economy - Industry).

There were many farm-workers' cottages on all farms in the parish, many of which were improved or renovated to some extent. Few of them were allowed to decay and were kept in reasonably good order. Now, however, because of reduced staffing of the farm some of the cottages have been let (or sold) to tenants who have little or nothing to do with the running of the farm. At Wolfstar, a row of farm cottages was demolished, and modern houses with greatly improved facilities were erected. At the old Wester Pencaitland Farm, the cottages and the farmhouse were converted into renovated dwellings, though the farmhouse was left more or less unchanged externally. The cart shed, probably the best vernacular building in the village, was converted into a house.

New houses have been built on the site of Lempockwells steading.

Standards of living – some recollections of homes in the parish

There is in the parish a row of three cottages (age uncertain) built of random rubble in which is included a fair amount of very hard whinstone. The walls are approaching three feet thick, with a pantiled roof.

Before the 1950s, two of the houses had been amalgamated to form one dwelling with all facilities. The remaining house was uninhabitable (though inhabited), with no water or toilet facilities, but in a short time the resident was removed to a hospital. His hobby, when he was living in his own house, was catching rats. The number of rats was quite considerable and he registered his catch on the wooden door of one of the three empty privies now demolished. A larger quarry that was trapped was his neighbour's dog.

The third house was then joined to the others making a dwelling with five rooms, a renovated kitchen, and bathroom with bath and shower. Many old cottages are now serving a useful and pleasant function, with a long life before them.

Ralph Barker, describing Rose Cottage in the 1950s

'[In the 1940s] at Beech Terrace, the bath was in the kitchen, the toilet separate, off the kitchen ... there was a stone wash boiler in the corner of the kitchen... piped water was heated from the fire. There was a bed recess with curtains in sitting room. Other newer houses had separate facilities'.

Janet Bassett

And on the changing profile of Pencaitland's residents

'In 1975, six stone cottages, originally built for miners about 1820, all belonged to elderly people who had lived in Pencaitland all or most of their lives. Each cottage had one to three rooms, and most had lean-to kitchens and bathroom extensions. Of the inhabitants, one was a retired miner, two the daughters of miners, one a farm labourer and one a retired lady's maid.

Now all the cottages have rebuilt extensions and/or loft conversions. The one-roomed one was first extended, then joined with the cottage next door. The owners are now all commuters, with the exception of one who is retired. The cottages change hands frequently, being very popular with first-time buyers, so they are continually being changed, redecorated and improved. They are now occupied by a nurse, a retired teacher, two computer whizz-kids and an air hostess.

In 1975, only one owner had a car, and the farm labourer the use of his tractor. He would park it outside his cottage at lunchtime, causing a considerable obstruction in the narrow road, but nobody seemed to mind. Now every household has one or two cars, making a total of eight'.

Liz Strachan, about Tyneholm Cottages

In the 1920s, Mr Reid of Tyneholm made available a portion of land for council housing in the area south of the present Queen's Drive. Thereafter the council kept adding to their housing stock until 1940. From the end of the war, housing was difficult so a few temporary houses (pre-fabs) were built. Council houses were built in each following decade until the available land was used up. Housing for the elderly was provided in Wester Pencaitland.

Homes (cont)

This description of the 1950s interior of a pre-fab, Institute Place seems quite novel today

'We moved in with my husband's parents when we married … [They lived in a prefab which] was detached in its own grounds, with a garden back and front. [The] back garden was quite large – used for growing vegetables, except for drying green.

The prefab was of metal construction [- even the] fitted cupboards in each bedroom were metal. [There were] two bedrooms, a large living room, a bathroom and a good-sized kitchen. [The] fitted kitchen [had] metal cupboards; a double sink (Belfast) – one deep for the washing; an electric cooker. [There was] no heating except an open fire, [on which we burned] coal and wood collected [from] nearby woods. [There was a] back boiler for hot water'.

Margaret Fairbairn

'[There were] no new houses so young couples had to live with parents. Houses now change hands frequently'.

Janet Bassett

Post-war, a small number of new houses were built.

At Park View (1940s) houses had

'Two sinks, one deep 'glass queen' ribbed glass washboard, no "poshers"[sic], and a big boiler in kitchen for clothes washing. Washing machines arrived in the late 1950s… a clippy rug (rag rug) was the only carpet when I married in 1955, otherwise lino. For cleaning, there was a Ewbank or a carpet-beater. Everyone used cast-iron bath, once a week, otherwise they sat on the draining board with their feet in the sink.'

Janet Bassett

Later, private housing developments on green field sites account for the increase in Pencaitland's population. A number of housing estates are scattered about the village, particularly in the east village and at Spilmersford. Building took place through the 1970s, 1980s and 1990s.

Wester Pencaitland

Lamberton Court	31 houses, early 1970s, Lempockwells Road
Bruce Grove	15 houses, early 1970s, Lempockwells Road
Dovecot Way	9 houses, c1976, by bridge
Old Farm Court	9 houses, completed and occupied in 2000

Easter Pencaitland

The Glebe	14 houses (pre-1976, near the school)
The Green	49 houses, built in 1988

East end development

Vinefields (1980s)	64 houses + others
Tyne Park (1990s)	31 houses
Mill Way (1990s)	17 houses
Limekilns (1990s)	48 houses
Spilmersford View (1990s)	9 houses

Homes (cont)

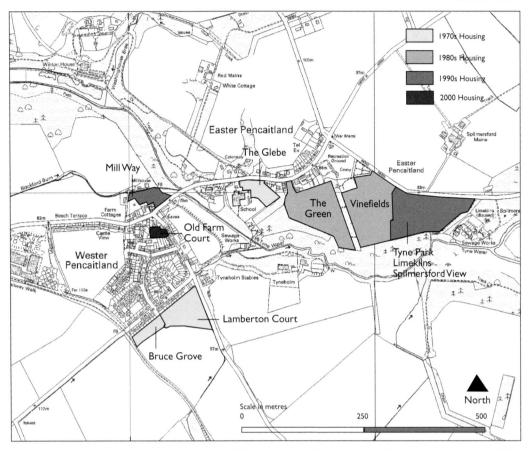

Pencaitland Housing

The increase in housing stems mainly from speculative building by private developers, including Wilcon Homes, Ideal Homes, Avonside Homes and Wimpey. The designs had no links to East Lothian. Indeed, they resembled the designs of 80% of the houses being built anywhere. The houses' lack of any particular architectural merit eventually resulted in the reduction of the designated conservation area of the village in the mid 1990s, when the housing areas of Vinefields, Mill Way and Limekilns were removed.

It took a while for the new population to merge with the older villagers but many of them participated in village affairs, partly through the church. Other people did not join in village affairs and merely commuted between home and work.

Private ownership gradually became the norm. In 2000, every house in the east village (except a small cluster of council houses in Easter Pencaitland) was privately owned, as were the Beeches houses. The majority of council houses are still council-owned in the estate in Wester Pencaitland, but a small number have been purchased by their owners under the right-to-buy legislation; these are fairly easily recognised, as the owners exercise their own tastes in windows, garden walls and doors. The opportunities for home ownership were just not there until tenants were able to purchase houses from council stock.

Utilities

There has been a public water supply available over the whole period. For sewage, a few homes still relied on private cesspits, but most had disappeared by the 1970s. At least one cottage - Rose Cottage, Lempockwells Road - had no sewage provision until 1952; there were probably more homes in the same situation.

Mains electricity is provided throughout the parish.

'All had electricity, very few were without. For heating ... mostly coal and kindling from the woods. Ranges went out, cookers came in. Bedroom fires to dry clothes – did not feel cold at time. Coal delivered to retired miners, others on coal van. Back to solid fuel in last 10 years [since the 1990s]'.
Janet Bassett

Mains gas was supplied in Pencaitland in the late 1980s. A very few residents use LPG.

Terrestrial television reception is good. Most residents can receive satellite TV. Mobile phone signals, too, can be received.

There are street lights in the main streets of the parish.

There is a regular rubbish collection (wheelie bins), and bulky items can be uplifted by arrangement.

Shops & Services

For other than 'everyday' shopping, Pencaitland residents travelled to the big Co-op in Tranent, where, twice a year, the 'divvies' (dividends) made it possible to afford new clothes; another occasion when clothes might be bought was at gala time. 'Luxury' goods were few and far between:

'In the 1940s and 1950s [it was all] sensible shoes (hardwearing), wellies, 'guthy rubbers' (plimsolls), hand-me-downs, coupons and rationing; then anoraks came in and winter coats went out – because of cars. Long coats came back in; hats, gloves and scarves were out. Umbrellas were rare in the 1950s, and Packamacs arrived in the 1960s.

We had Sunday clothes and working clothes; [they had to be] washable, as few could afford dry cleaning. [There was] no mail order, but firms came round the village with vans, which would take orders. Men have more clothes now, not just work clothes and best. Pullovers went out. Women [wore] aprons and wraparound, a little tea apron for entertaining in.

[There were] no bubble baths or shampoos until the 1960s, and no deodorants. [There was] a different soap for washing and washing-up - Lux and Palmolive. Perfumes of the time included 'Californian Poppy' and 'Evening in Paris'.

Post-war, men's hair was short back and sides, with Brylcream; in the 1950s, teddy boy [styles came in. Hair was] shoulder-length for women, older still in buns. A gents' barber went round the houses, and a postman cut hair in the evenings. Perms for women, tight ribbon around hair and roll; used metal curlers and pipe cleaners and rags, scarves around head'.
Janet Bassett

While there is no true 'commercial centre' to the village, there are and always have been a number of small shops serving the community. Premises changed hands fairly frequently but new proprietors usually carried on with the same wares. For many years, these shops were supplemented by a whole tranche of mobile services.

Many people were also able to be self-sufficient:

'Until the 1970s, some people kept hens [in the] very large gardens [of the houses] in Queen's Drive. Someone bred rabbits for food and fur. Everyone grew and swapped things…. fridges came in late in the 1950s – there was no place to put them anyway. In a fruit and veg. growing area, people ate what was in season, and the fruit and veg. van came round. We helped ourselves to turnips from passing horse and tractors. [We ate our] main meal at night, treats at weekends. Soups, stews, mince, roasts a luxury, large breakfast on Sunday, sausage, bacon, black pudding – no lunch – sat around table for all meals. TVs changed that, not so much baking'.
Janet Bassett

The local post office provided an excellent service with daily deliveries and collections. From 1990, it was located on the other side of the road from the previous building.

The Co-operative store operated until the late 1970s selling groceries, fruit and vegetables. The building was used after that (briefly) as a farm supply shop and then, equally briefly, as a bathroom supply shop. In 2000, the old Co-op building was being used by the local nursing home as offices.

A bicycle and motor repair shop (Rudkins) operated from a site to the rear of what was in 2000, the Spar shop, to 1992; it did not sell fuel.

The Spar shop opened in 1986, when Mr Ali Imtiaz took over from the Taylors; it sells general groceries, confectionery and lately, papers. Petrol pumps appeared at about the same time. It was extended when the repair shop closed in 1992. In the late 1970s, the building had been used as a general food shop, run by Bill and Elsie Taylor, and included a small delicatessen counter.

The Winton Arms shop (1945-60) sold general goods and groceries.

Papers were available from the White House, west village (Milligans).

From 1962-98, the several proprietors of the The Old Smiddy (formerly the blacksmith's shop and subsequently Dick Bailey's (joinery and building workshop and yard), offered food and drink, but the restaurateurs in general were fairly short-term. By 2000, it was empty, and the site is to be redeveloped for houses.

At the Boggs Holdings, several smallholders sold fruit, eggs and vegetables.

'[We shopped] once a week according to pay, [usually at] weekends. All the food was available in Pencaitland shops. Paper shop, post office and bakery, garage for bikes and shoes, Paraffin, Co-ops for everything'
Janet Bassett

The Winton Arms was a country inn, serving bar snacks.

'The men went to the pub at weekends. They tended to have a binge and get drunk when they got their pay packet, otherwise abstained. If they drank at home they were looked down upon and regarded as secret drinkers. Now, with fewer miners and manual workers and increased prosperity the pattern has changed. More drink at home through the week, not just at weekends'.
Janet Bassett

A wide range of mobile traders served the village over the period.

'Fish, bread, fruit, "Willy come early" (who was always late) the hardware van [with his] lamp in [the] dark, also sold treacle'.
Janet Bassett

Shops and Services (cont)

The following summary gives a feel of what vans called; the dates given are all very approximate:

Bakers:	Co-operative society van (1945-80s);
	Laidlaw of Haddington (1945-70);
	Wahlberg of Pathhead (from c.1970).
Boot repairer:	(1945-60)
Butchers:	Co-operative van (1945-90);
	Pow of Tranent (1945-90),

and there was another mobile butcher operating for a short time (1981-90?).

Coalmen:	J. Brand (1945-date);
	Fortune (1970-date);
	Turner (1970-date).

Coal deliveries were made to ex-miners in bulk.

Fishmongers:	Reekie (1945-date);
	Dickson of Prestonpans also called (dates obscure).
Fruit and vegetables:	Marr of Tranent (1945-80);
	Andrew Johnson (1980-date);
	Roots & Fruits (since the late 1990s).

Over the period, Pencaitland was visited (irregularly) by various ice-cream vendors. A chip van was a regular sight between 1945-70. The trader employed a portly boy reminiscent of the Dickens character in the Pickwick Papers. The van's approach was signalled by the trader leaning out the van window, wielding a heavy hand bell.

Pencaitland had a local library, in the old school. A mobile library served the village from 1970 on, operating from East Lothian County Council Library Service Headquarters in Haddington.

The services available in the parish included: Pencaitland Pest Services; the blacksmith/farrier; a caravan park – mostly for parking; childcare – small scale; a cleaning service – mainly window cleaners; electrician; joiner. By 2000, the public toilets were closed

Pencaitland's registrar for many years (before 1945) was John Cosser, followed by John Inglis Hepburn (1958-67), when the small districts were centralised. Pencaitland was then merged with Tranent.

Healthcare [2]

There was no surgery in Pencaitland village. Pencaitland patients mostly used that in Ormiston, which itself was part of the Tranent practice.

Dr J.S. Milne recalls a little of his work from his Ormiston practice, 1945-66

'The practice …extended from Haddington … to near Dalkeith … up to and into the Lammermuir hills. … all colliers, whether married or not, paid sixpence a week to the doctor of their choice for medical attendance and medicine for their families. We also allowed anyone … to join a club on the same terms as miners' families. … most of our income came from capitation payments and only about an eighth … from sending out bills. [Our] dispensing ceased in 1948 … if there was a pharmacist in the village, which there was, dispensing by doctors (except in emergency) was prohibited.

… there were very few motor cars … and all patients had to be visited who could not walk or cycle to

the surgery. Service buses were too infrequent to suit. We used to consult morning and evening, seeing about 15 patients each time. … no appointments …

Childhood illnesses were mainly not serious. We saw many throat, ear and chest infections. Wheezy bronchitis was common in small children. There was no geriatric service. … once an old person was on the visiting book we kept calling once a month. …the opportunity to tell us their troubles. The modern silent epidemic of dementia had not started…

In the 20 years from 1946-66, general practice changed a great deal…. demand … rose and continued to do so. In my time the demand was not unsatisfiable … in subsequent years increasing out-of-hours demand led to the creation of large rosters in which the doctor on call was up all night.'

Dr Gilbert Kennedy (1966-90) continues

'The Ormiston end of the practice was run by two partners, and staff increased to a secretary, two receptionists, and a visiting district nurse when required…. Infectious diseases had virtually disappeared by 1966 due to immunisation clinics. Bacterial infections … with the ever widening range of antibiotics. … Childhood ailments were rarely serious but … asthmatic problems seemed to increase…. we started an Asthma Clinic run by the practice nurse. …

By the 1970s the elderly in the practice were increasing and when they became dependant, they were not as readily looked after by the family as they had been in my early days in practice. "Old Folks Homes" were built to help the situation…

… smoking in the 1960s … still socially acceptable, but by the next decade … it was gradually becoming socially unacceptable. There were already many chest problems in the mining community such as pneumoconiosis and cigarette smoking added to these problems…'

And finally, Dr Andrew Davies (1990-2000)

'In 1990… the practice changed its area, drawing in its area considerably, hoping that with more patients being closer to the health centre, there would be easier access for patients to the centre and so reduce the need for home visits. This has happened in Tranent and also in Ormiston.

Workload has increased. Nursing homes have opened in Pencaitland and Tranent. … emergencies are handled by a co-operative of 11 practices (36 doctors) which covers west East Lothian.

Work in surgeries continues, looking after ill patients, many of whom are discharged from hospital early on many drugs and who need a lot of attention. Use of day surgery means increased vigilance and significant numbers of patients need readmitted. …

Our area has a high incidence of heart disease and stroke and diabetes (national average is 2%, ours is 10%), and cancer continues with levels of lung cancer in women approaching that of men. Infections still cause great problems, not least the upsurge in resistance to antibiotics and the onset of new lethal bacteria like E coli 157….

In general, children are very healthy but there is a new incidence of asthma and severe allergies eg to peanuts. Use of antibiotics has reduced in children. Most illnesses previously treated with antibiotics are viral and self-limiting….

Youth culture is an unknown area for many of us for the use of illegal drugs is greatly increasing. … Some patients in their late twenties have now been abusing drugs for 15 to 20 years. There is a definite incidence of long-term brain damage appearing….

Physical disability is less problematic and more is organised for disabled people … there is a shortage of places for respite for young, chronically disabled.

Healthcare (cont)

Older people are living longer and often alone.... There are lunch clubs and day centres in each village with added outings and activities. Families do try to maintain their old folk in their homes but cannot leave their jobs and the need for care plans is great.

Alcohol problems continue, with much evidence of over-indulgence.

Tobacco use is still very strong. ...

In summary, medical practice in the 1990s is expanding and is becoming more team-orientated to promote good health.'

And from a member of the public

'First aid was practised at home; [you went to an] old neighbour for old-fashioned remedies before trying the doctor. Another [neighbour] helped with childbirth and laid out the dead. Cascara [was given] to "clear you out". Treacle and sulphur (a teaspoon) for chests, once a year'.
Janet Bassett

Within the village, the WRVS (1945-date) did sterling work in delivering meals on wheels.

By the very end of the period, there were two nursing homes for the elderly in Pencaitland – that based in a new building (called Tyneholm Stables, because that was the original core of the building), and Tyneholm House, which closed during 2000.

From 1945-c1985, the 19th century Tyneholm House was used by the Dr Barnardo's organisation as a home for boys; there were about 30 residents. The house then became a nursing home for the elderly for about ten years; in 2000 it was for sale. A day centre was open once a week in the Trevelyan Hall.

'The elderly used to be cared for at home; [in the past they were] considered old at 60, now have to be 80. [It is] expected that social services will look after them, not the family. Now want them put in home, partly because children move away.

I can't remember many [people with a disability] in the village. The family took care of those there were. In the 1940s, handicapped children [were] taken away to Gogarburn. [They and their families were] largely just pitied and ignored. [Mentally handicapped people were] again tolerated but ignored; [their] family coped, otherwise despised'
Janet Bassett.

Pencaitland is one of several communities that fall under the Tranent Social Inclusion Partnership, a thematic SIP which is focussed on 'Youth with Community'. This partnership 'seeks to make a difference by breaking the cycle of inclusion which exists for many children and young people growing up in this ex-coal mining area.

... to involve and empower young people along with the wider community to take decisions and help deliver the kind of community and services they need' (*Sipped Up News,* summer 2001)

Based at Ross High School, this SIP is targeted at 16-25 year olds. Backed by government funding, the SIP was set up at the end of the 1990s.

Social issues

'Child molesters were known, so children were kept away from them, but [it was] not spoken about. Homosexuals – not spoken of or known – now probably prejudice exists, but as there are no obvious ones in village, not expressed.

Healthcare (cont)

Illegitimacy – war changed attitudes, but this was still a stigma. How would they manage financially? Now helped with money and a house and some have babies deliberately to get away from home…. Since the pill, mores have greatly changed. Promiscuity used to be despised. Increase in materialism – 'materials come before morals'.

Alcohol – drunks were scorned. [There was] no understanding of alcoholism but ordinary drunkenness was tolerated. Now the church has a visiting group. [In the] 1940s and 1950s neighbours and friends helped them.

Smoking – [socially] acceptable in 1940s and 1950s, then when cancer proved, gradually became unacceptable. Drugs – not [in evidence] at all until recently; now school children meet behind pavilion. Some get hooked when in the army'.

Janet Bassett

Education

In both schools – old and new – Pencaitland has been blessed, on the whole, by caring head teachers and teaching staff, and those pupils passing on to secondary school are well grounded in their various subjects.

Head teachers

1942-62	Charles Bruce
1962-79	John Archer MBE
1979-81	Thomas Couper
1981-97	James Marshall
1997-date	Miss Freda Ross

The move to the new school was made in 1976. It is a bright semi-open plan building and an additional three classrooms were built in 1998. By 2000, the roll was 225, plus nursery (20 morning and 20 afternoon places); East Lothian guarantees a nursery place for all three and four year olds. Pencaitland Primary School hosts an authority support base for young people from anywhere in East Lothian with social, emotional and behavioural difficulties. The maximum class size is six.

John Archer's years of teaching and his period as head teacher (1962-79) was a time of new methods of teaching; the following is extracted from an article in *Village School* (1994) pp19-20.

'… in the 1960s the changes … took place in primary education. They far exceeded all of the changes which had taken place from the occupation of the school in 1870….

The old school … The heating system was unreliable – with no janitor in attendance, the head teacher had to leave his class to stoke the boiler in the middle of the day. Toilets were situated in the playground …[until] the replacement of the old insanitary toilets by new mobile units…. The old dining hall… at one time a woodwork room, was damp and dingy and was replaced by a mobile unit, which was light, bright and airy. Meals were prepared at Ormiston school and brought in containers, which certainly did not add to their appeal.

With the increase in the school roll, a mobile classroom was then erected in the playground, making a total of four mobile units in a rapidly shrinking playground.

During the 1960s it was apparent that the old school was reaching the end of its days as a school… plans for a new school on land that had been previously purchased from the parish church….

Education (cont)

Old school at Easter Pencaitland (Ralph Barker)

In 1962 teaching was on a whole class basis, the teacher imparting information for the pupils to assimilate and to try to remember. This method took no account of the vast differences in intelligence, intellect and interests to be found within the range of pupils in a normal class. To change to a system whereby account was to be taken of individual abilities required a revolution in classroom practices. Henceforth the main function of the teacher was not to teach but to create situations and opportunities to teach a child to learn for himself. ... Although there were still occasions when class teaching was possible, the emphasis was to swing more and more to group and individual work.

Prior to the 1960s, parental involvement in the running of the school was non-existent. In 1963 the Mothers' Club was formed in the school. Parents also helped teachers prepare all the materials that were necessary for new methods. With so much parental involvement, discipline slowly improved and the use of the belt was no longer necessary. Another innovation made in the 1960s was the formation of children's clubs, covering a wide variety of activities, again greatly helped by the talents of parents'.

Mr Archer's predecessor, Mr Bruce, was an old-fashioned disciplinarian, but an excellent teacher.

Secondary education was provided at schools in Ormiston (junior secondary) and Preston Lodge (senior secondary) until 1954, when the Ormiston school became primary only, and secondary pupils went to Ross High, Tranent.

1947 was the last year for school leavers at the age of 14. Some of them were not too pleased at the lengthening of their school life, but most of the pupils soon came to terms with their new conditions.
Ralph Barker

There is little provision in the parish itself for adult and post-school education.

Transport

There was no change over time in methods of transport relative to Pencaitland parish. The trains had long gone – the passenger service in 1933, the one-a-day freight service in 1960; the line closed in 1964. On the buses, only service numbers had been changed for operational and administrative services as an attempt to make the public more aware of route numbering.

In 2000, bus services were provided by 'First Bus'. This ran a service to Edinburgh, basically at hourly intervals, with additional services in the early morning, but with an inconvenient gap of an hour and a half after the early services and the need to change buses in the evening. There was also a subsidised service on a circular route embracing towns and villages including Pencaitland and which made a link with Haddington. The community was well served by these buses.

In Pencaitland parish, more and more residents found that the possession of a car was an asset not only for commuting but for business purposes; shopping became much easier, and in the rural areas the sense of isolation was eased and some of the outlying parts of the parish were made more accessible. Conversely, parking the car became increasingly difficult; many cars were parked in the street, as there was, for owners of older houses, often no space available in the curtilage of the house. There remained, however, a core of people (mostly elderly or handicapped) who had no access to a car.

A section of the 17-mile Pencaitland Railway Walk (the land was purchased by the then council in 1971) passes through the parish. The walk is classed as a bridle path, and is used also by cyclists.

There is one right-of-way from Pencaitland to Ormiston. In 2000, Winton estate had begun work on a network of paths through the estate. There was public access along the Tyne to Nisbet.

Police

There was a police house in the village occupied by the local constable and his family; it had an added room, which served as a miniature police station. The local village policeman was always on the spot and was aware of everything that was going on, dealing with police duties ranging from petty theft to supervising the disposal of cases of anthrax in cattle. He was also a good community policeman, taking part and helping in various social events held in the village.

By the end of the period, times had changed. Some years ago (1971) the police station was closed. Policing post-1971 took the local policeman away to be deployed elsewhere; he was replaced by a police car which occasionally undertook a quick patrol through the village. Sometimes it parked in a conspicuous place near the garage when groups of teenagers were excessively noisy; of course they cleared out of the way when the police car arrived. There were infrequent visits by a community policeman, whose duties, however, covered a very wide area, almost reaching the English border.

Police finances were very stretched, which is no doubt the reason for the change in methods of policing, but it cannot be said that it satisfactorily replaced the 'on the spot' village bobby. There were, however, two special constables - auxiliaries - who were called when required.

There has been an apparent increase in crime in later years of the period, mainly house breaking and vandalism.

Police (cont)

Ex-bobby Joe Rowan shares just one of his experiences with the local poachers in the 1960s

'One weekend the local bobby was informed that poachers were intending to poach sea trout on a local river by unlawful means, (explosives and nets). A watch was set up by the police and eventually three men were seen to throw explosives into the river and after the explosion pull several fish from the water by means of nets. The men were arrested and the fish, nets and other equipment taken by the police as evidence.

As the police had no means of preserving the fish to retain them for production as evidence the only alternative was to sell them to a local fishmonger and retain the money received as evidence. A police report was submitted to the local procurator fiscal who decided not to take any proceedings against the poachers.

The outcome of the incident was that the money obtained from the sale of the fish was given to the owner of the stretch of the river from which the fish had been poached.

Unfortunately the nets and other equipment found in the poachers' possession and taken by the police as evidence had been stored in an outhouse which suffered storm damage and was seriously damaged beyond repair.'

Leisure

The ways in which people used their time changed over the period.

'Post-war, there were radios and very few TVs or cars. In general, mothers did all the [house] work, but children had to help. The family did the washing-up together. [In some households] a woman did not go out to work because the man didn't like it.

[That great leisure activity of courting] took place at local cinemas at Ormiston and Tranent, or at the dance halls – Trevelyan Hall, the Ballroom, Ormiston or Haddington. [There were] lots of places to walk, still asked parents for permission. Had to walk home, opportunities for courting'.
Janet Bassett

The unlicensed premises of the Miners' Institute (later a house) closed c1965 with the end of mining; it could be hired, and as well as the social club, there were weekly whist drives, snooker and darts. Outside the village, there is a small community hall at the Boggs, built in 1951 with money collected from the locality.

'Members met in the hall for certain social events – whist, carpet bowls and country dancing as well as the women meeting to prepare for the summer fete. They would do knitting, sewing and crafts such as basketry and pokerwork items for sale, along with the baking and preserves. This fete was the highlight of the year being held during August in the grounds of the Boggs farmhouse, although organised by the Boggs Community Association. It attracted large numbers of people from surrounding communities and was very popular. There was a children's party organised in the hall. Today the hall is used infrequently except for the Boggs Country Dance Association, which is still enjoyed'.
Beryl McNaughton

The Trevelyan Hall is now managed by East Lothian Council. For a number of years, it was run by the Pencaitland Community Association, and was available for hire to members of the public. From the mid 1970s the Church Centre was available; after 1992, this was succeeded by the Carriage House complex (see Belief).

These halls were used for dances; in the past there were dances every weekend, with the venue alternating between Pencaitland, Saltoun, Ormiston, Crossroads school and Humbie.

One particular dance band – that of Craig McVie – played all over the district until the 1990s. There are also many informal groups of pipers, accordionists, fiddlers and singers who perform on an ad hoc basis. An instructor in square dancing represented dance for a couple of years.

The halls were also used for parties, flower shows, as community centres and in fact all types of social occasions and small exhibitions. Up to the 1960s, the Rev George Morgan encouraged young people to appreciate music and several singers entered into musical concerts. Mr Morgan and others coached young people in drama and several shows were performed in the Trevelyan Hall, which boasted a small stage.

There were a few informal art displays in the parish. One was held in the Trevelyan Hall by the local amenity society in the 1980s, featuring paintings by L. David Levison (the minister) and by builder Richard Baillie who was largely a painter in oils and was a good minor artist. There were also photographic exhibitions of local scenes; in 2000, one was mounted for the Millennium, when a village calendar was produced.

Organisations and clubs came and went; brownies, guides, cubs, scouts, rover scouts and boys' brigade were all active 45 years ago; over time, some fell by the wayside but by 2000, scouts, guides and others were once again flourishing.

In later years, the primary school acted as a focus for the community. The cub scouts and rainbows all used the school, and the after-school clubs varied from year to year. Rugby, football, girls' football and netball were normally available. Youth clubs were run by East Lothian Council in the Trevelyan Hall from time to time.

In 2000, an application was being processed for an after-school club. This would be managed by a 'board' and located in the primary school. The hope was that it would cater for up to twelve children.

A playgroup also operates in the village, and play areas are sited in the public park and in the west village. Those at Woodhall Road and Lamberton Court date from c1975, and those at Trevelyan Crescent and the football park c1985.

Pre-war, Pencaitland organised a Children's Gala; suspended during the war, this was resumed in the 1950s. Unfortunately, by the 1960s, owing to insufficient helpers, it could no longer continue. It was replaced by a sports day each summer.

'The gala used to be a great treat. Daffodil teas – each person would set up a table and after cards or dominoes would serve elegant tea to invited guests'.
Janet Bassett

Groups for adults included the SWRI (established 1923, and re-started in 1947), which had an active bowling team in the 1970s. From the late 1980s, the Woman's Guild, a pensioners' club, and a lunch club all went well in Pencaitland.

Since c1985, the local horticultural society has arranged annual shows and plant sales. Other groups still active include the Pencaitland Amenity Society and the Pencaitland Art Club; there was also an annual pensioners' coach tour. The Pencaitland Lecture Society (established 1986) organise many and varied lectures and outings to places of interest.

At one time, the British Legion met in the Trevelyan Hall weekly.

Leisure (cont)

From 1978-85, the Pencaitland Music Club ran a season of concerts every winter, performed largely by gifted local musicians, but also by visitors from Edinburgh and elsewhere. The music performed ranged from folk to choral and chamber music.

Kind people lent their houses for the concerts, providing perfect settings for this small-scale music. The 50 or so concerts over the years depended entirely on the goodwill and generosity of musicians, organisers and hosts. Audiences were large and enthusiastic. The committee comprised: Penelope Ogilvy (flautist); Lionel Gliori (harpsichord maker and violinist); and organisers Ralph Wyllie and Liz Strachan.

Sport: locals have always fished in the Tyne; the Pencaitland Angling Club started in 1984 to encourage and instruct young anglers. By 2000, it had 30 members fishing ten waters each season. A weekly tote-lottery subsidises the cost of summer outings.

Sports facilities are available at the public park, limited to football, a bowling green and changing rooms. The bowling green has been used throughout the period, although the associated club closed in 1998, after falling into financial difficulties.

Pencaitland Amateurs (football), reached the final of the Amateur Cup played at Hamden in 1984; they merged with Ormiston Primrose and now their home ground is at Ormiston. There is also a youth football club, veterans' football club, tug-of-war team (who were Scottish champions five times & British champions six times). There is also a Sunday football team, which is run from the Winton Arms. There was a short-lived badminton club in the Trevelyan Hall.

From 1958-64, there was a cricket club.

Other leisure activities have had their followers, including table tennis (which had a fairly short life but was successful for a while), cycling, horse riding (in which there is an increasing interest), bingo had a period of popularity, being played in the bowling club to about 1990. Dominoes, pool and darts are played in the Winton Arms, which only had a beer and wines licence until c1955; since then it has had a full licence. It also holds weekly quiz nights, monthly ceilidhs and so on.

Gambling schools met 40 years ago (c1960s) in the park, and in the cart shed of Wester Pencaitland farm.

At the end of the war, there were six pigeon lofts, and pigeons were bred and raced; by 2000, there were only about two. From time to time there have been people walking greyhounds. There are serious bird watchers in the parish, and country walks were enjoyed by a large group of people during the late 1950s and early 1960s.

Swimming in the Tyne was popular many years ago but now with indoor pools in Haddington and Tranent there is not so much.

There was game shooting on Winton estate and the surrounding farms; some shoots were in organised syndicates but there was also informal 'walking-up' and pest control. In February/March each year large hare shoots were organised in the district where many guns would shoot 40-50 hares. Gundogs have been kept and trained in the parish up to the present time. The rifle club held its meetings and had a 15-yard range in the Old Brewhouse near the bridge, until it closed c1970.

Like other villages sited on the Tyne, poaching is a popular 'leisure' activity. Additionally, a large number of deer have been taken from various properties in recent years. This rather denies the claim that it was only 'one for the pot' (see Police).

Leisure (cont)

James Robertson, George Livingstone and Reg McVie share their memories of leisure times in the parish

'[People would] travel for up to 40 miles to follow a local dance band or regularly [go] six or eight miles for a Saturday dance by public bus, minibus or taxi; as a last resort [they went] on foot. On Sundays, only bona fide travellers could buy drink so there was quite a bit of to-ing and fro-ing. Taits in West Saltoun was an off-licence where it was possible to consume alcohol on the premises (under the counter).

40 years ago there was no trouble between the nearby communities and Pencaitland but then trouble started and continues at a low level, more than friendly rivalry, to the present day.

In 1945, holidays were just a few days and for farm workers had to be taken at short notice to fit in with the seasonal work. Later the 'trades' fortnight was taken although it is not so general nowadays. Camping was a great favourite with whole families going to Oxton or Longniddry etc. They would also visit relatives and stay with friends. Until 20 years ago Butlins was popular. It is only since then that families have been going abroad to the Costas.'

Economy - Tourism

Pencaitland is not a major tourist centre, but open days at Winton House and garden were, and remain, a major attraction, often coupled with visits to the parish church (open to parties by prior arrangement). Winton House has recently also become available for a range of commercial functions and has a long tradition of musical events.

The distillery at Genkinchie has a thriving visitor centre and museum of malt whisky (opened in 1968 - see below).

Economy - Industry

There have been a number of industrial activities in the parish, including mining.

The Pencaet Mine was privately owned; it ceased to be worked by William Gordon in the late 1960s or the early 1970s.

The Chancellorville Mine at Winton West Mains was opened privately by Mr Stein in the 1970s but closed after a short period of working under great difficulties. It was the last mine to produce coal in Pencaitland parish.

Glenkinchie distillery

Economy - Industry (cont)

Distilling and malting is a thriving local industry, with Glenkinchie Distillery (established 1830) producing lowland malt whisky. In 1939, the government severely restricted the supply of barley for distillery purposes; many distilleries closed but Glenkinchie was enabled to produce small quantities of whisky each year.

There was accommodation for horses at Glenkinchie. By 1956 the stables were almost empty except when Buchanan's Clydesdale dray horses came from Glasgow for their summer holidays. Two horses were kept, and barley and coal were carted from Saltoun station until the railway line closed in the next decade.

Bus loads of tourists come to view the distillery operations, see the museum, and no doubt to sample the wares. The permanent workforce – of some 10-14 - increases to about 23 during the tourist season.

Another very big user of barley is Baird's Maltings, which processes the barley. The market varies from year to year. In the 1990s, much of the output was shipped from Southampton to Japan, but by 2000, brewers in the north of England were the major customers. Sited to the west of the village in 1965, a new plant was built in 1978, and new drier in 2000; the buildings do little to enhance the village, but do provide some employment. The workforce is comparatively small, originally about 18, but latterly somewhat smaller. Annual malt production capacity is 45,000 tonnes.

Maltings under construction, 1964 (left)

Maltings after completion (below)

Economy - Industry (cont)

Other industries

When the mines and the pit were closed down and the Miners' Institute became redundant, it served for some years as a small factory making architects' models. This continued for a few years and then it closed down in the early 1990s; it was a loss to the village. The Miners' Institute has since then served intermittently as a furniture store, and is now being converted into a house.

Since the 1960s, a recording studio – Castlesound Studios – has occupied the old school at the end of Easter Pencaitland. It employs only a small number of staff, but a large number of musical groups (including Runrig) have recorded there.

There was a coach company that operated briefly from Pencaitland; by the 1990s, it had moved its headquarters to Edinburgh.

Economy - Art & Crafts

There were and continue to be many craft workers, artists and potters working in the area; a few are given below.

When he stopped teaching in 1974, Lionel Gliori started making violins and beautiful harpsichords in a workroom in his house. The instruments are works of art, not only musically but also artistically, being colourfully decorated with painted landscapes and other designs. Lionel has also made a few pieces of church furniture. He is partially retired.

Winton Pottery is located on the estate but is a completely separate entity. Marg Hall came to Pencaitland in the early 1970s, beginning her business in a small way and then full time in 1976. For three years she made miniature ceramic furniture, but since then has made hand thrown domestic stoneware and commissions such as commemorative plates and mugs. (Until 1985, her husband Chris Hall 'sculpted'. He is now based elsewhere).

Peter Stewart, who made hand-built ceramics and traditional stone musical instruments such as ocarinas, joined Marg Hall from 1994-2000.

The last bellows maker in Scotland worked in the village until late 1970s. His name is thought to have been a Mr Waldie. A saddler to trade, he also made leather rugby and foot balls for Edinburgh schools and dog collars and so on.

Economy - Agriculture

Pencaitland remains an agricultural and rural parish. However, farms became bigger, and moved from horses (phased out by 1958) to more sophisticated machinery requiring fewer men. In the 1950s, the workforce would be 10-15 strong, compared with the farmer plus one or two in 2000 (dependent upon the number of cattle). Owners of expensive machines such as combines are often contracted to work other farms.

Attitudes too changed; both Drew Cadzow (Huntlaw) and R.G. Ritchie & Son Robert (Jerusalem) emphasize that they did not overly use chemicals on their land (partly because of the cost, which could be greater than the benefit) and that they are keen to plant trees and take care of the hedges (although some had been removed to accommodate the larger machines). By 2000, the needs of the environment were being considered more. Farm paperwork was becoming increasingly computerised, and electronic 'tagging' of animals was coming. The farmers interviewed share a concern that the average age of farmers is 50+, and that fewer youngsters are entering the industry.

Economy - Agriculture (cont)

In 2000, three farmers own and run six of the parish's farms – Wolfstar, Huntlaw, Templehall, Pencaitland, Lempockwells and Glenkinchie. The remaining farms – Spilmersford Mains, Nisbet, Jerusalem, Redmains, Wintonhill and Broomrigg – are all rented from the Winton estate.

Owned farms
Kings have owned and farmed Wolfstar over the whole period; in 1950, they farmed 500 acres. By 2000, this had increased to 810 acres, with the addition of parts of Pencaitland and Lempockwells farms. Wolfstar used 180 acres of grass for 150 beef cattle; Alec King is the only farmer to have bulls to breed his own herd. Hill farmers sometimes (dependant on the year) over-winter their sheep on part of Wolfstar.

Huntlaw came into the ownership of the Cadzow family in 1982; their acreage in 2000 was 700 acres, and includes parts of the lands of Lempockwells and Glenkinchie farms. Huntlaw has a nucleus of 40 beef cows.

Since 1993, W. Barclay Hamilton has owned and farmed Templehall, 470 acres. Templehall produces top-grade certificated beef for Marks & Spencer and Tescos, buying in 200 calves to raise intensively indoors. Four new stores have been built since 1993: one for cattle, one for grain storage and cattle feed; one for machinery and one for potatoes when grown (these were only grown under contract). In addition, sheep (not the farmer's own stock) have been brought in to graze off one awkward shaped field.

In 2000, all of these owner-occupied farms grew similar proportions of the following: barley (spring & winter), sold to maltings (mostly Simpsons of Berwick) or for feeding cattle; winter wheat for milling at Chancelot Mills (Leith), or distilling, or for animal feed (sold to such as the chicken producers). Any 'set aside' was 10% of any arable acreage, and all the farmers used set-aside land for growing the industrial grade of oil-seed rape.

Rented from Winton estate
The Hoods have lived and worked Spilmersford Mains since 1939: they also farm part of Redmains, as well as owning some land outwith the parish. In 2000, they farmed some 320 acres, growing winter wheat (sold to Chancelot Mills) and spring barley.

Ronald Young took over Nisbet's 300 acres in 1969. Nisbet's spring barley went to Bairds of Pencaitland, its winter wheat to Chancelot Mills. Nisbet is the only farm in the parish to grow a commercial potato crop – about 25 acres.

In addition to their main farms, the Hoods and Ronald Young are also contracted to work Wintonhill's 500 acres. Both Spilmersford and Nisbet keep 200 beef cattle inside, grow oil seed rape and use around 25 acres for silage or hay.

The Ritchie family have run Jerusalem (where a few sheep were kept) and part of Redmains from 1936. In the early 1980s they also took on Broomrigg; by 2000, they farmed about 300 acres. At Broomrigg, beans and barley are grown for feeding, together with hay and silage. Bull calves are bought in, and kept entire until their sale (at 14 months) for beef.

Land use has not changed radically except at Redmains, where land used for market garden crops became arable. In 1962, Spilmersford was self-sufficient in fruit, vegetables and milk for the seven workers and their families, with dairy cows and pigs. The total weekly pay cheque was £87. Five days' rent now is equivalent to one years' rent in the 1960s.

Economy - Agriculture (cont)

Cart-shed at Wester Pencaitland Farm before conversion

House and workshop in converted cart-shed (Ralph Barker)

Economy - Agriculture (cont)

In the 1960s, Wintonhill had enough young men (under c18) to have its own football team, and 16-18 houses were occupied between Wintonhill and Spilmersford. By 2000, only four families lived off the 1500 acres of Spilmersford, Nisbet and Wintonhill.

Most of the farm cottages were rented out or sold, and steadings surplus to requirement were converted to homes, for example Wester Pencaitland farm cart shed was converted very successfully into a house & workshop (Lionel Gliori). When Lempockwells Farm was bought by Huntlaw in 1996, the steading was surplus to farm requirements; permission was granted for its demolition, and the stone was re-used to build six dwellings on the site – all attractive and designed in keeping with the rural setting. In 2000, Wintonhill Farmhouse was in the process of refurbishment by Winton estate after the tenant retired.

Beryl McNaughton (of Macplants at no 5) summarises life at the Boggs Holdings

'Many of the residents or their families have lived in the Boggs since the creation of the holdings by MAFF in 1933/34 (the date given varied depending who was speaking). Some families began in one holding and moved on to another if it became vacant and was considered a better holding. Approaching Pencaitland, the holdings on the right hand side were considered to have the better land. The left side was poorer and decreasingly good as it neared its boundary with Pencaitland, hence these holdings were mostly let with 10 acres and the right side with approx 7 acres. If the holder was proving good and enthusiastic he was offered it for buying from the Department of Agriculture. There is a general opinion that as people are not farming their land they are selling or leasing it to three local tenant farmers from the adjoining Winton estate.

Cuthills, no 17, at one time owned 24 acres but now have 9.5 acres, and still have a very small amount of fruit for PYO (pick your own). They have diversified to have a five van standing for caravans as a recognised Caravan Club site. After the war they grew raspberries, strawberries, black and red currants, gooseberries and potatoes. These were picked by children 'bus loaded' into the area from Edinburgh as well as local children from Pencaitland, Tranent, and Ormiston. The fruit was collected every night by large lorries and transported directly into the markets in Edinburgh, Newcastle, Manchester, Birmingham and Liverpool. Although some vegetables were grown for individual use, sprouts were the valuable winter crop and were grown by many holdings.

Most holdings had a cow for their own milk supply and some had calves for fattening. In the early 1960s pigs were considered to be a good idea, offering a quicker return on the land and at that time many holdings had large sheds built to house the pigs.

No 24 is across the road from no 17 and was bought in 1996 by a young couple with the intention of growing organic crops – they trade as East Coast Organic Boxes. They were able to begin their farming immediately as the ground had been unused except for a patch of strawberries. They have 2.5 acres and grow lettuce, strawberries and other salad crops. They keep hens for eggs. They use the usual holding brick built shed with its concrete floor as a packing and distribution area from which they send out 'boxes'. Having brought in organic produce to strengthen what they are able to produce themselves, they make up a mixed box of organic produce. This is then distributed to interested customers. In April 2000 they bought a further 7.5 acres from Cuthills directly across the road, to extend and diversify their activities within the organic field. Presently they are waiting for the land to be certificated for growing. They use a small tractor and rotovator for cultivation.

No 38 is owned by Mrs Main who has been a resident since 1934, when her parents acquired the 10 acre holding. She was absent from no 38 for 7 ½ years when she was first married. Like all Boggs children

Economy - Agriculture (cont)

she travelled by bus to school at Preston Lodge, Prestonpans. Her parents and later she herself grew fruit and some vegetables, much of which they sold at the door. They kept a small herd of calves for fattening.

Mr and Mrs. Yule live in the teacher's cottage adjoining the Old Schoolhouse and keep horses on their small piece of land. In the early 1990s they bought 1 acre from the Berrybank owner (Andrew Auld) for £10,000 to provide them with grazing for their horses.

At the present time there are approximately 80 horses stabled in the Boggs area. Mostly they are kept by residents for their own use although there is a livery stable, which homes approximately 25 horses. These can be seen being exercised along the roads or bridle paths. This stable has changed hands several times; its use has also changed – from livery to riding stable catering as a training school, and then back to livery.

No 5 – Berrybank – had been rented in 1958 by George Auld before being bought by him. It was run as an agriculture holding similar to most in the Boggs, cropping the usual raspberries, strawberries, gooseberries, red and black currants followed by the winter sprout crop. In 1981, Mr Auld not only sent produce to the market in Edinburgh, but also opened his fields to the general public for PYO. This practice continued for seven years until he sold his holding to his son Andrew. Mr Auld had a haulage lorry that he did business with and I believe when the son took over he continued running lorries from the site. The fields appear to have been put down to pasture at this time as young Mrs Auld owned several horses some of which she trained as trotters for racing. During the next eight years, Andrew and his wife considerably extended the house making a large kitchen, changing the main living area and adding on two rooms plus bathroom as well as a stair up to the attic space with a bedroom.

Suddenly the house was much larger so they decided to sell. In June 1996, Macplants, a nursery specialising in growing alpines and perennials, bought the holding of approximately 8.5 acres.

Gavin and Alison McNaughton bought the house, so Gavin works at home running the nursery, a family business having been in existence for about 20 years, which had operated on leased sites and was started by Beryl McNaughton in Edinburgh. There are three full-time employees as well as seasonal staff, who work alongside Beryl and Gavin producing plants for sale to garden centres, other nurseries, landscape firms, public bodies such as the National Trust for Scotland, the Royal Botanic Gardens, Historic Scotland and so on. In the brick shed a small retailing outlet is run for selling plants grown on the nursery and is operated by daughter Claire McNaughton.'

Local Government

Between 1975 and 1996, local government was, on the whole, efficiently administered. Mention should perhaps be made of Frank Tindall, the planning chief. He it was who improved the environment for most of the residents. His enthusiasm knew no bounds. Most of the other officers and their staff were very helpful. On the whole their decisions, with care and common sense, were made to the benefit of the parish and its residents, but of course some of those decisions were objected to, and these objections had to be addressed. Nothing is ever perfect. The parish was the centre of local government and the people in the parish looked to the local district councillor for help and guidance.

Local government appears to work well at parish level, with easy access to the local councillor who is ready with help and advice. Several improvements have been made to the parish because of pressure being exerted on the higher authority by the councillor, but most residents are eagle-eyed and are ever ready to air their views on the way the parish is progressing.

137

Local Government (cont)

Since 1975 a community council has been elected for the parish and some of its immediate surrounds. Community councillors are elected by secret ballot. The system works very well and to the benefit of the community. One of the most successful achievements was the organisation of the Millennium celebrations. All the members of the council are very dedicated.

The parish has been represented on the local council for 55 years through the varying changes to local government. Throughout the 55 years the various councillors have performed their work, on the whole, very well. They have not been dictatorial and, except for differences of opinions between 'the populace' and the district council on occasion, the electors have a good relationship with their representative.

The largest issue of importance in the parish has without doubt been the large number of residential properties being built. The local councillor addressed the issue well, but all opposition to the houses being built in such numbers was squashed by a public inquiry, which ruled that the development should go ahead. Ironically, the original owner of the land arranged for a lorry-load of stone to be tipped and levelled where the entrance of the estates were to be, and although that action was ten years before building started, it was ruled that the scheme had commenced.

Active political groups in the parish were the Labour party, the Conservatives, the Liberal Democrats and the SNP, with occasional sallies by the Green party.

Revisiting the Past

The Local History Group at Pencaitland is very small, being a branch of the local Amenity Society (established 1974) with only three or four members; it is about ten years old. The publication *Village School: the Story of Education in Pencaitland* was produced in 1994, and is still selling; the first run of 200 sold out, so a further 200 were printed. The driving forces behind this research were Ralph Barker, Julie Murphy and Liz Strachan.

Miscellany

Events

In 1948 the worst floods in living memory took place in Lothian and the Borders. Roads and fields were flooded, parts of the east coast railway line were cut and the river bridge separating the two parishes of Pencaitland and Saltoun was washed away.

In 1992 we had more flooding – not a particularly unusual event on low ground, but 1992 was worse than usual. What used to be called the August floods have now extended their presence to any time of the year.

Foot and mouth disease reared its head in 1967-1968.

People

Some writers are and have been residents of the village. Mona Macleod has written a number of historical works. Miss Chloris Wood is a poet of great repute in East Lothian and writes largely in the Scottish dialect. There is extant a poem dated 1920 by 'J.K.' describing a Pencaitland Sunday school trip to the sea; a valiant effort, but it can be classed as doggerel.

Hugh Buchanan is an established artist of architectural studies.

Spilmersford Bridge, damaged in floods of 1948

Jock Taylor was a noted motorcycle sidecar rider who was born and grew up in the parish. He was Scottish champion in 1977, and World Motorcycle Sidecar champion in 1980. He was killed during a race in Finland on 15 August 1982.

Archie Livingstone played football for Newcastle and Manchester United 1945-53.

Willie Young played football for Tottenham Hotspur and Arsenal late in the 1960s-early 1970s.

Ian Davidson played football for Newcastle in the early 1970s.

This account of Pencaitland parish was written by Ralph Barker on behalf of the local history group (part of the Pencaitland Amenity Society). Additional information, research and essays were provided by the following:

Dr I. Buchanan	Landownership; Population
Jan Bundy	Interviewer of Janet Bassett – standards of living
Dr A. Davies	Healthcare
Margaret Jones	Crafts; Economy – agriculture (interviewer)
Dr G. Kennedy	Healthcare
John Landon	Belief
Dr R.R.B. Leakey	Environment – Jerusalem
George Livingstone	Leisure; Miscellany – personalities
Ian Mackenzie	General
Beryl McNaughton	Leisure – the Boggs village hall; Economy - agriculture: the Boggs
Dr M. Matthews	Healthcare
Reginald McVie	Leisure; Miscellany – people
Russell McWilliam	General
Dr J. Milne	Healthcare
James Robertson	Leisure; Miscellany – people
Miss Ross	General
Liz Strachan	General; Interviewer of Janet Basset; Leisure – Pencaitland Music Club

and the recollections of Janet Basset (home life);Ralph Barker, Margaret Fairbairn, Liz Strachan (homes); Joe Rowan (poaching) and Drew Cadzow, Mr Hamilton, George Hood, Alec King, A. Ritchie and R. Young (farming).

FURTHER READING & REFERENCES

The Village School: the story of education in Pencaitland (1994) Pencaitland Amenity Society
Pencaitland Day Centre Looks Back; Reminiscences (1996), Pencaitland Day Centre Reminiscence Group
Land Use Consultants for the Countryside Commission for Scotland, CCS (later Scottish Natural Heritage, SNH) and Historic Buildings and Monuments Directorate, Scottish Development Department (first published c 1987, 1997 reprint) *The Inventory of Gardens & Designed Landscapes in Scotland: Volume 5: Lothian & Borders*
Snodgrass, C.P. (1953) *The Third Statistical Account: The County of East Lothian*
Tindall, F.P. (1998) *Memoirs and Confessions of a County Planning Officer*, Pantile Press

Notes

[1] Information from Newcastle University
[2] See CD-ROM for the full transcripts of essays by Drs Milne, Kennedy & Davies; their Tranent practice covered Ormiston and Pencaitland too. This material was contributed at the behest of Dr Matthews, Pencaitland.

SALTOUN
PARISH REPRESENTATIVE: *Julie Murphy*

Introduction

Saltoun is a small rural parish of 1473ha (3640 acres), lying almost entirely south of the river Tyne. The land varies in height from 200 to around 500ft, with the Skimmer Hills being the highest point. At the beginning of this period, tractors were replacing horses in the fields and there was an increasing reliance on mechanical implements. The size and complexity of farm steadings has increased, with larger cattle sheds, grain driers and more modern facilities.

By the 1990s the roads were full of cars, tractors, and heavy lorries; the only horses in the parish now are for recreational use. In the main settlement of East Saltoun there are now more parked cars, more houses, and more street furniture such as traffic signs and bollards, and painted markings on the road. Military aircraft regularly use the area to practice flying at very low levels. Nonetheless, the appearance of the parish is little changed from 55 years ago.

The area is mainly agricultural with a mixture of arable and livestock farming, and much of the land is still wooded. Saltoun Big Wood, the largest wooded area, is a working forest with regular timber extraction and re-planting. The Humbie Water and the Birns Water run through the forest to a confluence at its edge, and the Birns Water then runs into the Tyne at the north-eastern edge of the parish. The policies of Saltoun Hall and Saltoun House are parkland, with many fine specimens of mature trees. There has been no significant clearing of hedges in the parish.

The main settlements are the villages of East and West Saltoun. East Saltoun, the larger of the two with more than 400 people, a church, school and post office, is approximately at the centre of the parish. West Saltoun, lying one mile to the west, is much smaller.

At the end of the war, there was little effect on the parish other than continuing countrywide shortages. Five men from Saltoun were killed in the war, including Major Christopher Fletcher the second son of Captain Andrew Fletcher of Saltoun, who was killed at Anzio in 1944. Their names are read at the Remembrance Service each year, together with the names of those who died in the 1914-18 war. A memorial window to Major Christopher Fletcher was installed in the church after the war.

*Saltoun
Viaduct*

Environment

There have been no changes to the parish boundaries between 1945 and 2000. Saltoun sits on one of the largest blocks of limestone in Scotland, and although quarrying for lime has long been discontinued there are still traces of this activity, such as the limekiln and quarry at Middlemains. This now contains a most attractive pond with a large number of ducks and other wildlife, and much of the site has been restored to agricultural use. The quarry site on the Gifford road has been filled in and is now a community woodland project. This and other old quarries near West Saltoun have at one time been used as landfill sites for refuse disposal. All have now been filled, closed, and the surfaces restored and re-seeded.

Improving landowners made other changes to the landscape, including the joining up of some fields, the removal of a few hedges and the burying underground of many minor watercourses to ease cultivation.

Here and throughout the text, Julie Murphy comments on life in Saltoun
Houses at Spilmersford just beyond the parish boundary were flooded in 1948, and thereafter a river monitoring station was installed beside the walled garden at Saltoun Hall. This is still maintained by East of Scotland Water.

The parish retains a good variety of habitats for wildlife, as there has been relatively little destruction of woodlands, shelterbelts and hedgerows. With the active encouragement of the Farmers and Wildlife Advisory Group (FWAG), at field edges and corners, farmers have created many small new wildlife habitats. Roe deer are seen often in the wooded areas, and there are also foxes, hares and badgers. Red squirrels are still seen occasionally in the Saltoun Big Wood, but elsewhere, grey squirrels have moved in and are now common.

Numbers of rabbits were reduced as a result of myxomatosis in the 1960s, but they are now very common. Otters were not seen locally for many years but there have been recent sightings in the Birns Water. Bats are rare in the villages but may still be seen around Saltoun Hall.

There are good numbers of most woodland and garden birds, but birds in the open fields, such as skylarks, curlews and peewits, are now rarer than they were 20 years ago. There are also fewer song thrushes, swallows and house martins. More seabirds, such as gulls and oystercatchers are seen inland, and magpies and buzzards moved in during the 1990s. Herons, mallards, dippers, grey wagtails and moorhens are frequently seen in the Birns Water and elsewhere and goosanders arrived in the 1990s.

Butterflies, including red admirals, tortoiseshells, peacocks and orange tips, and moths including the goat moth are still seen, but not in such great numbers in recent years.

A rich variety of wildflowers are seen in woodland areas, on the river banks and on roadside verges. The council's policy of allowing them to seed before cutting verges has proved beneficial. Cornfield flowers such as poppies are seen less because of the use of herbicides.

Dutch elm disease affected many trees in the 1980s and 1990s but young elm survives (so far) as a hedgerow plant.

The grounds of Saltoun Hall hold many fine specimens of trees, including a large Lucombe oak, some very old sycamores, and all three types of cedars. Two of the Lebanon cedars date back to the 18th century.

Recently, Alistair Scott (with Walter Gordon) listed the following trees growing at Saltoun; the measurements given relate to the trunk circumference; this is measured at DBH (diameter at breast height - 1.3m above ground level, taken at the highest point of ground level).

Drive: sessile oak (*Quercus petraea* 13'7"); Lucombe oak (*Quercus x hispanica* 'Lucombeana' - a cross between *Q. suber* and *Q. cerris*, 12'6"); European larch (*Larix europaeus* 8'5"); and a young field maple (*Acer campestre*).

Forecourt shrubbery by garages: sycamore (*Acer pseudoplatanus*, 16'8" around burrs); sessile oak (*Q. petraea* 8'10"); Atlantic cedar (*Cedrus atlantica glauca*).

Behind house: Atlantic cedar (20 years old, growing well); silver lime (*Tilia tomentosa* ex-Markle Mains); whitebeam (*Sorbus aria* – young); coast redwood (*Sequoia sempervirens* – a young established tree); three cedar of Lebanon (*Cedrus libanii*) one 14'11", two at 20' circumference, both very long-established trees, possibly dating c1713; Deodar cedar (*Cedrus deodara* 11'5") - this tree was measured and was close to 100'tall; Japanese larch (*Larix kaempferi* 7'4"); European silver fir (*Abies alba* 11'5"); a young Weymouth pine (*Pinus strobus*); a large sycamore (*Acer pseudoplatanus* 16'10").

There was also a group of eight gean, or wild cherry (*Prunus avium*), and a young Norway maple (*Acer platanoides*) that has lost half its trunk. A recent tree was identified as a possible *Cunninghamia lanceolata*.

Going down to the river are: a red oak (*Quercus rubra* (borealis)); a third cedar of Lebanon, and another giant redwood.

There are no designated nature reserves in the parish. The Saltoun Big Wood is a popular area for walking dogs, and for riding.

Land Ownership

During the period 1945-2000, the Fletchers sold several of the farms on their estate. In 1954, East Saltoun, East Mains and, in 1956, Greenhead and Barley Mill farms were sold to the Hamilton & Kinneil Estate. Saltoun Hall and the surrounding land were sold in the late 1960s, and the house divided into nine privately owned apartments.

The Hamilton & Kinneil Estate then sold East Mains to the Morton family in the 1960s and the estate in turn bought Greenlaw from them. Greenlaw was later sold to Edward Irvine Reid, and later still to David Orr, in whose ownership it remains. Herdmanston Mains farm changed hands from Reid to Anderson R. Waddell in the 1960s, and Robert Sargeant replaced Miss Margaret Cadzow at Samuelston South Mains, which in 1981 was bought by William Logan, the current owner.

Saltoun Big Wood has changed hands several times over the period. Once run by the Forestry Commission, and then the Dumfries & Galloway Council Pension Fund, Sir Francis Ogilvy acquired it in the 1990s. Most of the Church glebe land in East Saltoun was sold for housing in the 1990s. So, in 2000, the vast majority of the land in the parish was still owned by families or companies engaged in farming. The Fletcher estate still owns Saltoun Home Farm and Middlemains. The farms of East Saltoun, Greenhead, Barley Mill and Upper Townhead are in the ownership of Hamilton Farming Enterprises Ltd.; this company was formed in 1987 on the reconstruction of the Hamilton & Kinneil Estates. Hamilton's also owns plantations at Dryden and East Saltoun (also known as Strawberry Wood) and the shelterbelt on the Gifford road.

Land Ownership (cont)

Aerial view of East Saltoun, 1966 (©Royal Commission on the Ancient and Historical Monuments of Scotland)

Family-run farms in 2000 were Herdmanston Mains (the Waddell family); Saltoun East Mains (Mortons); Blance (Scotts); Samuelston South Mains (Logans), and Gilchriston (Maxwells). The Maxwell family also own the Petersmuir Woods, and Saltoun Big Wood is still owned by Sir Francis Ogilvy of Winton House, Pencaitland.

Townscapes, Buildings & Landscapes of Distinction

The parish has lost or seen the decay of several of its 'treasures' over the years. Saltoun East Mains mill chimney was demolished in 1969 (Tindall, F. (1998) p165). Herdmanston House was demolished on 31 May 1969. The house had been used by the military during the war and thereafter was considered unsafe and uninhabitable. Herdmanston dovecot, just over the river Tyne, and close to Saltoun parish boundary, has become very ruinous over the past decades,

Townscapes, Buildings & Landscapes of Distinction (cont)

despite being a listed building. Herdmanston chapel (rebuilt 1840), also falling into disrepair, had originally what was thought to be a stone font. Current thinking is that it is a 12th century holy water stoup, as it was evidently originally built into a wall. The stoup is now in the Museum of Scotland, Edinburgh in the section on the mediaeval church.

Saltoun Hall was occupied by the Fletcher family throughout the 1940s and 1950s, and was sold in the 1960s. A sale of the contents of the house was held over three days in April 1966. The building was purchased by a private developer, Robin Jell who had a particular interest in preserving historic houses. It was divided into nine flats, which were sold to individual proprietors, the final flat being ready for occupation in 1972. All the major public rooms, except the dining room were retained intact in individual flats with the central saloon and dome, along with the gardens and surrounding land being owned communally by all the proprietors. Since the conversion further restoration and conservation work has been undertaken by the proprietors, including rebuilding some chimney stacks and replacement of some of the lead roofs.

The main feature of the past years has been the conversion of a number of buildings, including several listed buildings, into private homes. These are all prestigious conversions, which, in spite of the change of use, have retained the character and main features of the originals.

Although most of the parkland around Saltoun Hall has been retained, some areas are now ploughed, but care has been taken to retain the large parkland trees in these fields. The walled garden at Saltoun Hall was still in use as a 'pick your own strawberries' facility in the 1970s, but was subsequently planted with Christmas trees and has since been allowed to fall into disrepair.

The designed landscape around Saltoun Hall has for the most part been preserved. The gardens have been retained in their original form. A few of the mature trees have fallen victim to storms, notably on Boxing Day in 1998, but a programme of replanting is continuing. The wooded areas of the estate around Saltoun Hall suffered badly from Dutch elm disease in the 1980s. The dead trees have now been felled and there has been considerable replanting, mainly with native broad-leaved trees.

Population
By parish, from the General Registrar's office

1931	419	205M	214F
1951	355	173M	182F
1961	353	180M	173F
1971	360	184M	176F
1981	376	177M	199F
1991	365	167M	198F
2001	425	209M	216F

By parish, from ELDC

1991	364		
1997 (est.)	399	218M	181F
2001	NO DATA		

By settlement, from ELDC

---

235 East Saltoun 72 *West Saltoun*

NO DATA

Population figures are difficult to compare, as no two sources extract data in the same way.

145

Population (cont)

The population has remained at a fairly constant level. Housing built in the early 1990s in East Saltoun accounted for an increase of around 25, and further increases are likely.

There are a general mix of people in the parish. Some families have several generations still living in the parish or in the surrounding area, especially those connected with farming; some of the farms are now being run by the younger generations and employing fewer people, only bringing in extra workers at harvest time. Farm cottages therefore are often rented by young couples, for which council houses are no longer available. There are still some residents who have been born and bred in Saltoun but nowadays they are few; some were children of farm workers who moved around the area. Some young people from the parish still hope to continue to live in the area, and many do, but in many cases young people move elsewhere and others move into the parish.

The settlement of East Saltoun houses a good proportion of older people, some having lived there all their lives or moved in on marriage. There may still be some young mothers at home, but most women return to work once the children are at school, and often before that. There are some unemployed, but not significant numbers. Social activities attract a good mix of people, although long established events attract the long-standing villagers. Sunday morning congregations have all ages present, and encouragingly, there are many young families coming into the village willing to get involved, amongst them a good number of men. Distinctions between long-established residents and more recent incomers are there, but not pronounced. On the whole the people mix well, as for instance, in the church. You may hear more English accents and you will always get people who just live in the country but take no part in community life, preferring to travel to Edinburgh or larger towns for leisure activities.

There has been very little emigration or immigration. A few families emigrated to Australia. There have been travelling tattie howkers/turnip singlers working in the parish over this period, but they have not remained as residents. Itinerant workers are sometimes employed for the harvest.

A few Polish soldiers stayed on after the war and some Irish people who originally worked on farms. More English people and the occasional non-Europeans now live in the area.

Belief

The Church of Scotland has been and remains the principal belief system in the parish. The church, built in 1805 and A listed, and the graveyard, are still in use. The graveyard was extended in the late 1940s. Saltoun was united with the parish of Bolton in 1929.

'From 1959-79, church and community were closely involved, unlike today'
Nan Louden

The existing link was extended to Humbie and Yester in 1979; at this point the Saltoun manse was sold and a new one built in Gifford, where the minister is based. Services are held in Yester/Humbie/Saltoun or Bolton each Sunday – ie three each Sunday with Bolton and Saltoun alternating; this has been in operation since c1980. Previously both Bolton and Saltoun churches had held weekly services.

Day-to-day running of the church was mainly the responsibility of the beadle who saw to the heating, lighting, and so on:

Belief (cont)

'*My father was the church beadle. He would light the fire in the church on a Saturday evening, bank it up late at night and then get up early to rekindle it in time for a warm church service later in the morning*'. Margaret McCormack

Nowadays, there is no separate post of beadle and this work falls largely on the shoulders of the session clerk. With no resident minister in the parish since 1979, responsibility for the spiritual welfare of the parish is shared, to some extent, with the Kirk Session, which refers critical matters to the minister as necessary.

In 1994 on the 750th anniversary of the dedication of the church, a tree was planted in the churchyard to commemorate the event.

Ministers

1928-47	Robert N. Paisley
1948-58	Alexander Campsie
1959-79	George W.H. Louden
1979 Saltoun & Bolton linked with Yester & Humbie	
1979-84	Allan Scott
1985-97	John Wilson
1999-date	Donald Pirie

The celebration of Harvest Thanksgiving is less ornate and perhaps seen as less directly relevant to people's lives nowadays. The church is still decorated, but the tradition of providing sheaves of grain and seasonal produce has to some extent gone. Christmas sees the church decorated, including a tree, and the large involvement of children performing the Nativity Play. A candlelit service on Christmas Eve is popular with both churchgoers and non-churchgoers. Up until the 1950-60s most people worked on Christmas Day in Scotland but apart from essential workers this is now no longer the case.

The session clerk – Norman Murphy - set up a Bolton & Saltoun churches web page – www.ndhm.org.uk. The session/meeting room has been in existence since the 1970s. It is used for church meetings, Kirk Session meetings, Woman's Guild (since 2000 known as the Guild and open to both men and women), youth groups and occasionally for meetings of other village organisations.

Another part of the same complex was renovated in early 1970s to form one room used as the Tithe Byre, with a storeroom and a small museum. The Tithe Byre, started in 1972, provides an outlet and small source of income for many talented residents by selling home baking, crafts, garden produce and much else. A tithe, or 10% of takings, goes to the church. The museum (Bygone Byre) is a collection of old photographs and implements and artefacts from bygone days (see Leisure).

The meeting room next door opens for teas and coffees at the same time as the Byre – summer weekends and just before Christmas. Again, the tearoom is able to give considerable financial support to the church and village amenities.

Most of the glebe land was sold for housing between the late 1980s and 1997.

The church offers Sunday worship, a creche, Sunday school, Fish group (older children), the Guild, youth club (which originally started under church auspices, but now community-run).

Belief (cont)

There was a junior girls' choir that met in the manse c1960s-70s that performed in the church *'resplendent in red outfits with white ruffs'* (Nan Louden).

Change has impacted on all aspects of life; all Sunday school teachers are now required to undertake training in child protection. The position of Child Protection Officer within the church was felt to be very difficult in a village and is therefore covered by a single representative from the parishes of Saltoun, Bolton, Humbie and Gifford. The church has felt the legislation to be an unnecessary and intrusive burden on its work.

The Church of Scotland in Saltoun follows traditional/liberal (that is, mainstream) doctrine by means of Sunday worship and pastoral outreach. Membership has varied around 250 (plus or minus 25) for the last half-century.

Over the last 50 years the perceived role of the church has diminished. Churchgoing was far more socially important in earlier years, when people wore their Sunday best, hats and all. Services were longer. Most people, and particularly young people, stood in awe of the minister; residents have childhood memories of 'having to behave' in church.

Children were restrained. There were feelings of guilt and social stigma if not attending church. Nowadays it is not so. People attend from choice and personal conviction. There is a much more relaxed feel, gone are the 'Sunday best' clothes. Children are encouraged and noisy behaviour tolerated to a certain point! It must not however be felt to be a 'free for all'. The 'Sunday penny' - a child's church collection - still exists.

Today, the children will take a more active role in nativity plays and singing at Harvest Thanksgiving for example, and there are musical items by pre-teens, who have also presented drama in Saltoun church. The congregation is encouraged to applaud these performances, which would not have been the case in earlier years. At the same time there is a place for solemnity, for instance on Remembrance Day, at communion services, and so on.

Saltoun parish has a go-ahead youth section (although like everywhere else, the teenagers are missing and numbers are subject to demographic changes.) All these people must be encouraged if the church is to survive in its present form.

The influence of the church on morals has waned over this period. There is more acceptance of a more relaxed approach. Cohabitation prior to marriage has become more acceptable with fewer coming forward to membership of the church.

In the 1940s and 1950s young people were expected to join the church when they reached their late teens. However, it is not so now. An enthusiastic minister encourages people to consider becoming full members of the church. It is a fact however that it is often only considered prior to perhaps marriage, or the baptism of a child.

Julie Murphy comments here and throughout the text
On courtship, engagements and weddings

People met at school, at local dances and social events. Courting was often carried out on country walks and at the local dances. Only in the last 20 years or so have young people travelled into Edinburgh to work and socialise and therefore to meet a wider range of people.

Country girls tended to marry earlier in the past [55 years]. Engagement lengths would vary as they do today and many a young man would seek out the father of his intended bride. Church weddings [still] follow traditional lines, often with a piper in attendance. The ceremony of the 'poor oot' still exists, now and again.

Belief (cont)

The more established families often have family plots in the churchyard, so burials are still quite common, although the proportion of cremations has risen steadily in recent years. The Co-operative Society still conducts funerals to this day.

And on funerals

Although many deaths now occur in hospital or nursing homes, the body is often brought home before the funeral. Family and friends still occasionally walk with the body to church. Women only started to attend funerals in the last 50 years or so. Before that the event was for men only and the women stayed at home preparing the funeral meal. Although in the main black ties are still worn there is a gradual lessening of "funereal dress".

Since 1979, the Saltire Society has held an annual lecture to commemorate Andrew Fletcher in the kirk at East Saltoun usually on the first Saturday of September. With the restoration of the Scottish Parliament after 300 years, there has been increasing interest in this event in recent years.

Homes

Almost all of the homes in the parish are owner-occupied, with the exception of properties in the area owned by the Fletcher estate or Hamilton Farming Enterprises, which are either occupied by those who work on the land or rented out.

West Saltoun, c1970

Homes (cont)

East Saltoun is the main settlement in the parish. West Saltoun, one mile west, consists of one street of 15 houses. The only pressure for development is for new housing on a relatively small scale, mainly in the village of East Saltoun. More housing has meant a small reduction in farmland and more hard landscaping.

There has been little change in the location of housing since 1945. Council houses were built in East Saltoun throughout the 1940s, 1950s and 1960s, most in West Crescent; many of these have been sold, sometimes but not always to existing tenants. The council still owns a few pensioners' cottages.

Both Margaret McCormack and Jeannie Sandilands moved with their parents to West Crescent in the late 1940s – early 1950s as the farm cottages on Main Street were considered unfit for habitation.

'Living conditions in the late 1940s and 1950s were simple. There were many large families, often crammed into a small house. The living room would have linoleum on the floor with the occasional rag rug, the backing of which was easily come by. There would be a range or open fire with usually a kettle or a pot of soup quietly simmering. Fuel would mainly be wood, easily come by as there was a local sawmill, and coal. A primus stove would often be kept for emergencies.

These were the days prior to washing machines and often the washing would be laundered with a washboard over an open fire outside. Flat irons were still being used but were gradually being replaced by electric ones. Most food was home produced. Country gardens would hold vegetables and fruit, hens were kept - there is an old photograph in evidence showing hens grazing where the new churchyard extension is now.

Milk would be collected from the farm. The Co-op vans came round regularly, often taking your order and returning within a day or two with it'.
Margaret McCormack

The row of stone cottages on the main street was renovated in 1960/70s forming three houses.

The ruined cottage, The Lang Hoose, was restored in the 1950s (*Scots Magazine*, April 1975).

A house was built at the back of East Saltoun garage, and six on the Upper Saltoun/ Petersmuir road in East Saltoun. Three individual houses (Byre Court) were built behind the Tithe Byre in 1991.

The Glebe estate (mainly occupied by young families) in East Saltoun was built around 1990, with 20 houses owned by the Scottish Special Housing Association (ten fully, ten partly, plus three workshops). Despite much local protest, standard building templates were used. Four new houses were built in West Saltoun in the 1960s and 1970s; here too, the row of terraced houses was extended in 1970s. The Fletcher dower house at West Saltoun was turned into two flats.

There is less need now for housing for farm workers, and some of the cottages, including the Saltoun Hall lodge cottages, the gardener's cottage and the kennels cottages in West Saltoun are privately rented. Other rented properties include the Home Farm and Middlemains with a number of cottages, and Greenhead Farm and cottages.

One house was built beside the old walled garden at Saltoun Hall. Saltoun Hall itself was converted into flats (see Townscapes, Buildings & Landscapes of Distinction) and the former

Homes (cont)

Housing in East Saltoun

stable block there was converted into a private dwelling called Saltoun House in the 1970s. The former gas works for Saltoun Hall was converted into a private house in the 1970s.

There has been only one steading conversion in the parish, at Upper Townhead, which was converted into two houses in the early 1980s and one other in 1995. A bungalow was built beside Greenhead farm steading and also two cottages.

The Old Castle or Castle o' Cloots in East Saltoun, built in the 18th century - perhaps earlier - was restored in 1979-81. The restoration won awards from the Saltire Society and the Association for the Protection of Rural Scotland (Hedderwick, R. (1987) Vol XIX).

The Barley Mill in West Saltoun, built in 1712, was kept wind and watertight after being no longer required as a mill, but fell into disrepair in the 1950s; it was converted into a private house in the 1970/80s. The brownfield site at Middlemains (the old lime kiln site) was converted in 1985, creating two houses within the lime barn and a new house built on the site of the workers' cottages. Two new houses were built at Spilmersford Bridge, and a further two were built in the 1960s and 1970s close to East Saltoun Plantation in Lower Saltoun.

Typically for a rural parish, for many years homes in Saltoun relied mainly on open fires burning wood and coal. The weekly bath was common for many years; as in other parts of the county only the advent of electricity, and therefore easier hot water, and much later, showers, gave people easier access to more frequent bathing.

Farm workers wore clothing suitable for the job and in the years after the war this was often ex-Army clothing. Women, including female teachers, did not start wearing trousers until the 1970s, and even then only the younger and more adventurous ones.

The advent of the washing machine was a boon for the wives of agricultural workers who would labour over the washing of farm overalls, boiler suits and later on, jeans.

Utilities

The parish is served by the public water supply, with the water drawn from three different sources – Hopes (the biggest), Stobshiel and Fountainhall.

The main sewer from East Saltoun drains to processing tanks near Saltoun Home Farm. There are septic tanks attached to houses outwith the settlements; the council was responsible for emptying these until the 1990s. This is now the responsibility of East of Scotland Water, which charges occupants for clearing tanks.

At the beginning of this period some houses were still without mains electricity, but with a few exceptions, these were predominately outwith the settlements.

Mains gas is not available anywhere in the parish. A few residents use LPG.

Television came to the parish in 1953. Reception is reasonable, although Channel 5 is not generally available. Satellite TV is available through individual dishes, but there is no cable television.

There are no mobile phone masts in the parish. The service received is patchy. Some mobile phone operators provide reasonable reception, but the parish is on the black list for poor reception for several companies.

The main streets in East and West Saltoun are lit, but there is no street lighting outwith the settlements.

The council has a weekly general rubbish collection throughout the parish, but no collection of paper, glass or garden waste. Special collections can be arranged for larger items, but have to be paid for.

Shops & Services

The only shop in the parish in 2000 was the post office in East Saltoun. There was also a small general store until the early 1990s, and thereafter some basic items were sold in the garage. West Saltoun had a small general store run by Miss Jessie Tait until 1969.

Within the village, a range of services is now available. These include: childcare; building; plumbing; garage; post office; kennels and cattery; dry cleaning through the post office; blacksmith and farrier; garden tools maintenance; domestic help; gardening; play areas; public phone. East Saltoun's garage provided both fuel and vehicle repairs to the end of the period.

The old inn (uphill, adjacent to the manse wall) in the village was gone by the end of the war, and replaced by council housing; Swinton had owned it.

In the early part of this period, Co-op vans carried a wide range of items, and would take orders to supply specific items on request. They were the lifeline to communities and villages and settlements. In 1945 nearly 100 vans were on East Lothian roads. These vans were discontinued in early 1990s.

Clothing would often be purchased from Co-op vans, which would bring a selection out from the shop to the village. Otherwise people travelled to Tranent or Haddington to the Co-op stores, and perhaps to Edinburgh for something special. Haddington had a wider selection of 'boutique' type shops for the more fashion-conscious from the 1960s and 1970s onwards.

Travelling vans run by private businesses still supply fish, green groceries and milk. Recently, regular deliveries of boxes of organic fruit and vegetables have been introduced on request.

Shops and Services (cont)

*Post Office,
East Saltoun*

By 2000, the number of mobile services had been drastically reduced. A mobile bank operated until the 1990s, and East Lothian Council's mobile library was still visiting regularly. A hairdresser provided a service for people in their own homes.

Healthcare

There have been no healthcare facilities based in the parish throughout this period; there is no resident doctor, dentist, district nurse, health visitor, or home help.

'Country wines were produced in the parish, otherwise little alcohol would be kept in the house, perhaps a little for medicinal purposes'.

Margaret McCormack

Parish residents registered with GPs in Haddington, Tranent or Ormiston as these are on bus routes; the Ormiston practice has now merged with that in Tranent. Home visits by GPs are now mainly in emergencies; further treatment required (perhaps by nurses or therapists) is arranged through the practice, and usually takes place in the surgery, although home visits are arranged when necessary.

There were no special fears of illnesses in the parish, but perhaps more awareness of the possibility of accidents on the farms. Advice would be sought from family and neighbours and a doctor only called as a last resort in the 1940s and 1950s, before the National Health Service became fully established. Once people were more mobile they were more prepared to visit a doctor.

Home helps are arranged through GPs and local social services as required. Hospital referrals were usually to Roodlands Hospital in Haddington when it became a general hospital in the 1950s. It lost many of its facilities, including accident and emergency in the 1980s. The Vert Maternity Hospital in Haddington closed in 1974 and the Edinburgh Eastern General Hospital Maternity Unit in 1998. Maternity services are now provided either at the Simpson

153

Healthcare (cont)

Maternity unit in central Edinburgh, or the Borders General Hospital, Melrose or in Berwick. Antenatal care is available through doctors' practices.

In earlier times, mothers would often wait until they were sure of a pregnancy before visiting a doctor for confirmation. In the 1940s most births were at home, although a larger number than previously were going to the Vert Hospital in Haddington. This trend towards use of the Vert continued in the 1950s and 1960s until the hospital closed in 1974. From the 1970s most mothers had to go to Edinburgh, often choosing the nearer Eastern General Hospital but when this closed in 1998 it left only the Simpson Maternity Hospital. This is still the case although more mothers are now opting for the Borders General Hospital, and Berwick, and of course there will still be the occasional home birth. The most significant change over the years in childbirth has been in the role of the father, who is now far more involved than in the past, attending antenatal and parenting classes, being there at the birth and attending to the baby. People have to travel to these classes as they are not available in the village. Stays in hospital are now much shorter, with many mothers returning home very shortly after the birth. Unless there are complications it is very unlikely for a mother to stay in hospital for any length of time, unlike in the past when a week to ten days was not unusual. Following the birth the health visitor usually calls, but for routine weighing etc. of the baby mothers are expected to attend the clinic associated with the doctor's surgery.

Along with the national trend, there is likely to be some use of soft drugs.

There is no provision for elderly or disabled people in the parish. Volunteers provide transport to a lunch club at Humbie on Wednesdays. Regular deliveries of meals-on-wheels have been discontinued recently, and those requiring this service get deliveries of frozen meals and microwave ovens. One housebound resident in the village has a series of home helps who provide services, but none of these people live locally. Specialised support services and any adaptations to houses are generally supplied through the local council, but neighbours provide a good deal of general support.

Childcare was usually provided within the family or by neighbours until about 20 years ago. As more mothers returned to work in the 1980s and 1990s the demand for paid childcare increased and there were several childminders in the parish. As the regulation of childcare was tightened up in the late 1990s the number of childminders has declined. In 2000 there is one registered childminder in East Saltoun.

'I can care for three children under five, and two between five and eight in my own home; the premises have to meet health & safety regulations, and I and my family are checked out by the police'.
Christine Gillies

Childminding, and family support were the only childcare available until the playgroup started.

Education

A pre-school playgroup was started in the 1970s. It still meets Mondays, Wednesdays and Fridays in term time from 9 to 11.30am in the Fletcher Hall. It takes pre-school children of any age but, until they reach the age of two and a half, a parent or carer is expected to stay with them. There is a paid playleader with back up from a rota of parents Numbers have fluctuated over the years. In 2000 there were nine children, several of whom came from neighbouring

Education (cont)

Saltoun School, 1945

Saltoun School, 1965

Education (cont)

villages. A nursery class for three and four year olds attached to the primary school opened in 1998. It takes children every morning from 9-11.30am during school terms.

Primary education has been provided throughout this period in the old 19th century school in East Saltoun.

'Miss Cossar was our teacher. She cycled up to teach from Pencaitland – a long climb on a bicycle without gears'.
Margaret McCormack (late 1940s)

The roll of the school has fluctuated over the years, and there have been either two or three teachers depending on numbers. There was a threat that the school would be closed in 1984 in the interests of economy, and children bussed to Pencaitland, Humbie or Gifford. Closure was averted, however, partly due to vigorous local objections, and the school has now been modernised and extended.

The schoolhouse was incorporated into the school. The roll of the school was just 29 in 1989, but had risen to 63 in 2000, when there were three teachers. Children from outwith the school's designated catchment area can attend at their parents' request if there is room for them and parents arrange the transport. There has been a school board for a number of years working closely with the school. The school has a reputation over the years for doing well in national Burns competitions in singing and recitation. It maintains the village school atmosphere, at the same time preparing the children for secondary education outside the village.

At the start of this period secondary aged children attended either the Ormiston Junior Secondary School or, if they passed the qualifying exam, the Preston Lodge Senior Secondary School in Prestonpans.

'In the school, girls were expected to wear uniform including gymslips and the inevitable navy knickers. Socks, gloves and scarves were hand-knitted'.
Margaret McCormack

When the Ross High School opened in Tranent in 1954, children attended there instead of Prestonpans for senior secondary education. The secondary part of the Ormiston school closed in 1954, and all children then attended Ross High School, which had become a comprehensive school in the 1970s.

In the 1980s the rights of parents to choose their children's schools were extended, but free transport was provided only for those who attended Ross High School, Tranent. In 2000, secondary school children attended either Ross High School or Knox Academy in Haddington or travelled to private schools in Edinburgh.

There has been no provision for post-school education in the parish, apart from occasional informal evening classes, focusing mainly on leisure activities.

There is adult basic education provision in Haddington and Musselburgh. The council also runs an extensive programme of evening classes, which include both leisure and vocational activities. Although there is no further education college in the county, Jewel and Esk Valley College runs an outreach facility in Alderston House in Haddington in combination with East Lothian Council. This provides a variety of vocational courses that can lead to certification. More specialised classes, such as lip-reading, can also be provided for everyone but again are only held in Musselburgh, North Berwick and Haddington.

Transport

Buses have been the only means of public transport throughout this period. In the 1940s and 1950s, services were quite frequent, with several buses to Edinburgh daily. By the 1970s and 1980s however, buses had become quite infrequent and were little used. With deregulation of bus services in the 1990s, private bus companies have moved in to compete with publicly supported services: buses have become more frequent, but are still not much used. The nearest railway stations are at Longniddry and Wallyford. The council provide transport for secondary school children to Ross High School, Tranent.

There are no other privately-run transport services, although there is some sharing of cars by commuters on an informal basis. Parents often share transport arrangements for children attending schools in Haddington or Edinburgh.

As public transport services have declined throughout this period, and private car ownership has continued to grow, people have become increasingly dependant on private cars for getting about. Those moving into the parish over the last 20 years or more have been aware of this, and many families have two or sometimes more cars. The very few who do not have their own private cars are mainly long-established and often elderly residents who often get help from family or neighbours with shopping and so on. There is little evidence, as yet, that the recently increased frequency of buses has had much effect on people's travelling habits. With the increase in private cars, there are more parked cars on the street, and a need for off-street parking spaces within properties. More people commute by car to work outside the parish, mostly, but not always, to Edinburgh. The increase in commuters from Gifford has led to an increase in through traffic in East Saltoun, which is a cause of concern to residents, especially those with children attending the school on the main road.

Lack of road maintenance increasingly blights rural areas. Roads were in much better condition during the depths of the war than they are today. There are many (unavailing) complaints to the council.

Air pollution has probably increased with the rising number of vehicles, but as this is still a relatively sparsely populated area, this is not a serious problem.

The parish has a number of rights of way. Few of them are marked, and some are overgrown, especially in summer. Although not specifically barred, the general public are not encouraged by landowners to walk these paths. An exception is Saltoun Big Wood, where paths have recently been upgraded with improved signing.

Police

There was no resident police presence in the parish in 2000. Occasional police cars tour the area from time to time and a community policeman has responsibility for liaison, and can provide advice on security. Many properties have their own security alarm systems. False alarms from cars and home security systems are common and reduce the effectiveness of these as a deterrent.

A resident policeman lived in the police house in East Saltoun until 1954, the last one being Richard King who followed George Cockburn in 1947. The house was then let and later sold to Hamilton Farming Enterprises, and renamed as Fountain Cottage.

There is no evidence of an increase in crime, although the fear of crime has increased. Most crimes are of a relatively minor nature, such as vandalism, car crime and housebreaking. The post office was robbed in 1985. A Neighbourhood Watch group exists in West Saltoun.

Leisure

The Fletcher Hall in East Saltoun was built in the 1920s from funds donated by Captain Andrew Fletcher (1880-1951); the hall and the suite of rooms belonging to and opposite the church is available for hire. This accommodation is used for fund-raising events, private functions, exercise classes, the school and church groups.

'There were regular dances in Fletcher Hall and there always seemed to be buses to take you to another village should they be holding a dance. ... the Fletcher Hall dance was cancelled when Captain Fletcher died in 1951. The Fletcher family played a large part in the village in those days with Christmas treats for children up at Saltoun Hall. Villagers would be very respectful to the laird.'
Margaret McCormack

The school was used as a polling station for elections until the 1990s, but as elections have now become so frequent, the Fletcher Hall is used instead.

Organisations & Clubs: a youth club ran throughout the late 1960s and 1970s. From 1985 a new youth club has run in the evenings with voluntary leaders and support from the council. It meets in the Fletcher Hall on Thursday nights and in 2000 had around 40 members aged from ten upwards.

A group of parents has been running a summer play scheme for children since the mid 1980s. The council provides a grant to support this. The scheme operates every Wednesday during the summer holidays and organises outings and activities for both primary and secondary age children.

Fletcher Hall, East Saltoun

There are now no uniformed organisations for children that meet in the village, although there used to be brownies in the Fletcher Hall and a rainbow unit in the 1990s. Children from the parish now go to Gifford or Pencaitland for cubs, brownies and scouts.

Leisure activities have changed over the years, with many declining perhaps because of the advent of television. The Fletcher Hall was a hive of activity in the 1940s and 1950s with bowling, British Legion, recreation club, horticultural society, SWRI and Guild and weekly dances; country and highland dancing classes were held in the hall. Nowadays the Fletcher Hall is used for privately run classes in keep-fit and aerobics. Those attending come from all over the area and not just from the parish. Equally those who live in the parish travel elsewhere for a wide variety of leisure pursuits,

although in the early part of this period many people did not go away on holidays. Days out were more common. There were not the long holidays in the 1940s and 1950s. Children spent their summer holidays playing around the area.

The playing field beside the Fletcher Hall belongs to the village, but the council cuts the grass, and the school uses it. There is no regular football team, but the pitch is sometimes used for practice by teams from elsewhere. At one time a football team existed and there was also a rifle range attached to the hall used by the local miniature rifle club. The Women's Rural Institute, established 1923, ended in 1999 because of lack of support; in the past it entered a team for the Jubilee Curling Competition (1966). The SWRI booklet *The History of Saltoun* (1969) was published locally, with a very limited issue.

Saltoun Big Wood was used for orienteering, fungus forays, walks and, in more recent years, for companies' team bonding exercises. A bowling club beside the manse was in use until the land was sold in the 1980s.

'At the plantation in Lower Saltoun before the two houses were built, there was a pond (still there) and wild strawberries grew there. It was a great play area for the village children. The wood is known locally as Strawberry Wood and doubtless still used by the children of today. Children of the 1940s tended to play around the village, only going home for meals in the long summer holidays. Nobody worried too much about possible dangers in those days'.
Jeannie Sandilands

The museum at the Bygone Byre was established in 1972. The museum has old photographs, agricultural implements and kitchen utensils, school records, church and Fletcher family memorabilia. The material is displayed in an old stable with existing cobbled floor and bales of straw. It has changed very little since its inception in 1972. It is not advertised widely as a visitor attraction. People visiting the Tithe Byre will often wander into the museum; those revisiting the area, often find old school photos of interest as people try to remember names. The Bygone Byre museum is very much a display of implements and photographs of a bygone era in the parish. The children can sit on the knife grinder's seat and see such things as a working butter churn and a genuine ugly – the sun-hat worn by women (bondagers) in the fields. An ex-parishioner now in her 90s used to make these hats. The museum is checked over regularly.

Economy

Both Margaret McCormack and Jeannie Sandilands went into service in Gifford, on leaving Ormiston school in the early 1950s.

Nowadays, like many other rural parishes, most of Saltoun's population work outwith the parish. It is not known how many parish residents work outside East Lothian, but probably a significant number.

With the exception of the museum and tearooms, the parish has no facilities specifically for tourists. *The Haddingtonshire Courier Yearbook* of the early 1960s mentions a camping site but no one has any knowledge of this; the Fletcher estates apparently owned it.

Economy - Industry

Lime production for agricultural purposes - for 'gooding the land' (Tindall, F. P. p24) had been the main industry of the area but after 1960 it was no longer produced. It was extracted from a site on Gifford Road by opencast mining by the Co-operative Wholesale Society (C.W.S.).

A small sawmill on Petersmuir Road owned by Arne Albertson, timber merchant, was transferred to part of an old limekiln site in the 1950s. Later this became a coal yard, which closed in 1999. A plant hire business then rented space in part of the coal yard and is still in existence.

A large sawmill has existed at Petersmuir since 1950; it has had several changes of owners including (Edmund Leon and A. & R. Brownlee Ltd) but is still functioning. It was custom-built, and the buildings have extended over the years. It employed 15 people in 2000. Other than the presence of large timber lorries on the roads it has little effect on the parish.

East Saltoun Limeworks, 1974 (©Royal Commission on the Ancient and Historical Monuments of Scotland)

Economy - Arts & Crafts

People have been engaged in basket making, jewellery, soft furnishings, woodcraft, furniture making, knitting, metal work, painting and embroidery over the years. There is no outlet for craft work in the parish except for the Tithe Byre. Some craftwork, such as the two communion chairs for the church in Bolton, has been made to order.

Forestry: All significant woodland in the parish is long established. Saltoun Big Wood has been a forest in active timber production for much more than 50 years; it is currently owned by Sir Francis Ogilvy, having previously been in public ownership. Other areas of forestry production are Dryden (Hamilton Farming Enterprises Ltd.), and Petersmuir (the Maxwell family). There is a mix of nursery and mature stock, and of a range of ages. Petersmuir is mixed and deciduous; Saltoun Big Wood is mixed woodland, but mainly coniferous.

A small percentage (less than 1%) of local timber is processed at Petersmuir; the bulk of the wood processed by the sawmill is from outside the parish.

Economy - Agriculture

There are no agricultural smallholdings in the parish, although there is a smallholding just across the river at Milton Bridge beyond West Saltoun, which has goats and a good collection of peacocks, ducks, geese and exotic waterfowl.

Saltoun parish is rich in farms, which are the biggest employers locally. The last 55 years have seen a few changes of ownership, but no significant changes in farms; all the farms are owned, but some are operated 'in hand' by farm managers (see Land Ownership). There has however been a change of methods. There are fewer stock farms, and therefore less need for growing root crops and grass for food. Farms are turning to grain crops: barley is still produced for the brewing industry, but oat production has declined; the acreage of oil seed rape production increased from the 1970s. Of necessity, and to comply with EU legislation since the early 1990s, farmers make more use of set-aside.

Larger buildings have been erected for grain stores, to accommodate farm machinery, and for over-wintering cattle, leaving the original small buildings for storage. The use of bigger machines has improved the work rate and is more economical. The seasons are less well defined now, with harvests often starting in July and many a field will be cleared and ploughed by the middle of August. The use of chemicals has helped to give more winter cropping. There is no organic farming in the parish, but, with the influence of FWAG, many farmers are becoming more aware of environmental issues (see *The Farming & Wildlife Advisory Group in East Lothian*, Michael Williams, county volume).

The foot and mouth epidemic of the 1960s did not affect the parish directly, but farmers took the recommended precautions such as disinfectant at farm entrances.

Saltoun Home Farm/Middlemains – Fletcher estate (660 acres) is mixed arable and stock; it grows white cereals but no turnips, oats or potatoes.
Gilchriston – Maxwell (360 acres) is arable, growing mainly wheat, barley, oil seed rape, and some grass. (Today it is farmed with Cauldshiel in the next parish with a total acreage of 1040).
East Saltoun, Greenhead, Barley Mill, Greenlaw – Hamilton Farming Enterprises Ltd (756 acres) is mainly arable, growing cereals, barley, oil seed rape, some potatoes and forage peas.

Economy - Agriculture (cont)

Blance – Scott (370 acres) is a mixed farm.

Samuelston South Mains – Logan (200 acres) is arable, growing mostly potatoes, wheat, barley, and oil seed rape.

Saltoun East Mains – Morton (310 acres) is an arable farm.

Herdmanston Mains – Waddell (372 acres) is mixed stock and arable, growing mostly grain (more intensive) and turnips.

Others

McNaughton's Nursery Plants, located beside the river Tyne at Spilmersford grows, but does not sell plants. This is a family-run business linked to Macplants at Boggs Holdings (see Pencaitland parish).

From the mid 1990s, between East Saltoun and Petersmuir a kennels and cattery replaced two separate earlier enterprises of a fox farm (breeding silver foxes) and a breeder of Scottie dogs.

Local Government

Until 1975, Saltoun was linked with Bolton in having one county and one district councillor; the parish has never been very active politically.

At the reorganisation of local government in 1975, the representation was one district councillor (again linked with Bolton) and one regional councillor who covered the Tranent area. For some residents the distinction between the functions of Lothian region and East Lothian District Council has not always been clear.

Since 1996, the parish has been linked with East Linton and Gifford, and more recently with Haddington West, in having one East Lothian councillor.

Most administration being in Haddington was thought to make it easier, but every time the councils changed, in 1975 and again in 1996, additional expenditure seemed to be required, and wheels seemed to be re-invented. There was little evidence of economies of scale.

Saltoun shares its community council with Humbie and Bolton. Planning applications are checked out and public meetings called when necessary, for example, recently in respect of plans for more new housing in East Saltoun. Saltoun parish sends three members to the Humbie, Bolton, East and West Saltoun Community Council   Minutes of meetings are published on public notice boards in the two settlements and the public is invited to attend meetings.

The community council has organised 'Community Capers' biennially in recent years, and after many years has succeeded in improving the children's play area in West Saltoun. It organised fireworks for the Millennium, and has been involved in the Community Woodland Project.

Politics in the parish

There are no strong political influences in the parish. No SNP councillor has ever been elected, although a prominent nationalist resident flew the Saltire flag on a private house in the 1970/80s.

The parish was in the constituency of East Lothian and Berwickshire until the reorganisation of constituencies, and is now in the constituency of East Lothian.

A Conservative/Unionist Association was active in the 1950/60s   There are currently no strong political influences.

In spite of the fact that EU policies, especially those connected with the common

Local Government (cont)

agricultural policy, have a major impact on the parish, there is very little interest in politics. Numbers participating in elections have declined in line with national trends. Perhaps there are too many elections?

Revisiting the Past

Bolton and Saltoun church have a website: http://www/ndhm.org.uk

The Department of Economic History at Glasgow University has shown an interest in the bleachfield, which was established by the Fletchers and the British Linen Company in the mid 18th century in the grounds of Saltoun Hall. The location of this is just across the river towards West Saltoun, and beyond the parish boundary, but the development of West Saltoun may have been associated with the bleachfield as well as the barley mill. The use of the bleachfield was short-lived; it was discontinued with the introduction of steam power and the subsequent re-location of the linen industry.

Miscellany

Lottery money (about £1500) was given to the youth club in 2000; this was spent on equipment.

People

The Fletcher family played a dominant role in the life of the parish until the death of Captain Andrew Mansel Talbot Fletcher - JP, breeder of Shorthorn cattle, and sometime president of the United East Lothian Agricultural Society – on 16 February 1951 and of his wife on 25 June 1953. His funeral was a major local event, attended by large numbers of estate workers and tenants as well as family and many of the gentry of the county. His heir, John T.T. Fletcher, did not live permanently at Saltoun Hall, although housekeepers maintained the property.

Ruth Michaelis Jena lived in the Lang Hoose in Saltoun village. She is buried along with her husband in Saltoun churchyard. She was an author/writer/journalist famous for her work on the brothers Grimm, and an award is given annually in her name for contributions to the study of folklore or folklife in Great Britain and Ireland.

Professor Andrew Rutherford, Vice-Chancellor of London University, who lived in the drawing room flat in Saltoun Hall in the 1990s was a leading authority on Rudyard Kipling and wrote extensively about his work.

References

This account of Saltoun parish was written by Julie Murphy. Additional information was provided by the following:

Kathy Fairweather	Saltoun Hall; Interviewer of Christina Gillies
Julie Murphy	Interviews
The Saltire Society	Fletcher of Saltoun Annual Lecture
Alistair Scott & Walter Gordon	Saltoun Hall trees

And recollections of residents and ex-residents of the parish, including
Christine Gillies (childcare); Nan Louden (church); Margaret McCormack (home life; church; leisure –
dances); Jeannie Sandilands (education; leisure – play).

FURTHER READING & REFERENCES

Bunyan, Stephen A. (2000) 'The Fletchers of Saltoun' *East Lothian Antiquarian and Field Naturalists' Society Transactions* Volume XXIV pp67-76

Durie, Alastair J. (1976) 'Saltoun Bleachfield 1746-73' *East Lothian Antiquarian and Field Naturalists' Society Transactions* Volume XV pp49-74

Hedderwick, Rachel A. (1987) 'The Restoration of the Old Castle, East Saltoun' *East Lothian Antiquarian and Field Naturalists' Society Transactions* Volume XIX pp67-70

Lothian Regional Council (1995) *The Tale of the Golden Nail*

East Saltoun Primary School project – 16mm film (three minutes) concerning a local blacksmith and the Goblin Hall in Gifford

McWilliam, C. (1978) *Lothian: Buildings of Scotland* Penguin

Michaelis-Jena, Ruth (April 1975) 'A New Home in the Lang Hoose' IN *Scots Magazine* pp 12-19

Saltoun SWRI (1969) *The History of Saltoun*

Skinner, B.C. (1969) *The Lime Industry in the Lothians,* University of Edinburgh Dept of Adult Education & Extra Mural Studies

Tindall, F. P. (1998) *Memoirs and Confessions of a County Planning Officer* Pantile Press

Wylie, Margaret (1986) *A History of Saltoun and the Fletcher Family*

ABOUT THE EAST LOTHIAN FOURTH STATISTICAL ACCOUNT

It appears that East Lothian is one of the first of the Scottish counties to bring the run of Statistical Accounts (1789-93; 1845; 1953) up to 2000; in this it follows the third East Lothian account, as this too was one of the earliest of that series to be completed.

The driving force behind this work was the East Lothian Antiquarian & Field Naturalists' Society. At the AGM in 1997, the idea of a Fourth Statistical Account of East Lothian was considered; it was agreed to hold a meeting with representatives of the other (around 14) local history and amenity societies. The meeting was held on 18 March 1998, and was supportive; as a result, the East Lothian Fourth Statistical Account Society was set up at a second meeting on 21 May, and formalised on 5 August 1998 with an Executive Committee of Stephen Bunyan as chairman, David Moody as treasurer and Michael Cox as honorary secretary. Lottery funding was sought and £30,000 was granted in 1999 – to be matched by volunteer hours and input.

The editor, Sonia Baker, was appointed in November 2000, parish representatives sought and found by Christmas, and the structure document – a 94 page prompt sheet (or questionnaire) – was sent out to the parish representatives in February 2001. For the parishes with no organised history group, local history enthusiasts were approached for their assistance and input; occasionally, personal circumstances intervened and further support had to be found to complete the work.

A draft list of possible county wide topics was prepared, and authors located, with the last being approached in summer, 2002. The web site (www.el4.org.uk) was up and running by October 2002. Thus far, Volume One – the county volume, was published in July 2003, and Volume Two – the first of the parish volumes – in August 2004. The remaining parish volumes will be published in due course. Once the final volume – Volume Seven *Growing up in East Lothian,* which features a series of reminiscences from across the county – is published a CD-ROM of the entire work will follow. The CD-ROM will include everything that has been collected in full, and will be available for future researchers; the books and the CD-ROMs should not be regarded as the definitive work on the county's economic and social history, 1945-2000, but just a beginning.

For both the parish contributions and the county essays, the response was overwhelming. Material in all formats was welcomed and encouraged. Wherever possible, editorial intervention has been kept to a minimum, and the result is a lively mix of oral and written memories, together with researched material, graphics and photographs, around a specified structure. Local knowledge and access to personal networks were provided largely by the society's executive committee, as well as by other members of the society. In several parishes, the work was done by older members of the community, proving that age is no bar to enthusiasm and the wish to find out more. Without exception, the contributors have done an excellent job.

Once the society has completed its work, it will be wound up. The promised new Cultural Centre for the county in Haddington (due c2007) will hold the account's archive, and future researchers will benefit not only from an electronic version of the account, but room to research in comfort as well.

Volume Three
Biographies of Parish Representatives

Ralph W. Barker: an amateur botanist who helped on *The Atlas of British Flora* (1962) and also on *A Field Flora of the British Isles* (1999), both of which are relevant to Pencaitland.

'I became session clerk of Pencaitland Parish Church in 1961, and held the post for over 30 years. I am a member of the local history group, and have a particular interest in the carving and some of the tombstones in the parish church. I was a founder member of the Pencaitland Amenity Society, formed in the mid 1960s, and am still a member'.

John P. Bolton: MA (Cantab) M.I.C.E; retired chartered engineer, formerly lecturer in civil engineering and history of civil engineering at Napier University, Edinburgh. Humbie resident since 1970; member of the Fala and District History and Heritage Society.

Denise Brydon: *'I am a wife and mother of three boys and own the village newsagents in Main Street. My interest in the history of Ormiston was sparked by mnoving into Kinghorn House at the age of eight. The house had been largely untouched for years and as my parents renovated it, more history was uncovered. Today I have a strong interest in genealogy and was asked to help with the account by Annie Lyell, who wrote the Ormiston book 'You See it A' . David Fleming has been the unofficial village historian for many years and is my hero!'*

Kathy M. Fairweather CBE: Kathy is a former HM Chief Inspector of Schools, who retired in 2000. She is a member of the East Lothian Antiquarian & Field Naturalists' Society. Her first degree was in history at St Andrews University, so she welcomed the opportunity to re-engage with real history. She became familiar with the account through working with Julie Murphy on her home parish of Saltoun. Kathy then stepped into the breach when it became evident that there was no one available in the locality to both carry out the additional research necessary and to pull together the various contributions for Macmerry and the rural section of Gladsmuir parish.

Julie Murphy: has lived in the Pencaitland and Saltoun area for over 30 years and has always had an interest in local history. As a member of the Pencaitland Amenity Society she was co-author of a book on Pencaitland Village School, and has been active in recording tombstone inscriptions in several local churchyards. Prior to retirement she worked in adult education.

Jean Shirlaw: *'My interest in Gladsmuir parish was stimulated by the fact that my husband, Robert Shirlaw, had been minister of Gladsmuir from 1955-84. My research included church session minutes and heritors' records, also the Lamington and Elvingston records held by the NAS.*
When asked to help with the account, I felt a bit daunted as I had left the district for some years. However, having retained contacts in the parish, I agreed and was gladly given information of any changes that had occurred in the intervening years which were relevant to the project'.

David Robertson: has lived all his life in Longniddry. He pursued a successful career in education, and took very early retirement in 1996 to embrace a more congenial lifestyle. He has published a local history of Longniddry, and has a passionate interest in Scots traditional culture. He was not at first inclined to take on the job of writing up Longniddry for the account, but decided on reflection that it was better that the village he remembered should be described by a 'native' rather than by an incomer, which would have been the most likely alternative had he declined the invitation.

Michael Williams: retired army officer turned farmer. He farms at Eaglescairnie Mains, near Gifford (mainly arable). An enthusiastic conservationist, he practises a system of 'sympathetic' farming, which tries to fit modern farming into the countryside. Author of county essay, The Farming & Wildlife Advisory Group (FWAG) in East Lothian: 1993-2000.

VOLUME THREE
CONTENTS OF CD-ROM VERSION

The CD-ROM version of Volume Three also contains:

GLADSMUIR
   EXCL. LONGNIDDRY
Longer version

GLADSMUIR
   LONGNIDDRY
Longer version
Interview with Archie Mathieson
Interview with Gordon Morrison, plus extracts from a grieve's diary
Moray Welsh biography

HUMBIE
Longer version

ORMISTON
Longer version

PENCAITLAND
Longer version
Interview with Janet Bassett

SALTOUN
Longer version
Interview with Christine Gillies
Interview with Nan Louden
Interview with Margaret McCormack
Interview with Jean Sandilands
Information on the Fletcher of Saltoun Lectures 1979-2001

INDEX

INDEX (cont)

Index (cont)

INDEX (CONT)